Meher Baba

SEVEN COIN PRESS   SPRUCE HEAD · MAINE

Meher Baba
AVATAR OF THE TORTOISE

KENNETH LUX

Published by
SEVEN COIN PRESS
P.O. Box 477
Spruce Head, Maine 04859
PHONE: 207-594-0909
FAX: 207-594-0909
info@sevencoinpress.com
www.sevencoinpress.com

SHIPPING ADDRESS:
Seven Coin Press
146 Thomaston Street
Rockland, Maine 04841

Copyright © 2001 by Kenneth Lux
All rights reserved. No part of the material protected by this copyright notice may be reproduced or utilized in any form, electronic or mechanical, including photocopying, recording, or by any information storage and retrieval system, without written permission from the publisher.

PRODUCTION CREDITS
Editor: Constance E. Leavitt
Editorial Production Service: Bookwrights
Cover and Text Design: Lurelle Cheverie
Printing and Binding: Transcontinental Printing

Library of Congress Cataloging-in-Publication Data
Lux, Kenneth
  Meher Baba : avatar of the tortoise / Kenneth Lux
        p. cm.
   Includes bibliographical references and index.
   ISBN 0-9700974-0-9
   1. Meher Baba, 1894–1969.   I. Title
   BP610.M432 L89 2001
   299'.93—dc21
   [B]

00-063521
CIP

Photo credits and permission information will be found at the end of this book.

Printed in Canada
04 03 02 01 00   10 9 8 7 6 5 4 3 2 1

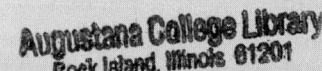

To the seeker,

who exists in

ever-increasing

numbers

CONTENTS

Preface viii
Acknowledgments xiv

1 FIRST CONTACT   1
2 HOW I CAME TO BELIEVE   17
3 HIS LIFE   28
4 AT THE CENTER —
  Meher Baba's Home in the West   49
5 DROPPING THE BODY   63
6 THE LAST DARSHAN   74
7 WHEN I BREAK MY SILENCE   89

8 THE MIRACLE WORKER   101
9 THE MAGIC FLUTE   111
10 KARMA SENSITIVE PSYCHOTHERAPY   121
11 EXAMINING THE POSSIBILITIES   129
12 ONCE IN A THOUSAND YEARS   146
13 IN THE AUGEAN STABLES   160
14 MORE TO COME   172

Endnotes   183

Bibliography   188

Index   191

PREFACE

I believe that we live in desperate times that are getting ever more desperate. Somehow, knowing there's an answer allows me to accept the extent of our desperateness. I also believe that's the way the human mind works. If a situation is truly desperate and no avenue of hope can be seen, the mind tends to deny the full extent of ominous things in order to preserve some measure of hope. It is so psychologically disastrous to be without hope that the mind recoils against it. Therefore, we should not lightly and callously condemn those who do not accept our state of crisis as being in abject denial.

Denial has the important function of preserving hope, although, ultimately, that cannot be its justification. To be without hope is disastrous because hope is actually part of reality; to lose hope is to lose reality. Reality is not just the "hard stuff"—the material world—but includes the human being. Hope is essential to the human being. Hope is not to be confused with wishfulness. Wishfulness can obscure reality, whereas hope opens us up to it. Had I not had hope, I do not believe that I would have recognized just how desperate these times are.

That's where Meher Baba comes in.

Baba physically came into this world in 1894 and left in 1969—a life of seventy-four years. For the last forty-four of those years, from 1925 on, he was silent—no words or sounds escaped his lips. All of his communications—and he communicated extensively—were by means other than speech and, amazingly, by means other than writing. When Meher Baba

IN THE OPENING SCENE OF A 1932 NEWSREEL, CHARLES PURDOM, SITTING NEXT TO BABA SAYS, "MEHER BABA HAS COME FROM INDIA WITH A MESSAGE FOR THE WEST."

began his silence in 1925, he wrote for about a year, usually on a slate. Then he abandoned the slate and began using an English alphabet board. He would communicate through the laborious method of pointing out, letter by letter, what he wanted to say. In 1954, Meher Baba dispensed with the alphabet board and relied on hand gestures.

It should be understood that Meher Baba's silence was not because he had little or nothing to say. Baba's words, expressed silently, are among the most profound and comprehensive that we have, as you will be able to judge for yourself from quotes that I have used throughout this book. One reason for Meher Baba's silence, he said, was that, "You have asked for and been given enough words—it is now time to live them." Who is the *you* in this statement? It is all of us. Then who is *he*? That is the subject of this book—and that is why I talk about hope.

This book began when I returned to Maine in August 1997 from a visit to the tomb of Meher Baba in India. Among the messages waiting for me was one from Connie Leavitt. I had not yet met Connie, but we had spoken once or twice on the phone. She and her husband own a book production studio on the coast of Maine and she told me that she was going to launch Seven Coin Press and was interested in publishing books with a spiritual or philosophical focus.

From our previous conversations, Connie knew that I had a spiritual orientation and had written in the field of alternative economics, although spirituality is not explicit in that work. When we first met, we discussed a book that I was then writing—a critique of the modern mindset and its resulting damage to both the environment and society. It sounded interesting to her, and so I sent her a copy of my previously published book, *Adam Smith's Mistake*.

PURDOM READING BABA'S MESSAGE TO THE WEST.

After reviewing *Adam Smith's Mistake*, she returned it with the comment that, with all due respect, it was not the type of book that appealed to her—it was too academic and intellectual. Rather,

her objective was to publish visionary, inspirational, and positive life-experience books that would reach out to a general readership. Well, I am not really an academic in that I do not teach at a college or university. Even though I do think that for society to change, a broader group than academia needs to be reached, the ability to do this kind of reaching was probably beyond me. I thought that Connie and I most likely did not have the basis for doing a book together. We wished each other well and said that we might meet in the future to discuss our interests in spirituality.

So, I was a little surprised to find a phone message from her on my return from India. In my everyday work as a psychologist, I advertise my approach as "Karma Sensitive Psychotherapy." It seems that she had seen my ad and wanted to know more about my method of therapy. In any event, when I returned her call, she was interested to hear that I had just returned from India, one of several trips since my first one in 1969. She had never heard of Meher Baba and when she asked about him, I stumbled around a bit and came up with a vague answer, such as the commonly used "spiritual teacher."

Despite what I felt was the blandness of my answer, Connie still wanted to know more, and she seemed intent about it. I might have brought in the term *Avatar* at that point, because I had just come back from India and Meher Baba's tomb and may have had the special energy that such a visit usually brings. Perhaps some of this came through to her. Finally she asked, "Did you ever think about writing a book about Meher Baba?" When I replied, "No," she said, "Do you think it's something you could do?" I said that it was something I could think about for the future, but for now I needed to finish my new book on the problem of the environment, and I left it at that.

IN THE FILM, BABA'S FINGERS CAN BE SEEN FLYING SWIFTLY OVER THE BOARD.

When I woke up the next morning, surprisingly, my head was full of thoughts on writing a book about Meher Baba. I somehow knew what such a book would be. I would use my life as a lover of Baba to present an account of him. My story would tell how I came to grips with Baba and who he is or is supposed to be. My encounter with Baba would, out of necessity, have to be individual, but I am also aware of the paradox that through the individual, we can reach the universal. As Charles Purdom, a lover of Baba who had numerous contacts with, and wrote a biography about, Meher Baba, put it:

> [Meher Baba's] work is with the human soul in general and equally with particular souls, for increase in consciousness is increase in particularness. It is a paradox that the more fully the soul knows itself and the more meaning it gives to the "I," the more completely it knows itself to be one with, not separated from, and having identical interests with all other souls.[1]

My story is the story of someone who never met Meher Baba physically, which will be the case for almost all readers of this book. If Baba is who he is supposed to be, then the physical meeting is not necessary. Indeed, the major work of such a one is something that only begins to unfold or become apparent after his physical death. It is by that continuity and eventual increase of his influence that history knows that such a one was real. Of course, his lovers know it outside the judgment of history, and that is precisely how they become his lovers. That process must always be a personal one.

To talk about the spiritual and universal and to connect both with reality is to allude to things that the modern world in its skepticism does not believe exists. To overcome such skepticism is one of the purposes of the appearance of Meher Baba. In this book, I will describe, as accurately and as honestly as I can, how this process worked and works with me. The reader can evaluate and judge for him- or herself. One of the reasons for this book is to give the reader an initial basis for doing so.

I have used the word *lover* several times. Meher Baba is supposed to be a spiritual authority. One who believes in an authority and adheres to that authority is seen as a follower of that person. Why don't I just say that I am a *follower* of Meher Baba? What is this business about being a lover of?

Meher Baba, himself, referred to his followers as his *lovers*. It was a term that Baba used first. Why did Baba do this? He was referring to *divine love*. He said that those who were being drawn to him were beginning to practice the highest spiritual art that is possible—that of divine love. This implies at least two things. One is that there is such a thing as the divine and that love is closely connected to it, and two, that Meher Baba, for some reason, is a worthy or appropriate figure to be associated with such a love. Both of these claims, as far as I am concerned, are outrageous within the context of the modern world. His claims and statements run against the whole tenor of modern mindset. The modern mindset, besides its skepticism, is particularly concerned with personal gain. That follows, of course, from its materialism, which is both philosophical and commercial. To talk about divine love, which is, of course, not sexual love and not the love of acquisition, is to talk about something that was left far behind in our past.

I am personally uncomfortable with the term *lover* of Meher Baba. It seems presumptuous of me to call myself a lover of Baba, which is to say someone capable of that kind of love—"pure" love. In fact, it would be just as presumptuous of me to claim that I felt that toward anyone, Meher Baba or no. After all, *pure*, four letters that it is, is still a very big word. Baba knows all this, just as Baba knows everything. By referring to his followers as his lovers, Meher Baba is in effect telling us that, as short of the mark as we are, indeed, as selfish and possessive as we are, through contact with him, in fact by the mere knowledge of his name, we are taking a step toward the path of pure love.

We start with where we are, as always. Our love can be as impure as love gets: possessive, selfish, lustful, you name it, but by contact with Meher Baba, in any form, even in name, that

BABA'S DIVINE LOVE CAPTURED IN A PHOTO.

love begins the process of its purification. In fact, the modern world is such that this concept of *pure* and *purification* will be looked upon askance. So, the other issue that the modern world looks upon with suspicion, *authority*, is joined with the concept of *purity*. We can say that Baba's authority, among other things, is the authority of purity, and, in fact, the authority of pure love. That is a vastly different association than the one we usually have with the idea of authority.

The question then arises, if Meher Baba is this, how come almost no one knows about him? Well, one answer would be that this world is just not very interested in purity or pure love. As Baba lets us know, and we are beginning to realize from our direct observations, this world will need to wake up to the necessity of these qualities if it is to get out of its current ominous condition. Meher Baba says that it is for this "awakening" that he has come, and that in time, this awakening will become clear. It's a question of timing. "I have come not to teach, but to awaken," he has said, and that is another way of understanding his silence.

So I asked myself that morning as I thought about my conversation with Connie, is it Meher Baba's timing that this has come about and that I now write such a book? I could only know by trying to go ahead with it. Perhaps the problem of the environment cannot wait, but a book by me on what the modern world is doing to the environment *could*. A book about Meher Baba, the Avatar, would be a more direct answer and source of hope than any analysis and recommendations that I could put forth as a social scientist.

I wrote a couple of chapters and then I met with Connie. I decided to bring a video of Meher Baba so that she could see who Baba is as a living, breathing, and moving about being and she could see how Meher Baba communicated in and through his silence. Photographs and film are central to conveying a sense of Meher Baba. After Connie watched the video, she told me that something inside of her "jumped." She was not sure why or what that meant. It was a good sign.

I hope, for the readers of this book, that something inside of them jumps. We all need something inside of us to jump. It is this inside—so vast—that has been closed off by the scientism and skepticism of the modern world, until it is nearly nonexistent. I, like many of you, personally know this. Therefore, I write about how life changed for me and the meaning and my understanding of this change. This is not, however, a story about me; it is a story about Meher Baba told through my experience.

My story allows you to connect with who Meher Baba is through your own story and leads you right up to this point.

ACKNOWLEDGMENTS

Even a little book from a small publisher may have a surprisingly large number of people who are called on to lend assistance and generously do so. Perhaps this time, it's because this little book is about a big subject. These people include the readers of the first two or three draft chapters, who, as a group, gave us the thumbs up on the project: Lois Anne, Carol Daigneault, Cheryl Evangelos, Beth Miller Long, Holly Smith, and Elizabeth Thorson.

When I had a complete manuscript, the following people invested their time in most carefully reading and indexing, making informative suggestions, and urging me forward: Robert Barton, Douglas Leavitt, Noreen O'Brien, Elizabeth Stewart, Angela Stone, and Peter Zeidenstein.

Among this same group were three whom I called on for more (and still yet more) feedback and input. Ann Conlon and Don Stevens were generously helpful and Naosherwan Anzar and his Beloved Archives lovingly contributed several precious photographs.

For expert editorial help, thanks are due to Cathi Reinfelder and my thanks to Mike McDade for his skilled technical expertise. I would also like to thank Lurelle Cheverie for her beautiful cover and text designs.

Sheila Krynski of Sheriar Foundation offered suggestions along the way and, with Wendy and Buz Connor, provided some rare photographs.

I want to thank Pat Sumner for facilitating the granting of permissions from the Avatar Meher Baba Perpetual Charitable Trust. I also extend my heartfelt thanks to Bhau Kalchuri for his personal approval as well as his continuing support in all things over the years.

Other exceptional photographs were provided by Meher Prasad, Sufism Reoriented, Lawrence Reiter, and Susan White. I am grateful to all of you.

As I indicate in the Preface, Connie Leavitt played an especially essential and actively involved role, not only as my publisher, but as my editor, too. This is perhaps one of the virtues of a small press.

I hope I haven't left anyone out, but I'm afraid I may have. If so, I extend my sincere apologies.

First Contact

Alas, alas,
I pity those who compare
a glass bead to a pearl.

HAFIZ

I first heard of Meher Baba in 1967. I was finishing my doctorate in psychology at Indiana University and was an assistant professor at the South Bend campus. An Indiana friend of mine had gone out to the San Francisco area to be a part of the doings of the hippies and the cultural revolution and he wrote to me of his observations—a report from the front, so to speak. In his letter was this sentence: "Have you ever heard of Meher Baba, he is too much for me."

I had no idea what he was referring to, and only the slightest curiosity about what he meant. But evidently the name Meher Baba lodged in my mind because some months later I recognized it as I was wandering through the stacks at the Notre Dame library. My eyes were caught by a book title and I stopped. The book was *God Speaks* by Meher Baba. I thought that this certainly had to be one of the strangest titles for a book. God speaks? God? What was this—monumental ego? I opened the book and the frontispiece was a photograph of Meher Baba. He was smiling, fifty or so, with a mustache, looking like an Italian organ grinder or a pizza chef, and sitting on a tiger skin. The photograph seemed as odd to me as the title.

Quickly perusing through the book, I noticed a series of charts that seemed to give a schematic account of spirituality and a comparison of the terminology from several different spiritual traditions. Feeling that I was already too much the intellectual, I concluded that I didn't need another intellectualized account of spirituality and promptly put the book back on the shelf. I thought, "Yes, this *is* too much."

MEHER BABA
2 AVATAR OF THE TORTOISE

MEHER BABA AS HE APPEARED IN THE PHOTO FROM *GOD SPEAKS*. AHMEDNAGAR, 1954.

Not long before this incident, I had begun to feel that I needed spiritual *experience*—not more spiritual concepts. I had read *Autobiography of a Yogi* by Paramahansa Yogananda, a marvelous account of this yogi's experiences and his coming to America in the 1950s to set up the Self-Realization Fellowship (SRF), a meditation school in southern California. I was fascinated with his book and the picture he posed of an entirely different universe than the one I was used to. Yogananda conveyed a sense of destiny moving through the events of one's life, the reality of extrasensory perception and occult phenomena, and reincarnation and karma.

Like many others of that time and generation, I periodically took LSD. Using LSD gave me a sense that indeed there was something more to this universe than what science and our education system taught. It gave me a feeling for the importance of experience versus theory and concepts, and led to my recent emphasis on spiritual experience.

After one of my LSD trips, a friend told me, "it's all chemistry." If so, for me, this created a conundrum. If there was another world beyond that of science, it had to be other than material because science defined and described reality as material. The paradox for me at the time was, if it is "all chemistry," that is, when you change your chemistry through drugs you change your experience, then perhaps spirituality has no independent reality. Perhaps spirituality is just another facet of one's material foundation. Moreover, if drug taking is a pleasurable activity and produces wonderful new experiences, then there is little reason to stop taking drugs. But that didn't sit quite right with me either.

Although I used drugs, I was always somewhat uneasy about it—at least as a way of life. I could not get past the feeling that there was something dissipating about taking drugs, and there was recognition of this in the hippie/drug culture. For these reasons, I became increasingly interested in meditation, which was a way to alter or "expand my consciousness" (the phraseology of the time) without drugs. Perhaps meditation did change body chemistry, but it did so naturally.

In my drug use, I often felt that I was on the verge of some kind of major breakthrough. I had that same sense in my meditations, only to a less intense degree. But the breakthrough never happened, and I became unsure what my ultimate purpose was and in what direction my meditations should go. I sensed that I needed a meditation teacher—a skilled and knowledgeable practitioner—to guide me.

I made plans to summer in California—stay with a friend, work on my doctoral dissertation, and perhaps visit SRF for two weeks. That is where I found myself in 1967—the "Summer of Love."

Soon after arriving in California, I journeyed by bus up the coast to see my friend who was now living in Berkeley. On the way, I stopped in Santa Barbara to visit other friends. I knew that there was a venerable swami at the Vedanta Temple in Santa Barbara, and during this stopover, I attended one of his lectures. The lecture was interesting, and I briefly considered concentrating my future spiritual efforts in Santa Barbara. From Santa Barbara I continued to Ojai and visited the Theosophical Center.

When I finally arrived in Berkeley, I found, ironically, that my friend had gone to Southern California, so I looked for ways to pass the time until he returned. I turned again to thoughts of finding a meditation teacher or school. Eknath Eswaran, an Indian professor at Berkeley, founded and regularly lectured at the Blue Mountain Meditation Center. I decided to attend one of his lectures. Just as in Santa Barbara, I was impressed by this teacher and thought that perhaps this was the place to obtain meditation guidance. On the other hand, I knew that when I returned to Southern California, I wanted to visit SRF because that might be the place to look for a teacher. The issue of needing to make some kind of choice was regularly in my thoughts, and I sensed that it mattered that I make the best or *right* choice.

Shortly before heading back to Southern California, I saw a notice for something called a Meher Baba League meeting. "Oh, here's that Meher Baba again. I wonder what this can be?" I was curious and thought that this must be one of the weirdest fringe aspects of the psychedelic/spiritual culture. Out of that sense, I went to the meeting at Sproul Hall on the Berkeley campus.

While I sat in the room before the meeting, I was surprised and even disappointed that there were no spectacularly strange people present. Everyone looked normal, at least as normal as anyone looked in those days. There were two speakers that night. One, Rick Chapman, was a psychology graduate student who had recently met Meher Baba in India. The other was Alan Cohen, a psychologist who had received his Ph.D. from Harvard. While I waited for the meeting to begin, someone came up to me and asked if I had attended a Baba meeting before. I said that I had not, and he then asked me if I had seen Meher Baba's messages about drug use. When I indicated that I knew little to nothing about Meher Baba, he gave me a booklet of those messages. It was titled, *God in a Pill?* Inside the front cover was a quote from someone named Hafiz, "Alas, alas, I pity those who compare a glass bead to a pearl." On the back cover was a quote from Meher Baba, "If God can be found through the medium of any drug, God is not worthy of being God."[1]

Again, these references to God. What is it with this Meher Baba? I thought. For me, God didn't exist. I believed that there was something called *enlightenment*, which is a state of mind. Buddhism and Buddhist literature described this phenomenon. The concept of *satori*, a Japanese term for enlightenment, was particularly emphasized in Zen Buddhism. In the classic book *Cosmic Consciousness*, Richard Bucke, a Canadian physician, wrote about individuals that he felt had attained this state of mind—figures as diverse as Buddha, Jesus, Walt Whitman, and Francis Bacon. Enlightenment made sense to me, and my psychology background, reading, and LSD experiences seemed to reinforce this concept, but not God.

I believed that the idea of God was, in reality, enlightenment or cosmic consciousness. I thought that many cultures had confused enlightenment with the idea of a great controlling being, someone who ran the show, and that for all the theological sophistication that had presumably been gained since biblical times, the idea of God still amounted to a great bearded figure in the sky.

So here was this Eastern figure, Meher Baba, who emphasized God. This seemed strange to me. I thought that spirituality was more sophisticated in the older cultures of the East than in the younger cultures of the West. Most Eastern religions, such as Buddhism, emphasize experience acquired through meditation and yoga, rather than what seemed to me a relatively childish projection of a parental figure elevated to a universal principle. Meher Baba seemed to me to be some kind of throwback—a rather odd spiritual teacher to come out of the East.

The pamphlet that was handed to me opened with these introductory remarks:

Many of those drawn to the use of LSD and other mind-changing drugs are prompted by the need to find out whether some enduring reality and purpose is to be found in life. The ideal is to experience such a sense of reality and purpose for oneself, if it is to be had. Many of those who have taken LSD trips are deeply affected by their experiences, regarding the use of psychedelics not only as a means of developing key insights into their own problems, but into the nature and purpose of creation as well. Certain individuals have become pioneers and in a sense prophets of the movement, largely as a result of the religious and even mystic implications that appear to flow from the use of drugs.

In this connection it is imperative to search for corroboration or refutation of these implications from persons credited with a high state of spiritual development through other disciplines. Meher Baba, of Ahmednagar, India, is such a one. Revered by millions throughout the world as a God-realized being and as Avatar of the age, he is doubtless the best non-acid authority available to compare the results of chemical stimulation of the deeper layers of being with those produced by techniques known and used throughout time by spiritual teachers.

Through an unusual series of events, Meher Baba has captured the devotion and imagination of a number of young thinkers and experimentalists who have been in the forefront of the psychedelic movement. Recognizing the authority of his statements concerning internal realization (inner experience of Truth), they have received oral and written descriptions from Meher Baba comparing the effects of psychedelics with the enduring states* of consciousness generated through inner development.[2]

The asterisk referred the reader to Meher Baba's book, *God Speaks*. The rest of the pamphlet was largely statements that Meher Baba had made in regard to psychedelic drugs and the value of the experience to be had with them. These included, "The experience is as far removed from Reality as is a mirage from water. No matter how much one pursues the mirage, one will never reach water and the search for God through drugs must end in disillusionment." The analogy of mirage and water was further explained by Meher Baba as "experiences of the shadows of the subtle (emotion, energy) plane in the gross (physical) world . . . even the most fantastic experiences thus induced are only the shadows of the subtle plane experienced in the gross world." Meher Baba was quoted as saying, "The experience of a semblance of freedom that these drugs may temporarily give to one is in actuality a millstone round the aspirant's neck in his efforts towards emancipation from the rounds of birth and death." Another strong statement followed. "In America it has become tragically popular among the young, used indiscriminately by any and many. They must be persuaded to desist from taking drugs, for they are harmful—physically, mentally, and spiritually."[3]

Time passed quickly as I read the ten-page pamphlet's detailed set of statements and spiritual description, and then the meeting began. I had two opposite reactions to the information in the pamphlet. On the one hand, these statements against the use of psychedelic drugs were the first and only ones I had ever read that made any sense to me. Because I was concerned about the effect and meaning of drug use, I had extensively read both pro- and con-drug literature. Most of the antidrug literature struck me as little more than government and Food and Drug Administration predictable propaganda. Almost none of it spoke to what seemed to be the value of the experience and the aspirations and questing that lay behind it. These statements by Meher Baba seemed to do this. They were strong and explicit against the use of drugs, but in terms that related to the motivations of the psychedelic drug user. I also found that it accurately and almost uncannily described my own experiences. On the other hand, the references to God and the implication that Meher Baba was a divine or God-like authority aroused my skepticism. I was more than skeptical. These opposing feelings were represented in this statement from the pamphlet: "To a few sincere seekers, LSD may have served as a means to arouse that spiritual longing which has brought them into my contact, but once that purpose is served further ingestion would not only be harmful but have no point or purpose."[4]

Cohen and Chapman, the speakers, had been students of psychology professors Timothy Leary and Richard Alpert while at Harvard, and Cohen had been active with them in the psychedelic drug movement. In the students' search for meaning and understanding through drug use, they came in contact with Meher Baba. Through personal experiences, Cohen and Chapman came to accept the legitimacy of Meher Baba's knowledge and authority and broke with the drug advocacy culture. They moved in a new direction—warning others about the dangers of drugs as explained by Meher Baba. Later, Cohen published a book called *Understanding Drug Use*[5] and worked with other followers of Meher Baba to develop spiritually based antidrug programs.

The reaction of Leary and Alpert to the apostasy of their young disciples was split. Leary remained in sharp disagreement with them, and Alpert was on the fence. After learning of Meher Baba through Cohen, Alpert went to India to try to meet him, but was unable to. He later found

BABA "SPEAKS" USING THE ALPHABET BOARD.
MEHERABAD, 1935.

and followed another spiritual master and took the name of Ram Dass. In his landmark book of the psychedelic and counterculture, *Be Here Now*, Ram Dass refers to Meher Baba and includes a line drawing of him. A number of Meher Baba's statements on drug use collected in the pamphlet were in response to letters that Alpert had written to Baba. In years to come, when some sought out Ram Dass for spiritual advice concerning drugs, he often recommended that the questioner read from the works of Meher Baba.

After reading the pamphlet, I suspended judgment and was favorably impressed by the speakers. In fact, as a doctoral student in psychology and a part of the psychedelic culture, I could identify with them. This was unnerving. I thought that what they said about Meher Baba was "wild." They said that Meher Baba was the *Avatar of the Age*, which meant God in human form—the incarnation that the world needed and was waiting for. Furthermore, they said, he had not spoken since 1925, and he no longer wrote.

While listening to Cohen and Chapman, a confusing buzz of questions developed in my mind. After the meeting, I spoke to Rick Chapman who, traveling to India on a Fulbright scholarship, was one of the most recent Americans to meet Meher Baba. I asked him what he thought of Yogananda. With a sympathetic sense, but with firmness and directness, he said,

"Why do you want to be a dilettante?" He told me he had read *Autobiography of a Yogi* and respected Yogananda. We discussed meditation, which was, after all, my reason for visiting California and my search up the coast. Chapman said that Meher Baba did not emphasize meditation. His followers, who I learned were called "Baba lovers," may meditate, for meditation has its own value, but it is not ultimately spiritually important. What was important, he said, was meditation in action. The point was that Meher Baba did not instruct his followers to practice meditation.

This was most strange to me. To me meditation was the essence of spiritual practice. Even with yoga, the ultimate purpose was to develop the ability to meditate. Meditation is sometimes called *raja yoga*, meaning the king of yogas. I could not imagine spirituality without meditation. But, then, various messages of the whole meeting did not fit my usual way of mentally structuring spirituality.

There was no opportunity to talk further, but I was told about a future Meher Baba meeting at a place called Sufism Reoriented, which was located across the Bay in San Francisco. The scheduled speaker was Don Stevens, a long-term American disciple of Meher Baba. I decided to attend this meeting before returning to Los Angeles.

This second meeting was held in a suite of rooms at the top of a hill on the cable car route in downtown San Francisco—a permanent meeting center for the Sufism Reoriented organization known as the Sufi Center. I had heard the term *Sufi*, which the dictionary defines as "Muslim mystic," but knew almost nothing about it. The center was formally and elegantly arranged—nothing scruffy or counterculture about it. The speaker was a middle-aged, conservative-appearing man who worked for Standard Oil. Although many in the audience were young hippie types, this was a different setting than I expected—again, to me, the surprising and enigmatic nature of Meher Baba was evident. I looked forward to hearing what this unexpected speaker was going to say about Meher Baba, but I was exhausted from traveling and as soon as I was comfortable and he began speaking—boom, out I went.

BABA, WITH ERUCH JESSAWALA AT HIS SIDE, REACHES TO CARESS DON STEVENS' CHEEK AT THE DELMONICO HOTEL DINNER PARTY. NEW YORK, JULY 16, 1956.

The next thing I knew I was waking up to applause at the end of his talk. I could have kicked myself. I had gone all the way to San Francisco for the purpose of hearing more about Meher Baba, and I hadn't heard a word. Because I missed the talk, I decided to buy a book at the meeting. I skipped over the hardback *God Speaks* and a three-volume paperback set called *The Discourses*, and settled on a thin inexpensive paperback, *The Everything and the Nothing*. I struck up a bit of a conversation with the person managing the book corner, and when he discovered that I was returning to Los Angeles, he gave me the address of Filis Frederick, a Baba lover who hosted regular group meetings in her home.

On the bus back to Los Angeles, I began to read *The Everything and the Nothing*. It consisted of short, one- or two-page messages, as well as poems and epigrams—a much different presentation than *God Speaks*. The first message by Meher Baba was entitled, "The Lover and the Beloved."

God is Love. And Love must love. And to love there must be a Beloved. But since God is Existence infinite and eternal there is no one for Him to love but Himself. And in order to love Himself He must imagine Himself as the Beloved whom He as the Lover imagines He loves.

Beloved and Lover implies separation. And separation creates longing; and longing causes search. And the wider and the more intense the search the greater the separation and the more terrible the longing.

When longing is most intense separation is complete, and the purpose of separation, which was that Love might experience itself as Lover and Beloved, is fulfilled; and union follows. And when union is attained, the Lover knows that he himself was all along the Beloved whom he loved and desired union with; and that all the impossible situations that he overcame were obstacles which he himself had placed in the path to himself.

To attain union is so impossibly difficult because it is impossible to become what you already are! Union is nothing other than knowledge of oneself as the Only One.[6]

"God is Love. And Love must love." And out of that impetus lies the creation of the universe. I found this message beautiful and eloquent. I thought that if God were indeed to exist, to have human form, and to speak, these were words that would be consistent with that image.

How intriguing that Meher Baba was actually silent; that is, if what I'd heard was true. The introduction to *The Everything and the Nothing* was written by Francis Brabazon, who was involved in compiling the book.

These Discourses were given over the last two or three years [this dated 1962] to his disciples by one who needs no introduction because he is the Self of every self and has his home in every heart; but because we have forgotten this he has re-introduced himself to men as the Ancient One who is before all things were and will be after all things have ceased to exist.

In earlier times he was known as Jesus the Christ and Gotama the Buddha and Krishna the Lover and Rama the King. This time he is called Meher Baba. Later, after he has dropped his mortal body, men will probably add "The Awakener" after his name, for he has said, I have come not to teach but to awaken.

Meher Baba asserts that he is God, Truth Absolute, and says he has taken form solely because of his compassion for suffering humanity. Man's suffering is great. Despite the propaganda programmes of "things were never better" man's suffering is so great that he has devised the means of self-annihilation, to extinguish himself and his seed entirely. The question that now occupies the minds of all thinking men is how this destruction may be averted—for the power for this destruction is in the hands of men who are not morally equipped to be the custodians of such power.

This thinking is not in clear streams, but is rather as the cross-currents of an agitated sea seeking a channeled flow toward *Something* that can guarantee continued existence. With religionists this *Something* tends to take the form of *Someone*, the world Saviour which all religions promise.

Meher Baba says he *is* this *Something* or *Someone*, "I am the One whom so many seek and so few find."

Naturally many will not accept this assertion. Indeed, while all men are praying for *Someone* or *Something* to save the world, some will be praying that this Man be saved from the gigantic deception of believing he is God!

But Truth has never waited for us to accept It, but, as the Wind listeth where It will, proclaims Itself according to its own sweet will and whim. It is as natural for God-Man to assert, I am God, as it is for us to assert, I am man. And it would be as laughable for God-Man to say, I am not God, as it would be for us to say, I am not man. Our ignorance of divine Truths is colossal and our ideas about God are so elementary.

It takes some courage to accept God as God-Man, for acceptance means surrender of one's individual ego-life. However, since our cherished lives are no longer ours but in the hands of the first one who will give an order for buttons to be pressed, surrender is not so difficult!

But more courageous than those who surrender themselves to God-Man would seem to be those, who, expecting a *Someone* or *Something*, remain true to their *expectation* by denying the occurrence of the Advent of God-Man *because they cannot prove he is not* what he proclaims he is.

And perhaps more courageous than these are those who continue to follow the westering false lights of material progress while the beautiful silent Person of God has already lit the east-sky with the Dawn of a New Humanity. Presently the Sun of his Word will break across the world, and his Glory will be manifest to all.

Meanwhile the Discourses in this book—dictated in silence by Meher Baba through hand-signs—may be said to be indications of the One Word of Truth that he will utter when he breaks his Silence and manifests his Godhood to men. *The Everything and The Nothing* constitutes a preparation of mind and heart to receive that One Word of Truth when he speaks it.[7]

These words, although articulate and moving, were confusing in some places to me. Meher Baba's statement about the "One Word of Truth" had been discussed at the first meeting I attended. Baba said he would eventually break his silence with one word or "The Word." Of course, he said this without actually speaking. As the introduction stated, the discourses in this book were given by hand signs.

After I returned to Los Angeles, I finally ran into my friend from Indiana. We talked of our lives and journeying during the past year, and how ironic it was that I had traveled up to the Bay area to see him, and he had, as I found out, come to Los Angeles to find me. I told him about my contact with the followers of Meher Baba, and I reminded him of his letter to me that mentioned Baba. I asked him what he meant by his statement that "Baba was too much" for him.

I expected him to say that the whole story about Meher Baba and his claims were too much—a sentiment with which I could certainly identify. I also wanted to tell him that I thought there were some things about Meher Baba that could not be easily dismissed. I was curious about his thoughts on Meher Baba. There was no doubt that his feelings were similar to mine, but what he said was, "He's too much for my ego."

Because I felt that Meher Baba could not be readily dismissed, and my mind was full of questions, I paid a visit to Filis Frederick, the person whose name I had been given in San Francisco, and later attended a meeting in her home. She told me her personal stories about Meher Baba and shared her photo albums with me. Again, I was impressed by the normality of this Baba lover and her utter seriousness and dedication to him as God or the Avatar. Over time, I learned more about what this meant.

The Sanskrit word *Avatar* is defined in one of the basic books of Indian religion, the *Bhagavad Gita*, where the Avatar, Krishna, says:

FILIS FREDERICK. CASA DEL ZORRO, BORREGO SPRINGS, CALIFORNIA, DECEMBER 1968.

> For whenever
> the law of righteousness withers away
> and lawlessness arises
> then I generate
> myself on earth.
> I come into being
> age after age
> and take a visible shape
> and move as man with men
> for the protection of good,
> thrusting the evil back:
> and setting virtue
> on her seat again.[8]

This text was paralleled by Meher Baba in 1954 when he said:

> Age after age, when the wick of Rightousness burns low, the Avatar comes yet once again to rekindle the torch of Love and Truth. Age after age, amidst the clamor of disruptions, wars,

fear and chaos, rings the Avatar's call: *"Come All Unto Me."*

Although, because of the veil of illusion, this Call of the Ancient One may appear as a voice in the wilderness, its echo and re-echo nevertheless pervades through time and space to rouse at first a few, and eventually millions, from their deep slumber of ignorance. And in the midst of illusion, as the Voice behind all voices, it awakens humanity to bear witness to the Manifestation of God amidst mankind.

The time is come. I repeat the Call, and bid all come unto me.[9]

In this appearance as the Avatar, Meher Baba explained more than was previously known or handed down through the centuries. He said that the Avatar appears on earth periodically—from approximately 700 to 1,400 years—depending on the needs of the world or the length of time it takes for his infusion of Love and Truth to dissipate. In our "cycle" of recorded history, and evidently there are many such cycles, he said that there were six appearances of the Avatar—Zoroaster (who also embodies Abraham), Rama, Krishna, Buddha, Jesus Christ, Mohammed, and now Meher Baba.

In another statement, Meher Baba elaborated on the 1954 message:

The Avatar appears in different forms, under different names, at different times, in different parts of the world. As His appearance always coincides with the spiritual regeneration of man, the period immediately preceding His manifestation is always one in which humanity suffers from the pangs of the approaching rebirth. Man seems more than ever enslaved by desire, more than ever driven by greed, held by fear, swept by anger. The strong dominate the weak; the rich oppress the poor; large masses of people are exploited for the benefit of the few who are in power. The individual, who finds no peace or rest, seeks to forget himself in excitement. Immorality increases, crime flourishes, religion is ridiculed. Corruption spreads throughout the social order. Class and national hatreds are aroused and fostered. Wars break out. Humanity grows desperate. There seems to be no possibility of stemming the tide of destruction.

At this moment, the Avatar appears. Being the total manifestation of God in human form, He is like a gauge against which man can measure what he is and what he may become. He trues the standard of human values by interpreting them in terms of divinely human life.... Avataric periods are like the springtide of creation. They bring a new release of power, a new awakening of consciousness, a new experience of life—not merely for the few, but for all. Qualities of energy and awareness, which had been used and enjoyed by only a few advanced souls, are made available for all humanity. Life, as a whole, is stepped up to a higher level of consciousness, is geared to a new rate of energy. The transition from sensation to reason was one such step; the transition from reason to intuition will be another.[10]

I was fascinated by Filis Frederick's photos, which spanned most of Baba's life. Meher Baba seemed to be a man of a thousand faces. The photo that I had seen in *God Speaks*—the pizza-man photo—seemed so unlike an image of God. Other photos that I saw at the meetings did, in fact, look like an image of Christ the Messiah. In most of these, Baba either had a very congenial, engaging smile or a serious penetrating look. I wondered why the pizza-man photo was chosen as the frontispiece for *God Speaks*.

Filis was in her early fifties—well out of the hippie-age range. She had been a fine arts and philosophy student at Cornell and Radcliffe and was now a toy designer for Mattel. She became a spiritual seeker and psychic at a young age. Before learning of Meher Baba, Filis attended a Vedanta lecture where she experienced a moving spiritual vision. She said that at some point the lecturer "disappeared" and in his place a beam of light pointed toward the East and she heard the words, "Seek the feet of the living Master."

In 1952, she met Meher Baba during his first visit to the Meher Baba Spiritual Center that had been established for him in Myrtle Beach, South Carolina. Baba had visited the United States several times during the 1930s—before the center was built. Filis met with him again on his subsequent visits to the United States in 1956 and 1958. In 1962, she was among a group of Westerners from the United States and Europe who visited Meher Baba in India during what was called the East–West Gathering.

Filis told me that often when people meet Meher Baba they sense that he seems familiar—that in a curious way they have always known him. She told me of a woman who, when meeting Meher Baba for the first time, was duly nervous about approaching one who could be nothing less than God. When she saw him, she found herself spontaneously saying, "Oh, it's you."

Filis said that without Meher Baba explicitly demonstrating it, the person in his presence intuitively realizes that Baba knows their every thought. Nevertheless, Baba is warm and human, has an excellent sense of humor, and puts people at ease. She described an incident that occurred the first time Meher Baba came to the West in the 1930s. The leader of the welcoming group equated spirituality with meditation and had urged everyone to close their eyes and meditate even when Meher Baba was with them. Sitting in a group around Baba in their meditation postures, they heard a thump, and something landed on the floor. Opening their eyes they found that Baba had mischievously pulled a book out of the bookcase and dropped it. They could read the title: *All Quiet on the Western Front*.

As I talked with this warm, open, generous-spirited woman, I began to sense and to feel what it may have been like to be with Meher Baba. Was this just some sense of suggestion generated by my own mind?

I returned to Indiana at the end of the summer with the three-volume set of *Discourses*, a small booklet of photographs, and scant work done on my doctoral dissertation. A seed had been planted. I did not yet know that Baba had said he had come to sow the seed of love.

How I Came to Believe

*The thing happened one summer afternoon,
on the school cricket field, while I was sitting
on the grass, waiting my turn to bat.*[1]

A BOY OF FIFTEEN
AS HE EXPERIENCED THE TRANSCENDENTAL

When I returned to the South Bend campus of Indiana University for the fall semester of 1967, the Vietnam War and the protest movement had escalated. As a student I had been actively involved in protesting the war. Now as a faculty member, I was pleased to accept the position of advisor to the campus chapter of Students for a Democratic Society (SDS), which had contact with and support of the chapters at Notre Dame and its sister school, St. Mary's.

These three universities had established a "Free University," which was a popular alternative institution. The Free University offered noncredit courses in topics that were alternatives to the regular school curriculum. I signed up to teach a course in mysticism. I structured the course to begin with some of the classics of spiritual and mystical tradition, the *Tao Te Ching* and the *Bhagavad Gita*, and later move on to the modern "mystic," Meher Baba.

This mysticism course was truly an alternative for me. My regular psychology classes focused on the scientific approach to psychology and included laboratory methods and statistics. This alternative class had a lively energy and was one of the high points of an intense and busy semester. I was also surprised and a little bit intimidated when a couple of priests signed up.

When the course study progressed to Meher Baba, the book I assigned was the one that I had first read—*The Everything and the Nothing*. On my own, I read other works by Meher Baba in order to expand my knowledge, and I finally borrowed *God Speaks* from the Notre Dame library.

I found that different works authored by Meher Baba had somewhat different writing styles depending on the method of his dictation and to whom he was dictating. In all cases his books had to involve other parties because in addition to not speaking, he did not write. When it is said that Meher Baba "wrote," it must be clear what is meant. In some cases, he spelled out every word on the alphabet board. In others, he sketched key lines and a general outline on the alphabet board and then a close disciple wrote the complete text.

In 1954, Meher Baba stopped using the alphabet board and all his writings were produced through hand gestures. In all cases, however, when Meher Baba "authored" a book, he was scrupulous in his instructions to the disciple involved in changing certain words and phrases. Many of these writings by Meher Baba were dictated on the run—on trains and riding in cars—and disciples wrote on the top of suitcases and typed on typewriters on their laps.

I found these messages profound—among the best that I had read in the area of spirituality—and consistent with my first impression of what I would expect to hear from God. I was amazed at Meher Baba's forty-two years of silence. Clearly this man had something to "say"— and keeping silence was not a technique to create an aura of profundity and wisdom. In a biographical account, I read that long-time disciples who remembered his voice described it as "juicy." They said that he loved to sing and often woke them up in the morning by singing to them and from time to time spoke to them of the meaning of life. It seemed clear that his silence was a severe restriction, but one that he was apparently able to overcome in other ways. Despite total silence, his life as a spiritual master was active and diverse: opening and running schools and clinics, feeding the poor, meeting with many thousands of spiritual seekers, and making close personal contact with people all over the world. He traveled around the world a number of times and established two spiritual centers, one in Myrtle Beach, South Carolina, and the other in Australia, north of Brisbane. His was not a life of silence in a cave or alone in the Himalayas, but rather a life fully in the world, even if not *of* it.

I was confronted with a dilemma by bringing Meher Baba into the classroom. Even though I presented him as a modern mystic—an all-encompassing and vague general term—I knew that Baba claimed to be, and was accepted by his followers as, the Avatar—the incarnation of God. Meher Baba was most explicit about this:

> I was Rama, I was Krishna, I was this One, I was that One, and now I am Meher Baba . . . I am that Ancient One

whose past is worshipped and remembered, whose present is ignored and forgotten, and whose future (Advent) is anticipated with great fervor and longing.²

And using Western terms, and speaking within the Western religious tradition, he said:

> The true Messiah can arouse the highest ideals in men and touch the hearts of millions . . . If you love me as St. Francis loved Jesus, then you will not only realize me, but you will also please me.³

And here I was in one of the most prominent institutions in the world of Christian learning—with two priests in attendance. What was I supposed to do? I certainly had no idea if Meher Baba was what he said he was. But, I also didn't think that such a claim, as outrageous as it may sound on the surface, should be dismissed outright. I did not envision this mysticism course as an exercise in weighing evidence and figuring out who Meher Baba was— although to some deree that was what I was engaged in. If I was pondering the facts, I saw it as my personal task— not as a task for this class.

I decided to stick with the text of *The Everything and the Nothing*, allowing the book to speak for itself on this matter, and let the chips fall where

DURING BABA'S VISIT TO PORTOFINO, ITALY IN 1933, HIS SPIRITUAL WORK INCLUDED SPENDING SOME TIME IN A CAVE USED BY ST. FRANCIS OF ASSISI.

they may. I found, to my surprise, that who Meher Baba claimed to be was largely ignored by the class. Even though *The Everything and the Nothing* did assert that Meher Baba was the Avatar, no one seemed to pay much attention to it. I surmised that structuring the class as one in mysticism and Meher Baba as a mystic had worked all too well, allowing the class to read a claim of being the Messiah and letting it go in one ear and out the other.

Something happened several times during class that I and the others found uncanny. Because the messages or essays in the book were short, we read a number of them in class. Someone would ask a question, either about Meher Baba or some other spiritual theme, and we would discuss it and attempt an answer. We found that when we moved on to read the next message, that message would speak directly to the previous question and provide an answer. It was a marvelous coincidence.

For me, the coincidences continued. In addition to reading the writings of Meher Baba, I read other spiritual and mystical literature. Norman O. Brown, a prominent author renowned for his book, *Life Against Death*, was recognized for advancing strong and fundamental critiques of the reigning psychological and philosophical paradigms. His next book, *Love's Body*, was a remarkable book, not only for its theme and title, but for its structure. It was composed of quotes and excerpts from an array of literature and was a tour de force of Brown's scholarship. The objective of *Love's Body* was to demonstrate how literature converged on the main theme of spirituality and that the world was indeed, Love's body—the Christian Body of Christ. At the conclusion of the book, Brown quoted Lama Govinda, a respected Western authority on Tibetan and Eastern spirituality:

> It is not the audible word through which people are converted and transformed in their innermost being, but through that which goes beyond words and flows directly from the presence of the saint: the inaudible mantric sound that emanates from his heart. Therefore the perfect saint is called *Muni*, the Silent One.[4]

It was my choice of timing in reading *Love's Body*—during the period that I was reflecting on Meher Baba—that startled me. One of the most prominent aspects of Meher Baba's life was his total silence. Buddha is called *Sakyamuni*, which means the silent sage (*Muni*) of the Sakya family. Lama Govinda, through Norman O. Brown, seemed to be telling me that becaus of Meher Baba's silence, he could be recognized as Muni, the perfect saint. With a seemingly accidental play of events, here was a strong independent sign to me that Meher Baba could be the true One.

Meher Baba's writings clarified the term *perfect saint* in a way no other previous spiritual literature did. Meher Baba stated that *saint* can be used in a technically precise way that differs from the word's general usage. His writings referred to the seven planes of advanced inner consciousness or awakening that is familiar in spiritual and occult literature. He said that the seventh plane is equivalent to God Realization, and various students of mysticism have pointed out that the Bible describes the seven days of creation and says God rested on the seventh day. God exists on the seventh plane of consciousness. Meher Baba uses *saint* to refer to one who is on the fifth or sixth plane of consciousness. He explains that the fully God-Realized or Self-Realized being should not be referred to as a saint. Thus, Theresa of Avila, for example, was a saint but her Beloved, Jesus, was not a saint but the Avatar. Therefore, if one is perfect, that one should not be referred to as a saint. As far as I knew, only Meher Baba had made this delineation. The Perfect One is either the Perfect Master or the Avatar and nothing less than God incarnate. Baba was not vague about this or his own status.

> In the world there are countless *sadhus*, *mahatmas*, *mahapurushas*, saints, yogis and *walis*, though the number of genuine ones is very, very limited ... I am neither a *mahatma* nor a *mahapurush*, neither a *sadhu* nor a saint, neither a yogi nor a *wali* ... The question therefore arises that if I am not a *sadhu*, not a saint, not a yogi, not a *mahapurush* nor a *wali*, then what am I? The natural assumption would be that I am either just an ordinary human being, or I am the Highest of the High. But one thing I say definitely, and that is that I can never be included amongst those having the intermediary status of the real *sadhus*, saints, yogis and such others.[5]

During this period of teaching at the Free University and spiritual reading, I found that I no longer had any desire to use LSD despite its ongoing use in my circle of friends. I lived in a commune that was a center of political and alternative activity in South Bend. Although I did continue to smoke marijuana and had been moderately sexually active, as a professor I now felt a certain responsibility toward restraint and setting a nonpromiscuous standard.

In the spring of 1968, the Democratic National Convention was looming as the sight of a major antiwar protest. Indiana University was not far from the location of the convention site in Chicago, which gave the antiwar movement in South Bend an increased intensity. We were certain that at least one FBI agent would attend some of our meetings. The issue of violent activity directed toward draft boards was a topic of debate and controversy, and at a rally on the Notre Dame campus, I stated that I thought this kind of action may be appropriate.

The SDS chapter at Indiana University decided to hold a rally—illegal by University rules—in a major campus building, Northridge Hall—the administration building. Because the University was a commuter campus with little open campus area and no dorms, we felt that the only way to get the attention we desired was to hold our antiwar demonstration in this main building. Our campus was not exactly a hotbed of political or social involvement. As a commuter campus, not having enough parking was a major problem, so we adopted the slogan, "There's No Parking Lot Problem at the Pentagon."

I felt that I was living in two worlds. One world's focus was spirituality, mysticism, and Meher Baba. The other's was SDS and politics. These two worlds were far apart. The phrase "You cannot serve two masters" was in the forefront of my mind. I felt that each of these worlds was vying for control. There seemed to be two different basic worldviews. One view saw the world in spiritual terms, with all else, including politics, following from that and existing only in the overall context of spirituality. The other view seemed to exclude spirituality. The Marxist as well as the Freudian view declared that religion was the opium of the people or an illusion; religion or spirituality kept people from engaging in the issues of the day and fighting against injustice. Often the institutions of spirituality were in alliance with the forces of authoritarian conservatism and social repression. The spiritual point of view seemed to counsel patience; the affairs of the world were in the hands of forces greater than human beings—a higher power, if not specifically God. The political point of view counseled urgency—"If not you, who? If not now, when?"

The day of the campus demonstration came. With apprehension, but with "revolutionary courage," as we called it then, our small band marched into Northridge Hall. To dramatize the event, we supplemented our parking lot theme with "The New Spirit of '76." Three people marched in front of the demonstrators: one playing the flute, another the drum, and the third holding the flag. I was the one holding the flag. As we marched, I noticed something curious. The signboard in the promenade hallway announced something like, "Welcome Congressmen," and gave the room number where a committee meeting of the Indiana State Legislature was scheduled. I gave the notice slight thought as we proceeded.

Before I knew quite what was happening, a figure dressed in a dark business suit ran out of the crowd and tried to grab the flag from my hands and a tussle ensued. Other dark-suited figures arrived and the SDS students pressed onward toward the building. The president of the South Bend campus appeared and valiantly yelling above the crowd, told us that we needed to break up the demonstration. In those days, the president of this campus was well liked and respected. With what I suspect may have been a measure of relief at seeing a way out of this melee, we complied.

This became a major I.U.–South Bend incident. The dark-suited figures were the state legislature committee members that were meeting on campus the day of the demonstration. When they learned that I was not a student radical, but a faculty member—a faculty radical, let us say—they strongly expressed their opinion to the administration that I be removed from my position. Many of the students and faculty were outraged by such a demand and rallied to my defense. The issue was debated in the faculty senate and a party was held where I was the cause célèbre and guest of honor.

I later became aware of another interesting coincidence. It seems that a student in one of my psychology classes was also the daughter of one of the disgruntled congressmen. She had assured her father that I did not speak against the war in my class and she asserted that my teaching in the classroom was beyond criticism. That may have put a damper on the congressmen's ire and the intention to have me removed from the faculty.

Despite the congratulations and cheers from my supporters, I was acutely aware of the role the congressmen's presence played in making this the issue that it was: the attention and notoriety concerning me, as well as causing more public discussion of the war issue at the university. Had it not been for the reaction of these congressmen, the demonstration may well have been a bust and perhaps seen as a silly, adolescent dramaturgy—with me being the grown-up adolescent as well as one of the instigators. It seemed that no one else saw the coincidence. Many thought that it was brilliant timing of our demonstration. But I could not overlook the unintentional synchronicity.

I came to realize how the attention I received by being in the center of this local political tempest satisfied my ego. I sensed, rather suddenly, that I had an unconscious need to be recognized and lauded and that at least some part of my political activism was driven by this need. I recognized this same need in other activists and political participants of all stripes. It was a sudden lesson in the role of the unconscious needs of the ego and how it plays a starring role in political activity. This is not to say that this need discredits or eliminates the value and significance of politics any more than it would of art or any other public human activity, but the issue of ego and power is certainly central to politics.

With this realization, I sensed that Meher Baba's hand was behind all of this, that my personal lesson in the affair was brought about by him for my edification. It was a startling sensation. It meant that there was a guiding force behind all phenomena, including human events—that the Avatar/Christ was the same as this guiding force. On the other hand, I was a psychologist and I knew that the experience of a directing force behind events was consistent with paranoid schizophrenia. Indeed, as an intern at Connecticut Valley Hospital, I examined patients with various forms of such belief systems. So what was going on? Was this an insight into the essential nature of things, or was I having a mental breakdown? I naturally preferred the former alternative.

I marveled at how my inner questioning concerning serving "two masters" was so dramatically and clearly answered. Not on an intellectual level, as I might have expected, but through an unfolding and seemingly spontaneous experience of intense energy and feeling. I suddenly understood that if God exists, the political must, of course, be below God. For the first time in my life, I felt that God may indeed exist. I was curious as to how the phrase about two masters had occurred in my mind in the first place. Because I did not read the Bible, I did not recognize the correlation. Later, I learned that the biblical metaphor of the two masters referred to the choice between God or mammon[6] (wealth), and that suggestion was to have further significance several years later when I worked in the field of economics.

After the faculty Senate debate, the school administration decided to censure me, but not to fire me. At spring break, I went to New York City where I was born and grew up and where my parents were. I planned to attend a Meher Baba meeting that was scheduled to be held in the city and also visit a South Bend friend of mine who was now living in the East Village—the East Coast equivalent of the countercultural Haight-Ashbury district in San Francisco. I wanted to tell my friend that God really existed and that he had previously taken human form as Rama, Krishna, Buddha, Jesus, Mohammed, and now as Meher Baba.

On the way to New York, I read for the first time a Discourse by Meher Baba entitled, "The Problem of Sex."

> Like everything else in human life, sex comes to be judged through the opposites, which are the necessary creations of the limited mind. Just as the mind tries to fit life into a scheme of alternatives—such as joy or pain, good or bad, solitude or company, attraction or repulsion—in relation to sex it tends to think of indulgence and repression as alternatives from which there is no escape.[7]

Meher Baba then talks about the state of inner freedom, which is a life that is free from either of these ultimately dissatisfying opposites. In practical terms, he says that:

> It should be borne in mind that the life of freedom is nearer to the life of restraint than to the life of indulgence (though in quality it is essentially different from both).[8]

One thing this means is that promiscuous behavior is to be avoided, as this leads to inner binding and not freedom.

Sex is a sensitive and subtle issue that arouses some of our deepest passions and reactions. Often what one says about it is readily subject to misunderstanding. I hesitate to give my own interpretation of what Meher Baba says on these matters and prefer to quote directly from him. That is not easily done because there is the question of selection from a fairly substantial body of material. All of Meher Baba's words and counsel about sex have been written down, but some material exists only in verbal form related by Meher Baba to various individuals in personal discussions and passed on by those disciples who lived with him.

An acquaintance, who was inquiring about Meher Baba, read this same Discourse and promptly lost his interest in Baba. I remember him saying to me, "Sex is not a problem." Reading this Discourse delivered a jolt to my contemporary value system and lifestyle. It was like the message about drugs. Meher Baba spoke against indulgence in a way that managed to get my assent. In this regard, his effect was different from any other previous counsels of restraint and abstinence that I had encountered.

When I arrived at my friend's "pad" in the East Village, I found that he had stepped out, but a couple of his friends, or roommates, or just "crashers" were

MEHER BABA'S LOVE FOR ANIMALS WAS ALWAYS EVIDENT. ALWAR RAJASTHAN, FEBRUARY 8, 1938, DURING THE BLUE BUS TOUR.

there and invited me in. While waiting, I picked up a book of poetry and turned to a sexual poem. It was written by a woman who began by saying that her lover had lost interest in her. One day he said to her, "You're different" and this "you're different" was arousing to him. Midway through the poem, I put the book aside. Influenced by Meher Baba's words, I, myself, did not want to get aroused, something I would not have done in the past.

Suddenly, I began to feel a welling up inside of me that came from my heart area. It felt like a fountain had opened. What came out of this fountain was a sensation of love, but it was a pure love and did not have the sexual elements that I had always associated with love. I had never had a feeling like this before. I thought, "Ah, so this is Meher Baba's love." *Meher Baba's love*. That was his essential nature—as God is love, and Love must love. And he had said, "Not only in this incarnation, but every time I come, I stress that love is the remedy," and, "I am the Ocean of Love. I have only love to give and all I want is love."

I came to New York believing in the possibility that Meher Baba was God, and that is what I wanted to tell my friend—to deliver the Good News. This experience of spiritual love happened again in perfect timing, like an ultimate confirmation, strengthening my belief just before I planned to announce it in a public way for the first time.

My friend had been a student on the I.U.–South Bend campus and had been active in SDS. When he returned, I began by telling him about the events of the demonstration and its aftermath, which naturally he was eager to hear about. Then I proceeded to tell him about the coincidences and about Meher Baba. I was surprised that his reaction was not what I expected; naively I thought that in some way his reaction would match my own. Instead, I found he was not interested in what I told him and my interpretation of the coincidences left him unimpressed. This was my first awareness that the news about the Avatar's reappearance on earth was not automatically believed upon the telling.

Perhaps I should not have been surprised, but it took a long time after that for me to understand what was involved. To realize or, let us say, to accept that Baba is the Avatar is momentous. If it is true, can there be anything bigger? Maybe it's too big. Or it needs to be put on hold. Someone receiving the message may not necessarily be ready to deal with it further at that given time. Their focus and what is important to them may be elsewhere. As I was beginning to learn, readiness is everything in the matter of the divine and readiness means timing. My time had come. Nevertheless, the significance of the Avatar's advent is that the world's time has come and it is the purpose of this book to present and explore this event.

Meher Baba explained that it is not important to the real master whether one believes in him or not. What does matter is the disciples' integrity of purpose and commitment to live by truth, whatever they take that truth to be. Meher Baba said, "The Master is unconcerned whether the disciple doubts him or has faith in him. What he tests is whether the disciple is or is not sincere and wholehearted in his spiritual search and pursuit." This is not to say that belief or faith is unimportant, rather that what is needed is "living faith." Meher Baba makes this distinction:

> Living faith, on the other hand, has the most vital and integral relation with all the deeper forces and purposes of the psyche. It is not held superficially; nor does it hang, like mere intellectual beliefs, in the periphery of consciousness. On the contrary, living faith becomes a powerful factor that reconstructs the entire psyche; it is creatively dynamic.[9]

At the time, I had no understanding of this issue. With my experience of a "movement" as the way society changed, I expected the news of Meher Baba to spread like wildfire and transform the world—a Meher Baba movement. After all, the world seemed to be in desperate need of a transformation. This need seemed so obvious to me. If there was a God and he could descend on earth when he was needed most, it certainly seemed like the time for a movement was at hand.

When I returned to South Bend to finish out the semester of teaching, I decided to resign my position for the coming year. I felt that the incident surrounding the campus demonstration would most likely influence my future on that campus and I wanted to finish my Ph.D. With money I had saved from teaching and, for the first time in my life, no plans or expectations for the future, I headed down to Myrtle Beach, South Carolina, to the Meher Baba Spiritual Center.

To understand the significance of the Center and its unique founding, the story of Baba's life needs to be narrated. After all, Meher Baba's claim to be the Avatar must at the minimum rest upon such an examination. So we turn to that story first.

·3·3·3·3·3·3·3·3·3·3·3·3·3·3·3·

HIS LIFE

He who knows does not speak.

LAO TZU

There have been two comprehensive biographical accounts of Meher Baba's life published since the 1960s, each a series of several volumes. *Glimpses of the God-Man* by Bal Natu has six volumes beginning with Meher Baba's life in 1943, the year that Bal Natu first heard about Meher Baba, and continuing to April 1955. The second series is one of the most remarkable and complete biographies ever written about anyone. *Lord Meher*, originally published as *Meher Prabhu*, was written in Hindi by Bhau Kalchuri shortly after Meher Baba dropped his body in 1969. The expected twenty-volume set is being continuously translated into English and published year by year.

Meher Baba's life was extensively documented and published. One of the reasons for this is because Meher Baba requested that people close to him take notes and keep diaries of their experiences. Others wrote on their own volition. *Lord Meher* is nearly a day-by-day account. Therefore, to questions such as, "Was Meher Baba really totally silent?" the answer is "certainly." Meher Baba was almost never alone, and even while he slept at night, there was a watchman nearby. There is little doubt that Meher Baba did not utter a word after he began his silence in 1925. All his actions and non-actions were carefully noted and documented.

Meher Baba's father, Sheriar Mundegar, was born in 1853 into the ancient Zoroastrian religion in what was then Persia. Despite his Zoroastrian background, Sheriar would often visit a Muslim spiritual master, which was puzzling to his fanatical Muslim neighbors because at that time the Zoroastrians were persecuted by the Muslim majority.

In his teens, Sheriar left home to further his spiritual search. At the age of twenty, he emigrated to India, as had many others of his faith, and joined an older sister who lived in Bombay (now Mumbai). Later, he moved about one hundred miles east of Bombay to Poona (now Pune).

In India, Sheriar lived as a wandering dervish and did not intend to marry, but his sister constantly implored him to get married, raise a family, and live a normal life in the community. In 1892, he finally agreed and married Shireen, a girl from a Poona Zoroastrian family.

Shireen was educated and described "as intelligent as she is fair." Sheriar, on the other hand, had not been schooled and, in order to raise his family, taught himself to read and to write. He eventually learned four languages and became known as a poet and a singer. Meher Baba later spoke of his father's remarkable life saying, "There was none like him. It was because of him that I was born as his child."

Merwan Sheriar Irani, the birth name of Meher Baba, was born on February 25, 1894, the second of six children. (The surname Irani indicates that Iran is the family homeland.) Although Shireen was practical minded and not as overtly spiritual as Sheriar, she had some unusual dreams during the period preceding Merwan's birth and during his infancy. While in the hospital awaiting his birth, she saw a glorious person, shining like the sun, sitting in a chariot as thousands of people passed by gazing at him in his radiance. Several months after Merwan's birth, she was frightened by her dream of a goddess, a *deva*, in a green sari rising out of the family well and saying to her, "Give me your son."

Despite these dreams, Merwan's childhood was relatively normal and happy, although he was somewhat precocious. He began walking before his first birthday, and his mother was challenged to keep him contained and safe. He was an attractive and charming child, good hearted but mischievous, and family and neighbors took pleasure in looking at and playing with him.

He would sneak coins from his father's pockets and give them to beggars, who then would come knocking at the door. Those who knew Merwan during his early school years called him "a good student . . . a good sportsman . . . a respectful son . . . a model child . . . an excellent singer . . . a high idealist . . . compassionate to the downtrodden . . . a moralist . . . a purist . . . a lover of poetry . . . possessor of a gifted mind . . . a pragmatist," and above all, "soft-hearted."[1]

He attended St. Vincent's High School, which was considered the best high school in Poona. It was run by missionaries but, unlike most Roman Catholic schools, religious instruction was not mandatory. Discipline, however, was strict, and punishment for mischief often meant strikes with a cane.

Merwan liked poetry, literature, and writing. At fifteen, a story of his was published in the British monthly magazine, *Union Jack*.

Later, under the pseudonym *Huma*, his poems were published in several Bombay newspapers.

In 1911, he entered Deccan College in Poona, where the British poet and writer Edwin Arnold once taught. Arnold was the author of *The Light of Asia*, published in 1879, which was an account of the Buddha. *The Light of Asia* gained substantial popularity in English-speaking countries even though Arnold was criticized for being sympathetic to a "heathen" religion.

Deccan College was close to Merwan's home, and he traveled to and from school on his bicycle. He immediately reaffirmed the promise of his high school years; he was admired as a student and active in sports, particularly cricket.

In 1913, during his sophomore year, all that changed.

Hazrat Babajan, an old woman who was regarded as a saint by many in the local Muslim community, had her "seat"—a place under a tree—alongside the road Merwan used to travel to college. She was called *Hazrat*, the Muslim name of veneration for a spiritual teacher, and was reputed to have been born between 1790 and 1800, which in 1913, would make her an incredible 120 years old.

Merwan knew who she was, but as a nineteen-year-old student, had no occasion to pay any attention to her. One day in May, however, as he rode by on his bicycle, she beckoned for him to come over to her. Out of respect he did so, and when he came close she embraced him and tears streamed down her cheeks as she said, "My beloved son, my beloved son." Meher Baba later said that he felt a blissful current going through his body during the embrace. After that day, he came often to spend time with her under her tree.

One evening in January 1914 as he was about to leave, Hazrat Babajan held his face between her hands and kissed him in the center of his forehead. At that moment, he almost lost consciousness and mechanically walked home.

His mother found him in bed the next morning, staring outward in a sightless daze. Merwan behaved like an automaton for nine months. As this state continued, his upset and worried mother took him to various doctors in Poona, to no avail. She also confronted Babajan, and to Shireen's consternation and anger, Babajan repeated that Merwan was *her* son and that he would one day shake the world.

Sheriar's awareness of his son's spiritual destiny may have somewhat eased the situation. During Sheriar's wandering as a dervish, he had heard an inner voice telling him that what he was seeking he would find in his son. Perhaps this spiritual message induced Sheriar to accept marriage when it was eventually thrust on him.

Merwan never resumed life as a college student. Babajan later told followers that she had stationed herself at that place in Poona because of Merwan. Meher Baba later explained that this kiss from Hazrat Babajan removed the veil of normal and ordinary consciousness that covered him as he was growing up, and he had plunged suddenly into the Beyond.

At the end of this nine-month period, Merwan intuitively began to travel, but his journeys were far from random. In April 1915, he traveled by train to a village about thirty miles south of Poona and asked to see a spiritual master, Narayan Maharaj. In contrast to Babajan, who was always under her tree no matter what the weather, some of Narayan's wealthy followers had built an ornate throne of silver for him. When Merwan arrived, Narayan came down from his throne, took Merwan gently by the hand, and led him back to the throne to sit. Merwan stayed with Narayan overnight and then returned to Poona.

A few days after this visit, Merwan spoke to several young men who had been friends since boyhood, saying, "Come with me. I am going to meet certain very great saints. They are very holy. The men I will let you meet with me all belong to God."[2]

Merwan then went north of Poona to meet Tajuddin Baba, a holy person of the district who, in his youth, was thought to be mad. Many thought this was certainly true after Tajuddin walked naked across the tennis court of an upper-crust British family, an incident that caused his confinement to a mental asylum. Eventually the overseer of the asylum recognized Tajuddin's spiritual status, became a devoted disciple, and released Tajuddin.

As Merwan approached Tajuddin, the fragrance of roses was in the air, for this is what Tajuddin was holding in his hands. Tajuddin got up, moved toward Merwan, waved the roses over his head and around his face, and said, "My heavenly rose."

Later Baba explained that each personage that he visited was more than a saint; each was a *Sadguru*, a "Perfect Master," one who has completed the journey of consciousness and has become a fully God-realized being. As Baba later explained, there are five Perfect Masters in the world at any one time, although they are not readily known to the world at large, and they almost always exist in the East. When the Avatar is born into the world, his appearance is precipitated by these Perfect Masters. They and the Avatar are one in perfect consciousness, but each has a different role and function.

The Avatar plays a larger worldwide spiritual role. Meher Baba later said that because his is the last incarnation of the Avatar in this cycle of time, his work and its effects will be on the widest scale of all. It was not a coincidence, but spiritually arranged, that all five Perfect Masters were found in close proximity to Merwan's birthplace: Hazrat Babajan, Narayan Maharaj, Tajuddin Baba, Sai Baba, and Upasni Maharaj. These last two Perfect Masters were to play the greatest role in Merwan's coming into his destined mission as Avatar of the Age.

Probably the most widely known and revered spiritual master of India was Sai Baba of Shirdi, who at this present time, many years after his death in 1918, far surpasses the populace's knowledge, even in India, of Meher Baba. In fact, a European scholar of Eastern religious thought and a biographer of Sai Baba of Shirdi only refers to Meher Baba as "an important figure of the Sai Baba movement."[3]

When Merwan came to see Sai Baba, the latter was on his way back from attending a call of nature. This most earthly of human acts was always celebrated by Sai's followers as a great occasion with a large procession and a band playing. As Sai Baba was about to pass by, Merwan, in an act of complete prostration, stretched full length on the ground in front of Sai Baba. Seeing him, Sai Baba called out one word in a deep voice, *"Parvardigar,"* which means *Preserver of Creation* or *Avatar* in Persian.

Following that meeting, Merwan was directed to travel a short distance to a small temple where Upasni Maharaj, the leading disciple of Sai Baba, stayed. In 1915, Sai Baba brought perfection to Upasni, now a Perfect Master, the fifth of the Age, and the last that Merwan visited. This visit to Upasni was a longer stay because Upasni supplied the major work that fully brought Merwan into his Avataric role.

On the surface, the first meeting between Merwan and Upasni Maharaj seemed to have been less than congenial. When Upasni saw the young man approaching him, he picked up a stone and hurled it at him with great force. This act had great spiritual significance. The stone struck Merwan on the forehead and drew blood in the same spot where Babajan had kissed him. As Bhau Kalchuri writes in *Lord Meher*, this was the first blood that the Avatar, the Messiah, would shed for the world.

Meher Baba said that the impact of this stone, especially on an inner level, began the process that ended the dazzlement induced by Babajan's kiss, and brought him back to function as a world-oriented and "normal" human being. This process and the work with Upasni lasted about seven years.

YOUNG MEHER BABA IN TURBAN. POONA, 1917.

In January 1922, Upasni said to him, "Merwan, you are the Avatar and I salute you." With a handful of disciples, Merwan, now given the name *Meher Baba*, "Compassionate Father," departed from his long-term tutorship with Upasni and began his work in and for the world.

Meher Baba's first disciples were either boyhood friends, who recognized his new status, or disciples directed by Sai Baba and Upasni Maharaj to go with Meher Baba. Later that same year, Meher Baba's group had grown to forty-five and comprised a range of religions and ages, some of them considerably older than their twenty-seven-year-old spiritual teacher.

In the spring of 1922, Meher Baba told his group of disciples that they would undertake a foot journey from Poona to Bombay and remain in Bombay for a year. He asked each of them to consider whether they were prepared to give up all of their previous attachments to the world and undertake such an arduous and dangerous expedition. The attendant danger was possible arrest by the British for being anti-empire revolutionaries. The previous year, Mahatma Gandhi had been jailed with a six-year prison term. All organized bands of wandering men were highly suspect. Claiming they were spiritual aspirants would be viewed with suspicion by the British authorities, but with faith in their young leader they set off. In early June, they arrived safely in Bombay and began to renovate a large residence that they had rented on a year's lease.

They named their new home *Manzil-e-Meem*, "House of the Master." Those disciples who expected Manzil to be a typical or traditional Indian ashram, with the standard spiritual disciplines of meditation and yoga, were in for a surprise. Instead of these practices, they found themselves dealing with an austere and rigorous life: going to bed and rising early; doing carpentry and masonry work on the house; taking various jobs in the city to support themselves; and recreation consisting only of games, outings, and other mundane activities. This clean, healthy, ordinary life, however, was suffused with an increasing awareness of the spirituality and joy that was inherent in everyday living.

Meher Baba referred to his disciples as *mandali*, which means circle. Later, he referred to his followers with the word *lovers*, meaning lovers of him as God in human form. Other words he retained but endowed with new developed meaning were *Avatar* and *sanskara*. Sometimes translated as "ritual," Baba used *sanskara* to mean impressions.

Bhau Kalchuri summarizes some of the other important aspects of this early stay in Bombay:

In Manzil-e-Meem, they had also accepted being away from their homes and thus remained detached from their families. They were given the opportunity of living with men of different religions and communities—something none of them had ever done before. In Meher Baba's comraderie, they were inspired to shed the various individual differences, prejudices and respective likes and dislikes, for the general benefit and welfare of all. During this phase of their discipleship, Meher Baba prepared the mandali for future strenuous training which would not have been possible without having spent these preliminary months living with him in Manzil-e-Meem.[4]

Baba's unique way of unexpectedly changing plans became evident during this period. Baba told the mandali that they would live in Bombay for a year and, indeed, the Manzil building had been let for that period of time. After a difficult renovation to meet their needs and with two months left in the lease, Baba surprisingly instructed them to disband the home and move to Ahmednagar, a moderately sized town 120 miles west of Bombay. From Ahmednagar, Baba took the mandali about six miles away and settled in an abandoned British military base, using the few remaining buildings and constructing others. This site came to be called *Meherabad*, "Meher flourishing." Despite Baba's many travels and different living situations in the future, Meherabad came to be the central home base to which he always returned.

The mandali may have missed doing yoga while in the Bombay dwelling, but Baba aptly called their work *Gamela yoga*, "the yoga of labor." While in Bombay, Baba himself lived more austerely than the mandali. He often fasted—for months at a time on liquids alone—and later on in the Ahmednagar area, lived in a man-made cave, underground in a pit. Despite this strict discipline, he had extraordinary energy. Waking before the others, he sang and danced in the dawn and roused them to their tasks. He ground the group's daily grain and tended to the ill and poor in the surrounding area. At one time, Baba explained that he "never fasted" in the sense that saints and yogis do in order to deny their bodies and build their spiritual powers. Rather, he was engaged in spiritual work that made it physically impossible for him to accept food, even though weakness and suffering under such conditions were felt as intensely by him as by any ordinary person.

At Meherabad, Baba had a cramped boxlike table structure built and would stay inside it for long lengths of time. During this period, he was involved in writing a book in longhand that contained previously unrevealed spiritual secrets. The manuscript was locked in a steel box that Baba kept with him when he traveled.

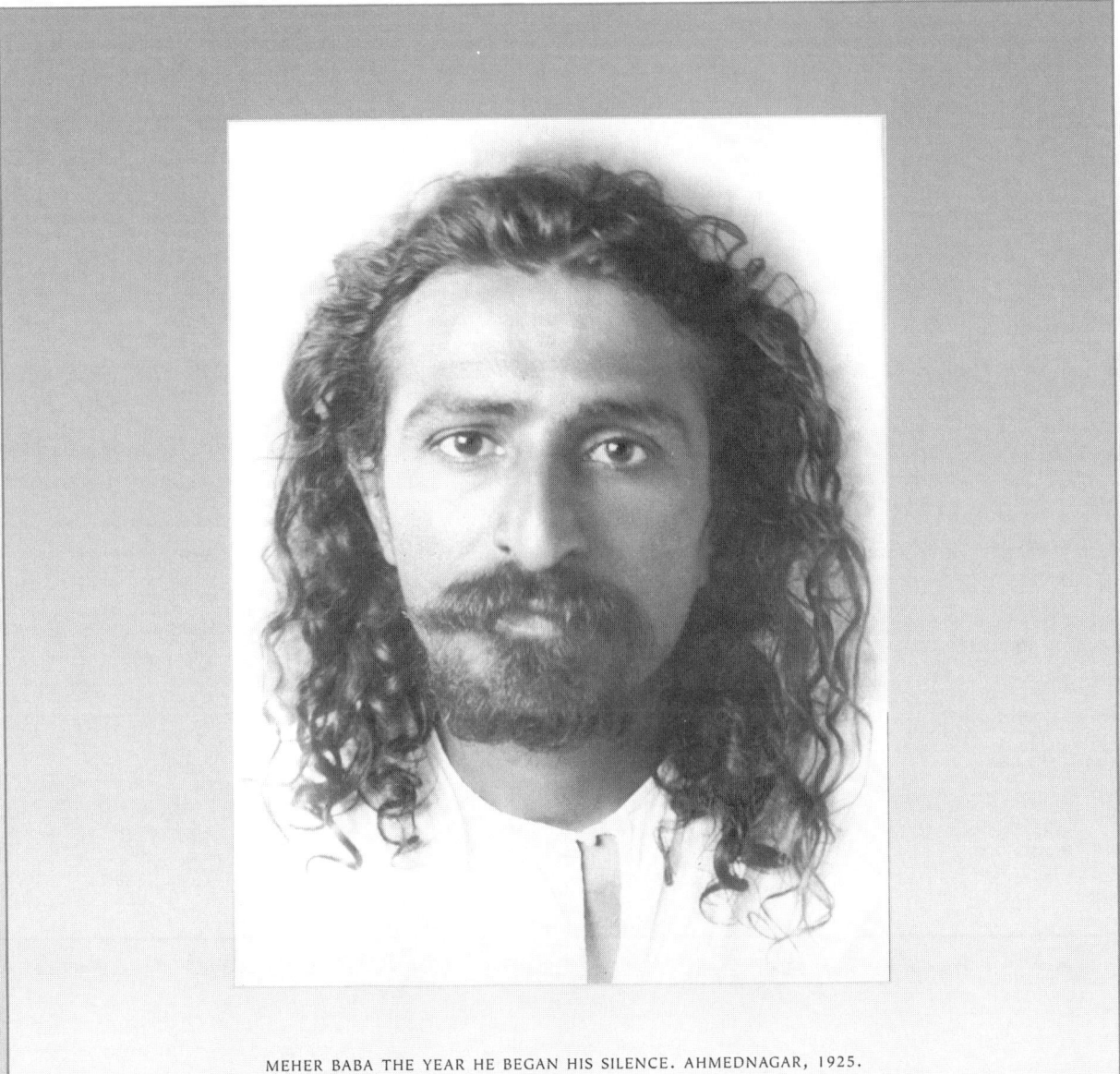

MEHER BABA THE YEAR HE BEGAN HIS SILENCE. AHMEDNAGAR, 1925.

Late in the evening of July 9, 1925, Meher Baba told the mandali that he would keep silence for a time, perhaps for as long as a year, beginning the next day. The mandali complained, "If you do not speak, how can you teach us?" Baba replied, "I have come not to teach, but to awaken."

On July 10, his silence began. In place of speaking, he used a writing board or a slate. Near the end of that first year, Baba wrote that his silence would continue beyond the year. At that time, the mandali could not have conceived that Meher Baba's silence would endure for over forty years. In January 1927, he abandoned writing and wrote only his signature on necessary documents such as his passport.

Instead of the slate, he used the laborious method of an English alphabet board to spell out, letter by letter, what he wanted to say. Slowly at first and later more extensively, Baba developed his own language of hand gestures that close mandali translated. In 1954, Baba abandoned the alphabet board and relied solely on hand gestures.

Some indication of the meaning of Baba's silence, as well as his progressive abandonment of the usual outward means of communication, is given in his last message on the alphabet board:

There is no reason at all for any of you to worry. Baba was, Baba is, and Baba will also be eternally existent. Severance of external relations does not mean the termination of internal links.

It was only for establishing the internal connections that the external contacts have been maintained until now. The time has now come for being bound in the chain of internal connections.[5]

Baba's elimination of outer methods of communication seemed to emphasize, as he continually did from 1925 on, that he was preparing to break his silence and utter the "one Word" to signal his public manifestation and precipitate the world transformation.

Baba often said not to worry. In several extended messages he said that worry is one of the main impediments to the advancement of the spiritual life and the attainment of personal happiness. From the 1930s on, this message was summarized by him in the phrase "Don't Worry, Be Happy." In the late 1960s, when I first heard this phrase, I saw it as Baba's own inimitable and light way of putting things; it sounded rather la-di-dah. Little did I know what was to become of this phrase.

In 1927, a new phase of Baba's work began when he opened a free children's school in Meherabad. Spiritual instruction was given in addition to academic subjects. Initially, it was called the Meher Ashram; when older students were added, it was renamed the Hazrat Babajan High School. As with all of Meher Baba's work, the school featured a mix of young people from different religions, nationalities, classes, and castes. The school was undoubtedly the most advanced in India. As Baba made clear from the beginning, spirituality was not verbal or intellectual concepts, but everyday experience seen in a new light and trying to see the one in the many. It was also learning the value and meaning of tolerance for others who are outwardly different from oneself.

When various children at the school began to have unusual experiences (such as swooning, apparently losing contact with this world and experiencing worlds beyond) reminiscent of Baba's own experience after the kiss from Babajan, Baba put these children in a special section called *Prem Ashram*, "the ashram of love." A detailed and enchanting account of these schools, *Sobs and Throbs,* was written by Ramjoo Abdulla, one of Baba's mandali.

The Meher Ashram, which began with ten or eleven students, had grown to over a hundred two years later. Despite a few interesting crises, the school was a thriving, successful institution. One incident occurred when a father pulled his son out of the school because of religious mixing. Several times the boy escaped from his home in Bombay and made his way back, a journey of 120 miles, to Meherabad. Despite its success, Baba announced in 1929 that the school would close. Everything would be shut down, and the children would go back to their homes and their regular schools. Again, Baba appeared to suddenly change plans with no apparent or logical reason.

Baba explained that the nature of his work was different from what people would ordinarily expect. His work was not to establish institutions or a new religion. He said that his outer activities, such as setting up free clinics, working with the poor, opening an ashram and schools, although good in themselves, were used by him as scaffolding for his real work, which was inner and directed toward changing the consciousness of humanity. When his inner purpose was accomplished, the scaffolding of the outer institution, program, or plan was taken down.

"Love calls me to the West" were the words in a telegram that Meher Baba sent to Englishman Meredith Starr in 1931. Starr was one of the first Westerners to visit India and meet Meher Baba, and how he came to meet Baba is perhaps indicative of Baba's enigmatic ways. During the heyday of the schools, Baba sent a close mandali, Rustom Irani, to England to find English children who would attend. Rustom was unsuccessful; he was not able to recruit a single child for the school. Besides, he found England lonely, cold, and generally inhospitable and may well have wondered why Baba was sending him on such a fruitless mission. In the course of his visit to England, however, he told a number of people about Meher Baba. One was Meredith Starr, who strongly felt that there was something special about Rustom's master and wanted to meet Meher Baba. In 1929, he went to India and stayed with Baba for six months. When Starr returned to England, he published the first book in the West about Meher Baba, a book of poems called *Arrows of Flame*. He also established a retreat in Devonshire that Baba promised to visit.

Meher Baba left for England on a ship, the *Rajputana*, in 1931, two years earlier than Starr had expected. The coincidental circumstances of this trip are quite interesting: Baba told his mandali several years before this trip that Gandhi would one day meet with him. As Baba set sail on the *Rajputana*, it turned out to be the ship on which Gandhi was also traveling to England for the Round Table Conference on the future status of the British colony of India. In order to play his political cat-and-mouse game with the British, Gandhi had not decided until the last minute to go.

Jamshed Mehta, the mayor of Karachi, was a Baba lover and had arranged for Meher Baba and the mandali's passports, so he knew that Baba was traveling on the *Rajputana*. Mehta was also an acquaintance of Gandhi, and when he discovered that Gandhi had boarded the same ship, he cabled Gandhi on board and urged him to meet with Baba. Gandhi knew of Baba, and had read some articles about him in an early Indian publication, *The Meher Message*. Gandhi had also met with Upasni Maharaj after Baba had instructed one of his mandali to send an Upasni biography to Gandhi.

On September 8, 1931, Gandhi met with Meher Baba for the first time in Baba's cabin. Present was his secretary and Baba's, Nariman Dadachani. Gandhi said to Baba, "I have read much about you and wanted to see you one day when God willed it; but I never expected it to be so soon." Interestingly, when Gandhi finally decided that he would attend the conference, he had said to reporters before embarking, "I must go to London with God as my only guide."

The meeting with Gandhi lasted for several hours and ranged over topics from spirituality to politics and the issues of the upcoming conference. When he was told of the book that Baba had written by hand before he began his silence, Gandhi asked if he could read it. Baba told him that no one had read the manuscript, but he would select a few pages for Gandhi to read. The key to the steel box was in India, but Gandhi said that he could try to get the lock open and Baba gave him permission to do so. Thus, Gandhi was the only one to read any of that unpublished manuscript written by Meher Baba. To this day, it has not been published and its whereabouts is unknown.

Gandhi and Baba met two more days. At one point Gandhi asked Baba, "When will you break your silence? I am very eager to hear the first words you speak. Will you speak soon? I hope it won't be long. If your influence is so great that you can impress people so deeply without talking, I can imagine what you will do when you speak. You should speak soon!" Baba dictated in reply, "I am just waiting for that. I will speak soon. The time is near."[6]

Baba agreed to meet again with Gandhi in London on October 2, 1931. Some of the London papers referred to Baba as Gandhi's spiritual advisor or guru. But this was not correct. Gandhi spoke with Baba about staying with him as a disciple, but Baba said that Gandhi should only do this if he gave up politics.

This first trip in 1931 was one of thirteen trips that Baba eventually made to the West. He visited many countries around the world, often traveling incognito, and, with a few exceptions, the premise of these visits was to personally contact people who were drawn to Baba. Meher Baba said that his travels "laid cables in the unseen." There were three visits to the United States in the 1930s and three more in the 1950s.

Baba's visits were low key with little publicity. One exception was his visit to Hollywood in 1932. The 1932 summer Olympics coincided with Baba's arrival in Los Angeles and many reporters were in town. Baba's disciples arranged a press conference, and Baba delivered a powerful, extensive message. The first and the last paragraph are as follows:

So much has been said and written about the "Highest Consciousnesss" and God-realization that people are bewildered as to the right process and immediate possibility of attainment. The philosophical mind wading laboriously through such literature only ends by learning a few intellectual gymnastics. The Highest State of Consciousness is latent in all. The Son of God is in every man but requires to be manifested....

I eternally enjoy the Christ State of Consciousness, and when I speak, which I intend doing in the near future, I shall manifest my true self. Besides giving a general spiritual push to the whole world, I shall lead all those who come to me towards Light and Truth. This, in short, is my mission in the world.[7]

Meher Baba continued his visit in Los Angeles and proceeded with his work, but he confided to one of the mandali, "I am not happy here." He met numerous people connected with the film world including well-known actors and actresses Tallulah Bankhead, Gary Cooper, Virginia Bruce, and Cary Grant. All seemed to be moved by, and in many cases, entranced with him. He was invited to a gathering at Pickfair, the twenty-two room mansion of Mary Pickford and Douglas Fairbanks. Pickford, who was spiritually inclined, had written the book, *Why Not Try God?* While at the social, Baba dictated the following message:

> The whole universe and its structure, I have created. The universe is my cinema. But just as an audience becomes absorbed in witnessing a drama on the screen, and the film engages their emotions and sways their feelings by its influence, causing them to forget that it is not real—in the same way, the spectators of the world are charmed by this worldly film show, forgetting themselves and taking it to be real!
>
> So I have come to tell them that this worldly cinema in which they are absorbed is not real. I have come to turn their focus toward Reality. Only God is real, and everything else is a mere motion picture![8]

At a gathering of over 1,000 at the Knickerbocker Hotel, people stood in line to meet Baba in a side room and then filed out a different door for refreshments. Some of their comments were recorded:

> If Christ were alive today, he would look like him.
> What a divine glow on his face.
> He does not seem to belong to this world.
> Can any man be so beautiful?
> He is the living Christ!
> I feel like looking at him forever!
> I just cannot leave. For the first time in my life, I have seen divinity![9]

On June 4, Baba lunched with Marie Dressler, who had received the Academy Award for best actress the previous year. They were soon sharing stories and joking like old friends, and she said to him, "Baba, if you permit me, I would like to take you out to the woods and dance with you. And even if you want to speak a few words to me, I promise not to tell anyone." Baba replied on his alphabet board, "Before breaking my silence, it is essential for me to proceed to China. On my return, I will break my silence on July 13 at the Hollywood Bowl." Dressler said, "When you break your silence, I will be at your side."

Meher Baba had told his new Western mandali that he would break his silence in the Hollywood Bowl and a radio hookup was arranged. He proceeded to China, but once there he told his mandali that he would travel on to Australia and New Zealand and then back to India. He asked them to send a message to California that he was not going to break his silence in the Hollywood Bowl after all.

When this news was received in California, many were devastated and immediately dropped away from Baba, seeing him as a fraud. The stir that Baba caused with his visit to Hollywood was over and his name essentially vanished from sight. A few, however, kept their faith in him and continued to be among his close Western lovers.

One couple, Jean Adriel and Malcolm Schloss, had been instructed by Baba to have a gathering and to tell people about his imminent return from China and that he would break his silence. The evening of the party, they received the message that the Hollywood Bowl extravaganza was off. Out of deference to their hostess, they attended the party and the next day informed those involved of the disappointing (to say the least) news. They reported, "Overnight, practically all of the newly-made friends became ardent enemies!" But the next day a cable for them arrived saying, "I knew you two would not fail me. Love, Baba."

An English actor, Quentin Todd, who had accompanied Baba to the United States and initially arranged the Hollywood contacts, struggled with this rescission, but then thought, "No ordinary man would behave like this." Several years later when the agony of this time had passed, some of these Western disciples joined Baba in India, and he made them laugh at the absurdity of his silence being broken over a microphone in the Hollywood Bowl!

BABA WORKING WITH AND SERVING THE MAD AND THE MASTS.

In the 1940s, Baba's focus, sometimes to the exclusion of almost anything else, was his contact and work with those people in the East who are known as *masts* (pronounced "musts"). The masts were known as "God intoxicated" souls—people who were absorbed in God and thus had little or no concern for the mundane affairs of the world. Meher Baba referred to them as total and absorbed lovers of God, and he always displayed unceasing love and solicitude for them. They were people who, to one degree or another, appeared to the rest of the world to be mad or deranged. Some walked around naked. Others dressed in multiple layers of tattered clothing. (One of these, for example, was known as "twelve coats.") Some had metal wire wrapped around different parts of their body.

Often they would remain in one place for incredible lengths of time—weeks, months, years—hardly moving. Others constantly moved about, never seeming to remain stationary. Some essentially lived in latrines.

While one might wonder how those with such bizarre behavior could be anything but demented, Baba explained that if carefully observed, their inner spiritual status could be detected. For instance, in their presence, one might be unaccountably happy. Another time, their strange and often incoherent utterances might suddenly reveal something eerily coherent and of deep significance. This could be especially striking if they were near Baba. On October 14, 1946, when the mast Azim Khan Baba saw Meher Baba he said, "You are Allah. You brought forth the creation, and once in a thousand years you come down to see the play of what you have created."[10] Certain masts, the *jalali* or "fiery" types, when in a *jalali* mood, became fearsome and unapproachable by people who feared physical abuse.

Some mandali were skilled in their mast work with Baba and were referred to as "mast hunters." William Donkin, an English doctor who was extensively involved with Baba's mast work, kept remarkably detailed records; he essentially recorded every mast contact. Statistics show the scope of this work: the intensive period covered thirteen years from 1936 to 1949; there were about 20,000 mast contacts (many were repeats); virtually every part of India—every major city, many smaller ones, and hundreds of remote villages—were visited; and about 75,000 miles were traveled.

Donkin, a doctor, writer, and spiritually sensitive person in his own right, was the perfect individual to document this unprecedente and almost unfathomable spiritual work. The record was eventually published as an encyclopedic, anthropology-like study entitled, *The Wayfarers: Meher Baba with the God-Intoxicated*. Donkin wrote, "... only the imagination can bring to life the brief notes of so many contacts between Meher Baba, the Perfect One and these strange wayfarers on the path to the Infinite."[11]

BABA BATHES A LEPER. PANDHARPUR, NOVEMBER, 1954.

Donkin was attuned to the difference between the ordinary mad and the masts, and gave this capsule description: "They do not exhale any of that subtle antipathy that seems to emanate from the insane, but actually kindle a sense of harmony in one's self." And this despite the *jalali* aspects. The mandali understood that the reasons there were masts in India and a few other parts of the East and almost none in the West was because the East is where these souls chose to incarnate and India was a spiritually central place on Earth. Baba indicated that his work with the masts was both for their benefit as well as for the assistance he could get from them in his world-renewing mission. "I work for them, and they work for me," is how he sometimes put it. The mandali's part in assisting Baba often taxed their physical endurance to the limit—yet Baba's presence sustained them. Donkin relates a beautiful description of this effect:

> His physical presence and the brilliance of his leadership have that impossible quality of the philosopher's stone, that, by their magic touch, they transmute the base metal of the most commonplace routine into a treasure of loving service. This is perhaps an ornate way of describing something that is at once so real that one might think it easy to describe quite simply, and so transcendental that the spirit of it eludes the grasp of words. But this magic, this imponderable something, weaves itself like a golden thread into the fabric of everything that Baba does, and when the factual details of a phase of Baba's life are buried so deep in the ashes of one's mind to be almost forgotten, the memory of this splendid thing is there still.[12]

In 1949, Baba indicated the end of the thirteen-year-intensive phase of the mast work by announcing to the mandali that almost everything that was listed as in his possession was to be sold or given away. The list included land where ashram buildings had been constructed, houses, furniture, cars, small power plants, cattle, and so forth. Baba essentially never had any real personal wealth. In fact, he never touched money, except when giving it to the poor in symbolic amounts (symbolic of inner work in dealing with world poverty). His life was one of physical austerity, discomfort, hardship, and never indulgence. All money that seemed to come his way when it was needed was quickly used for his work. But with this announcement, even these minimal property ties were to be eliminated. He mysteriously said, "I am becoming *ghatt* (hardened), *naffat* (callous), and penniless. Remember the proverb *Nanga-se-khuda-bhi-darta-hai* (even God is afraid of the naked)."[13]

Why the reference to God in this way? Wasn't Meher Baba supposed to be God in human form? The answer soon became clear. Baba had been the Master. Now he was to play the role of the seeker.

The mandali were invited to join him in this new phase if they wished, but to do so they had to continue to obey him as their Master. He told them that they would lead a life of "hopelessness and helplessness" in which they would rely "wholly and solely upon God." It was to be a life of complete honesty. He termed it the "New Life." Before this time, he had been the Perfect Master; now he was to be the perfect seeker. The mandali were his "companions," and, in any public contact, they were to refer to him as their "elder brother."

Twenty companions joined Baba in the New Life. They traveled in a modified bus that was drawn by two bullocks—a New Life Caravan—as well as on foot. For a time, a colorful assortment of animals went with them, giving them the appearance of a small traveling circus. They lived with no thought for the morrow, which Baba described as living in "the active present." Everyday was a penniless fresh start. They begged for their food, with the phrase *Premsa Bhiksha Deejayi*, "Please give with love," written on their begging bowls. It was a life of hardship, but it was also a life of joy in freedom sustained by the company of their elder brother. Despite their hardships,

MEHER BABA WITH ENGLISH DISCIPLE, MARY BACKETT. NASIK ASHRAM, 1937.

Baba emphasized that they must strive to be cheerful and not give in to "moods"—another declaration of "don't worry, be happy."

Meher Baba defined the New Life in terms of four aspects: (1) the gypsy life, which meant wandering; (2) the begging phase; (3) *langoti*, which meant the life of the simplicity of the loincloth; and (4) the labor phase, which meant the everyday life of working (at times the companions took jobs and even started a small business manufacturing butter). Baba participated in all of this, and said that because he carried out the first three phases, others no longer needed to be engaged in them, and that one's ordinary life—that is, the labor phase—was now a spiritual path. He said that this was a life of complete dependence on God—a life of honesty, cheerfulness no matter what the conditions—a life of being natural. Meher Baba said, "This New Life will live by itself eternally, even if there is no one to live it."

Meher Baba, with the mandali, formally began the New Life on October 16, 1949, and ended it on February 13, 1951, and again went into extended seclusion. He called this seclusion work, "Man-O-Nash," the annihilation of the limited ego-mind. He said,

> Manonash results in this glorious state in which plurality goes and Unity comes, ignorance goes and Knowledge comes, binding goes and Freedom comes. We are all in this shoreless Ocean of Infinite Knowledge, and yet are ignorant of it until the mind—which is the source of ignorance—vanishes for ever; for ignorance ceases to exist when the mind ceases to exist.[14]

In messages and discourses, Baba explained that the development and acquisition of the ego-mind over the course of the evolutionary journey was necessary. The purpose of that journey, which is the journey of creation, is to develop full consciousness, which is achieved in the human form. But that achievement means that full consciousness that already exists in the human is covered over by the *sanskaras* (impressions) that were accumulated during creation and evolution. These impressions need to be eliminated, which means the elimination of the ego, and then full consciousness will shine forth in inherent glory. Nothing from outside needs to be acquired. All that is needed is to eliminate the false.

After this four-month seclusion, Baba, now fifty-eight, entered what he called "The Free Life." He had been the Master and then became the seeker. In this last phase, he was now "free." His age did not stop his activity; rather in some ways it increased. This became a period of public appearances, with Baba formally letting the world know that he was the Avatar, the world savior, the one expected and waited for. "I had to come and I have come," he said. "I am the Ancient One." Much like Christ's saying, "Before Abraham was, I am."

These announcements were given during a whirlwind tour through two areas of India—Hamirpur in the north, which Baba referred to as his "heart," and Andhra in the south, which he said was his "head." Even though Baba had made no public appearances since the early 1940s and had been doing all of his work incognito (known only to his small group of mandali and close lovers), many thousands, sometimes estimated at over 100,000, were drawn to him on these tours by the magnetism of his love. To be sure, not all became his devotees or lovers, but because of these tours, centers for him were established in India, and Meher Baba's presence as one who claimed to be the Avatar became public knowledge.

Awareness of Meher Baba spread outside India as Baba traveled to the West for the first time since the 1930s, visiting Europe, England, and Australia as well as the Center that was created for him in Myrtle Beach, South Carolina. Western Baba lovers were given the long-awaited chance to see and be with him again. A relatively small number of people, hearing about him for the first time, generally through others, were able to meet him. During these appearances, Baba explicitly said he was the Avatar "in every sense of the word." He also said that he would soon break his silence and that would be the signal for his "public manifestation." His manifestation would usher in a new world age, a "New Humanity," based on love, social harmony, and cooperation. He said, "Now is the time for all to know that I am God in human form," and "Love me, love, me, love me, for when I break my silence it will be too late." This latter statement apparently meant that when he broke his silence, there would no longer be any special charm in "coming to him." Some disciples wondered why Baba had not made similar appearances at an earlier age, when he was young, attractive, and looked like the classical conceptions of the Avatar or the Savior. These questions were part of the enigma of Baba's ways.

This issue of whether Baba could be the Avatar was more pronounced after Baba's two automobile accidents, one occurring in Prague, Oklahoma, on May 24, 1952 and the second in 1956 in Satara, India. In the first accident, his left side was badly damaged from head to foot, and his right side sustained even more extensive injuries in the second accident. In both accidents, mandali traveling with him were seriously hurt and one died instantly in the 1956 accident. Baba's appearances and announcements of being the Avatar continued during this period when, often, he could not walk and had to be carried around in a lift chair.

How could it be that one who was presumably the world Savior could not even save himself and others from the mundane disaster of car accidents? Whatever doubts these events might have caused his lovers, those who knew the details of Baba's life saw these events as intimate with and part of his work. In 1928, Baba had warned that a "personal disaster" would befall him. He had also indicated that he *must* spill blood on American soil as well as in the East. Like other apparently enigmatic statements by Meher Baba, these were noted and put aside.

Elizabeth Patterson, one of Baba's first U.S. disciples, was the driver of the car in the Oklahoma accident. She had met Meher Baba in Harmon-on-the-Hudson, thirty-five miles north of New York City, during his visit to the United States in 1932. During a walk with him in the woods one day, he picked a small pink flower and gave it to her. He then spelled on the alphabet board that she should always keep it, note the date, and someday she would know the meaning. She pasted it inside the front cover of her Bible and wrote down the date. Several years after the accident, she discovered the Bible while unpacking an old steamer trunk, and read the words on the cover, "Baba—May 24, 1932"—twenty years to the day before the Oklahoma accident. (The Bible and note are now displayed at the Center in Myrtle Beach.) Baba later indicated the significance of these accidents when he said that his "physical bones [were] broken so as to break the backbone of the material aspects of the machine age (*Kali Yuga*), while keeping intact its spiritual aspect."[15]

Baba said that in a new era of humanity, the material West and the spiritual East needed to come together to promote "a happy blending of the head and the heart." In November 1962, at sixty-eight, he held a *sahavas* (a period of companionship) in Poona, India, which was called the East–West Gathering. Approximately 3,000 lovers from the East joined 140 of his lovers from the West for four days of *darshan* (seeing and being) with Baba. The sahavas was held during a time of intense world political crisis. China had invaded Tibet and had launched its armies against India. On the other side of the world, the United States and the USSR were engaged in the Cuban missile crisis.

Following that sahavas, Meher Baba again went into seclusion, but like past seclusions, it was not a withdrawal *from* work but a withdrawal *into* work, referred to as his "Universal work," and seemed to be concentrated on inner planes. Correspondence with his lovers throughout the world was severely limited, and there were few meetings with visitors. There were exceptions, and one was a 1965 darshan for Easterners that lasted several days. From time to time, Baba referred to his continued suffering from the crippling affects of the accidents and the suffering of the world as being linked. All of this, he said, was in preparation for the breaking of his silence.

During this time, President John F. Kennedy, Senator Robert Kennedy, and Martin Luther King, Jr. were assassinated. The Vietnam conflict became a full-scale war and the Six-Day War between Israel and the Arab nations erupted. India, at odds with both China and Pakistan, experienced large-scale crop failure, famine, other natural disasters, and the death of its two leaders, Jawaharlal Nehru and Bahadur Shastri.

In the United States, the hippie movement, the anti-Vietnam protests, and the psychedelic drug era began—the 1960s counterculture. Despite his outward seclusion, Meher Baba issued warnings about the use of drugs and personally contacted Western lovers such as Rick Chapman in the United States. Chapman notes that despite Baba's forty-plus years of work in the world, thirteen trips to the West, and the establishment of centers like the one in Myrtle Beach, he did not begin to be recognized by the Western public at large until the 1960s when he spoke out against the use of drugs in the quest for expanded consciousness.

As described in Chapter 1, it was in that context that I first learned of Meher Baba.

At the Center —
Meher Baba's Home in the West

O Beauty so ancient and so new.

AUGUSTINE

I think that many people visit the Meher Spiritual Center in Myrtle Beach for the first time to check out Meher Baba, to learn more about him, to determine who he is. I went already believing, but had I been on the fence, visiting the Center would have swayed me.

The Center is located on 500 acres of beautiful, natural, virgin forest, marshlands, and wetlands, which are designated by South Carolina

MYRTLE BEACH GAZEBO.

as a wildlife sanctuary. The area includes a pristine lake and white-sand frontage on the Atlantic Ocean at Grand Strand Beach. The Center, which remains open even though Meher Baba is gone, is a place for those who know about him, or want to know more, come for a rest and retreat. The accommodations are simple cabins nestled among the trees. Cabins for families have their own kitchen, and other cabins share a large common kitchen. There are nature trails that weave through the woods, dotted with gazebos and similar resting places. Other buildings include a library, a meeting room, and Meher Baba's home in the West. The atmosphere is one of peace, stillness, and natural beauty.

NORINA MATCHABELLI AND ELIZABETH PATTERSON WITH BABA. RAHURI, 1937.

How did the Center come to be? In 1941, Meher Baba asked two Western women mandali, Norina Matchabelli and Elizabeth Patterson, who were living with him in India, to go to the United States to find property for a center. He told them that he wanted "a home in the West," where he could live and work and others would visit. He spelled out five conditions that the land for the center had to meet: (1) the climate should be equitable; (2) it should have more than ample water; (3) it had to be on virgin soil, never before built upon; (4) it should be land that could be tilled; and (5) it should be given "from the heart." This, of course, was quite a daunting task. How could they possibly find a place that could fill all of these conditions? But, as Meher Baba's mandali, they trusted him and were confident of his directions.

When they arrived in the United States, they thought that the natural place to look would be California, so that's where they began their search. Nothing turned up, however, that met Baba's requirements. Over a three-year period, they searched throughout the country, including visits to Wisconsin, Washington, and New Mexico—wherever there was a lead or mention of a site that might be a possibility. No suitable site was found.

During this period, having no luck finding a site for the center, the two visited Elizabeth's father, who lived in Myrtle Beach. While there, Elizabeth suddenly remembered a tract of land along the beach that her father owned. She had camped there years before and was surprised to find that she had completely forgotten about it. She and Norina inspected the property and found that it matched all four of the physical requirements stipulated by Meher Baba.

Elizabeth's father gave it to her as a gift, and she wrote to Baba, "You may be sure it will be 'given from the heart.' I am pleased to say that Father gave it to me 'from the heart' and knows the fact that it will be used for your spiritual and humanitarian purposes eventually." She continued, "We find a vast amount of work will have to be done in clearing the underbrush because with virgin land there are so many insects and crawling things—like the first day of Creation," and then also, "When Baba, whom you think is far off in India, projects an idea for a Center it comes to pass."[1] It is interesting to note that the land is the site of an ancient Native American trail along the coast that was known in colonial times as the King's Highway. Stagecoaches traveled this route and George Washington passed through it.

Elizabeth and Norina were called back to India to be with Baba in 1947, and using blueprints of the land, he selected the spot where they would build a brick house for him. It was expected that he would live there for considerable periods of time. Near a picturesque lagoon, inhabited by an occasional alligator, a small cabin was constructed that Meher Baba used for private interviews.

At the end of 1949, Baba indicated that he would come to Myrtle Beach in 1951 to stay for a year. This visit was delayed until April 1952 when Baba, with eleven of his mandali, arrived at the Center for the first time. One of the eleven was Katherine (Kitty) Davy, a Western mandali living in India with Baba during the search for land and construction of the Center. She knew some details about the Center project through letters and cables that went back and forth and "wondered what it was all about."

Meher Baba stayed at the Center for two weeks and then arranged for a car trip to the West Coast before returning to Myrtle Beach. It was during this trip that Baba had the first car accident. Elizabeth, who was the driver of the car, was seriously injured, and, as a result, Baba asked Kitty to stay and help at the Center, while he returned to India to finish convalescing. He asked that she remain at the Center until he called for her.

In 1956, when Baba visited for the second time, Kitty was still at the Center. Meher Baba's second visit lasted only six days, and again he asked Kitty to remain in the United States to help manage the Center with Elizabeth.

But few visitors came. In a letter to Baba's two closest women mandali in India, Mehera and Mani, Kitty wrote, "Yet, in spite of the lovely weather, I feel depressed because when I think of Baba coming here twice and the time Elizabeth and Norina have been here and I now for five years, there should be more love and faith here for Baba. Large numbers know of Baba and their number grows, I know; but where to look for that love and faith that mean so much to Baba. I just have to repeat those words, 'Neither he that planteth nor he that watereth but God that giveth the increase.' So, one must just wait. Results may not come with this generation down here."

Meher Baba returned again in May 1958 and stayed for twelve days, receiving visitors, having meetings, and so forth. Before leaving for India, he requested that there be more activity at the Center. Elizabeth asked him who could or would come, and she recalled that "Baba gave me a very illuminating smile, and said, 'Those who love and follow Me and those who know of Me and want to know more.'"[2]

In 1962, when Kitty next saw Baba in India at the East–West Gathering, he once more told her that he wanted her to stay in Myrtle Beach and help Elizabeth. Then, on her birthday in 1963, Baba sent her this cable:

BEING WHERE I WANT YOU TO BE
YOU ARE NEARER AND DEARER TO ME.
MY LOVE TO YOU TODAY AND ALWAYS.[3]

So the person who years ago had "wondered what it was all about," was wondering about a

BABA, SURROUNDED BY DEVOTEES, SPEAKS WITH DON STEVENS.
MEHER SPIRITUAL CENTER, MYRTLE BEACH, 1956.

location and work that was to be a major destiny of hers as a disciple of Meher Baba.

In October 1963, Kitty wrote to Baba's sister, Mani, and concluded her letter with these remarks, "Well, I must not bore you. Cannot think of anything amusing to say—unless it be the latest sensational news in many of the illustrated papers, that young students are experimenting with different types of pills and experiencing 'Union with God and Mysticism states' —can you believe it? Anything so absurd!"

What she didn't realize at the time was that this absurd situation would lead to a wave of new people discovering Meher Baba and the beginning of a marked increase in visitors to the Center.

That is where I came in.

When I met Kitty and Elizabeth in 1968, I knew only that they were two matronly ladies who had lived with Meher Baba in India. Each had a distinct personality. Elizabeth was austere, dignified, even regal. Kitty, on the other hand much like her nickname, was warm, personable, and profoundly interested in those she met and spoke with. I immediately liked them both and soon observed that all the close disciples of Baba were natural and human, each in their own way.

I met their assistant, Jane Haynes, a woman in her early forties, who first visited the Center shortly after Norina died in 1957. Jane, like Norina, had been an actress and a stage director and had moved to Myrtle Beach with the actress Zasu Pitts to open a regional theater. When I first met Jane, she was active in a project called "Happy Club," which invited children from the local black community to the Center once a week for a fun visit. Perhaps sensing my activist values, she took me with her when she visited several of these children from extremely poor families and invited me to attend the dedication of a playground in that neighborhood in which her teenage son, Charles, participated in the ceremony. I was overwhelmed with the pain of life and the vibrant love demonstrated by these followers of Baba. I sensed the inner message, "You see, this is the love that it takes to be really able to help people."

ELIZABETH PATTERSON AND KITTY DAVY. DILRUBA, 1976.

The atmosphere at the Center was one of beauty and spiritual peace that was evidently Meher Baba's. His house and his bedroom, although only open for a few hours a week, were special places. The little Lagoon Cabin was open all the time and was an intimate place to be with "him." When Meher Baba visited the Center and a larger number of people gathered for various events, The Barn was used.

The Center's directors and Baba lovers who were staying there were waiting for the next opportunity to see Baba. There had been talk about another visit since the East–West Gathering in 1962. But Meher Baba had been in seclusion since then—the longest period of seclusion yet. During this time period, Pete Townshend of the rock band The Who became a Baba lover. Townshend's rock opera, *Tommy*, was dedicated to Baba.

While in seclusion, Baba released statements that central to this work was his preparation to break his silence. Those in Myrtle Beach hoped that when Baba came out of seclusion, he would visit again. Some thought that he might break his silence in seclusion and everything would change. Some long-time Baba lovers hoped he would not break his silence so that he might come to Myrtle Beach again. Also at issue was his fragile, disabled condition—the result of the two automobile accidents. While visiting the Center ten years earlier, he had been carried everywhere in a lift chair with four people holding poles at each corner. Now Meher Baba was seventy-two years old. Could he even travel again?

At this time, in 1968, I unexpectedly felt impatient to see Baba. Strangely enough, although it had been over a year since I heard of and accepted Meher Baba as the Avatar, I had not been anxious to see him. Perhaps it was fear or an uncertainty of what my reaction would be if and when I did meet him. Furthermore, I believed that if he were God, He was present everywhere, as he had stated: "I am not this body; I am really everywhere. I use this body as a cloak to make myself visible to you." I didn't think I needed to see him; I just needed to be able to feel him wherever I was. I thought that seeing him might, in some way, blunt the fact of his omnipresence. And then, suddenly, all this changed. I felt an urgent desire to see him. I became concerned with and focused on his seclusion ending. Would it end in Myrtle Beach or India? Would I, could I travel to India?

JANE HAYNES. MEHER STUDIO, 1994.

I heard that a Baba lover, Nikos Colias, was preparing a small project at the World's Fair, in San Antonio, Texas. The theme of the fair was "Confluence Cosmos." Colias had set up a booth and was planning a daily program about Meher Baba that was to be presented at one of the fair's presentation theaters. As an activist, this project appealed to me. Here was a chance to spread the word about Baba; to announce to the world that the one we have been waiting for had arrived. So, with several other young Baba lovers, a car full of literature, and a tray of slides for a public presentation, I was off to San Antonio to lend a hand.

We were able to set up the booth, but we immediately ran into problems about using the theater. The manager did not support us and then left without appointing a replacement with the authority to make decisions about the theater.

After we set up our booth, we languished in the hot summer sun. We did go to see the popular epic film, *2001*, a futuristic story with a society-stirring appearance of a monolith that ended with a suggestion of reincarnation and spiritual realization. We thought of it as an unconscious Baba film. What cinched this thought for us was the dramatic theme music, Richard Strauss' *Thus Spake Zarathustra*, with Zarathustra being the German name for Zoroaster. Baba had been born into a Zoroastrian family and said that Zoroaster was the first incarnation of the Avatar in our cycle of time. The word, *spake*, came from Nietzsche who was one of the founders of modern secularism. Nietzsche, at least in his own genius, was an unconscious harbinger of Baba's world-renewing word. Again, I saw that God worked through design—apparent "coincidence," or what Carl Jung termed *synchronicity*—as well as irony. Perhaps of all of these, irony was the surest sign of His hand.

But despite this new way of looking at the world, I was saddened and disturbed by two events. The first was the death of Beryl Williams. Beryl, a New Yorker and long-time Baba lover, was the keeper and dispenser of Meher Baba photographs. She had a marvelous collection of photo albums of Baba from his early years to the current time—photos with numerous mandali and at various locations: the canals of Venice, in front of St. Marks Cathedral, at the Great Pyramid of Giza, and at the center in Myrtle Beach. She was one of a relatively small number of Baba lovers who were African American. When I first "came to Meher Baba," I visited her in New York. We met on a magical afternoon at one of those small squares embellished with pigeons, a large monument, and public clock, in old lower New York. Being with her, seeing her pictures, and hearing some of her amazing stories of life with Meher Baba was an experience that affirmed my belief in him.

While we were in San Antonio, we received news of her death. As foolish as this may seem in retrospect, I was shocked. Did I expect that Baba lovers would not die? Well, that couldn't be it. Intellectually, I knew many had died since Baba began his work in 1921. But, Beryl was the first Baba lover that I knew personally. Somehow that made it different for me. So, what was so disturbing? At the time, I was not able to voice my inner feelings. I now know that my inner conflict was connected with the fact that Meher Baba had supposedly come to redeem the world. He certainly had not done that yet. That would happen when he broke his silence. But Beryl was a Baba lover, living in a corrupted and disintegrating world, holding on to him, on to his *daaman*, the "hem of his garment" as he put it, waiting for the silence breaking and worldwide spiritual renewal. Yet she died before this happened.

The second disturbing event was that we were not able to use the theater at the World's Fair as we had expected. If Meher Baba was the Avatar and his purpose was to renew the world, if he had the infinite power of God to do so, why wasn't he pulling strings to make this happen so that we could spread the message about him?

Finally, somehow, near the end of the summer, we were given permission to present a program in the theater. Despite our nervousness, we had been pushing for and looking forward to this for a long time. Our talks were planned around a slide presentation of Meher Baba and an illustrated account of the cosmology that he presented in his book, *God Speaks*. The slides had been prepared by Filis Frederick for presentation at spiritual gatherings in California.

The big day arrived. There were a lot of people at the fair and the programs in all the theaters usually filled up—ours certainly did. The theater filled for each show, and we presented our program, full of youthful spirit and joy, knowing that we were presenting to the world the essential message of our time. Thus, I was quite chagrined that at each of these shows, people would get up and leave about halfway through. It wasn't just a few either; it seemed like *The Exodus*. What was going on? Nevertheless, we continued to pass out literature, present our program, and tell our friends about Meher Baba.

It was then we got "The Telegram," delivered to our door. It was from India and it was from Baba! It read:

BY SPREADING THE MESSAGE OF MY LOVE YOU MY LOVERS WILL ONE DAY ENTER THE DOMAIN OF MY DIVINE LOVE STOP MY LOVE BLESSING TO YOU[4]

Then it mentioned our names and the names of two Baba lovers from New York, Adele Wolkin and George McCuen, who encouraged us to go ahead with the project and helped print the literature we were using.

Not only the words of the telegram, but its very existence took our breath away. How did Baba know? And about us? And the timing? Now, after a summer of frustrated attempts to produce the program? Now, as we were finally presenting them in the theaters? It seemed like Baba's infinite and divine knowing.

Despite his omniscience, Baba worked in natural ways as the mandali have well noted; In fact, Meher Baba worked hard to hide his omniscience. We never were able to confirm it, but it seems that Adele kept Baba apprised of the situation throughout the whole project; she probably told him that we had finally started the theater presentation.

Long-time Baba lovers like Adele, Filis, and Jane Haynes had amusingly experienced this issue of public presentations about Meher Baba. In 1964, they received Baba's permission to have a booth at the World's Fair in New York. At first they thought their booth should be placed in "The Hall of Religions." But Baba cabled, "No." He said, "I am not one of the many, but the one in the many." Eventually they wound up setting up the booth in the apparently totally irrelevant presentation hall of house and living quarters design. It was called "American Interiors." One day Richard Nixon and his entourage came by the exhibit. One of Baba's lovers handed him a brochure of Baba's messages. Nixon took it, got out his pen, autographed it, and gave it back.

Public presentations of Meher Baba were something new. Except for a brief period in the 1930s, Baba never sought, never wanted, and took significant pains to avoid publicity. From the beginning of his work through the New Life of the early 1950s, he nearly always traveled incognito. To paraphrase his attitude, "If I am what I am, I don't need publicity agents." The Avatar would accomplish his mission regardless of whether the world recognized him. Nevertheless, he did state that his mission was renewing the world, and his appearance as Avatar was the last incarnation in this cycle of time, which included the six previous appearances on Earth as Zoraster, Rama, Krishna, Buddha, Jesus, and Mohammed. When he broke his silence, "all life in creation will know, feel, and receive of it."

This stance of avoiding publicity and recognition began to change after the New Life, at which time Meher Baba began to publicly announce himself as the Avatar. Before the New Life, he would never have given permission or approved of his lovers giving a public presentation at a World's Fair. By the early 1960s, Meher Baba stated that "Now is the time for all to know that I am God in human form," and it was in this new phase of his life, when he was more than sixty years old, that programs such as these were allowed. But, as described, the effect of these programs was hardly earth-shaking. Today, the world still knows little about Meher Baba.

After that summer in San Antonio, I returned to live in Myrtle Beach so that I could have ready access to the Center. No one is allowed to live on the Center. Even Dilruba, the house where Kitty and Elizabeth lived, was adjacent to, but off, the property of the Center.

I had completed my Ph.D., but supported myself by doing odd jobs in town. I found that I could not get these jobs unless I hid my credentials; no one would hire someone with a Ph.D.

to drive a linen delivery truck. At this time, there were perhaps twenty or so Baba lovers who moved to Myrtle Beach to live near the Center. We were mainly preoccupied with when Baba would come out of seclusion to meet his old and new lovers. Would it be in India or in Myrtle Beach? With the seclusion and limited communication with Baba, the main source of information about Baba's life and work were letters from Mani, Baba's sister and close mandali. Mani wrote to central places around the world, and these letters were copied and distributed to individuals and at group meetings. Mani's warm, witty, and detailed letters of happenings in and around Baba began in 1956 and continued regularly until 1969. They were typed and often ran for several pages. The letters were referred to by Mani as the "Family Letters," meaning they were addressed to all of us in the "Baba family."

If and when Baba came out of seclusion, it would be announced in a Family Letter, so one advantage of living near the Center was that we would get this news immediately.

In September 1968, word quickly spread throughout the Baba community that a Family Letter had arrived. Kitty and Elizabeth called us to meet at Dilruba where the letter would be read. The intensity of my desire to see Meher Baba continued to build, and I could hardly wait to hear that we would see him. A part of me could barely believe that this would be possible; God in human form, the special and rare appearance of the Avatar in human history, and I might be able to see him!

With overwhelming anticipation and pin-drop silence, we listened as the letter was read. The style of Mani's letters can be conveyed by quoting directly from the opening lines:

> By the many calendars at Meherazad [15 miles from Meherabad and where Baba and the mandali lived], and other gentle reminders, I know that you are waiting to receive this letter. I, too, have been waiting to write it, waiting till I might capture the only news that you are waiting to receive: that Baba has announced that He will give Darshan. But alas, this much wooed announcement continues to elude, appearing joyfully close at hand and painfully out of reach, seemingly near but far off as the horizon. While the world of Baba-lovers is suspended in the vacuum of a breathless waiting, while the lovers yearn for His smile and strain for His call, Beloved Baba gives no indication yet as to when they will see him. He tells them:
>
> BE PATIENT. WAIT IN MY LOVE. THOSE WHO WAIT FOR ME NEVER WAIT IN VAIN. YOU WILL SEE ME, BUT WAIT TILL I CALL.

HOLD ON TO MY DAAMAN—AND WAIT FOR MY CALL.[5]

The letter continued for seven pages and relayed a lot of information, some of which would only become clear later. But the essential disappointing message was—no darshan. For me, the letdown was immense. As some people drifted out, I felt immobilized and unable to leave the house. Finally, Kitty came up to the few remaining, and in a nonchalant and cheery way said, "Come on, let's go for some ice cream," and we drove to the nearest parlor.

At the time, I thought that Kitty was able to respond this way because she had spent so many years in close company with Baba that this disappointing news wasn't as significant for her as it was to those of us who had never met him. Years later, I realized how wrong I was.

Seeing and spending time with Baba does not lessen one's desire to be in his physical presence, but rather increases it. This is one of the essential characteristics of one who is the Divine and Eternal Beloved, the supreme object of love. A drop of this Divine Love only increases one's desire for more of it. That longing, that increase in longing, is the fuel that drives the lover's engine of seeking.

Kitty's and Elizabeth's disappointment was certainly much greater than ours. Meher Baba was their true Beloved; one could say they were dying to be physically with him again. It was not because she lacked disappointment that Kitty was able to be so carefree in her response to the bad news. As I discovered later, her response came through tremendous discipline and control of mood that the mandali learned by being with Meher Baba for years. It was the detachment, "Don't Worry, Be Happy," learned from Baba that was a compensation and counterbalance to the continuous stoking of the fire of longing which increased by being with him. It was the former that enabled one to survive the latter, but, without the latter, there is nothing. So the "let's go for some ice cream," so simple, so practical as a way of dealing with the news, was a profound spiritual achievement. I was receiving an early lesson of how the Master uses disappointment as a weapon in his arsenal to increase the lover's longing—to have that lover become aware, slowly, over time, that he or she is in fact a lover of the Divine Beloved.

Because I now knew that if and when darshan was announced, it could well be in India, I recognized that I needed money for the trip. And who knew when that would come? I couldn't drive a linen truck forever. So when several Baba lovers from the Washington, D.C. area came to the Center and told me they had room in their "commune" (yes, hippies), and that there were job opportunities in the D.C. area, I decided to join them.

My first job in D.C. was with the "countercultural" *Washington Area Free Press*—peddling papers on the streets of the city. I was even interviewed for an article about Baba that appeared in the paper. The counterculture was in full force; protests against the Vietnam War were happening regularly at the White House. I was now a nonextreme participant; my political activism was tempered by my following of Meher Baba. After all it was he, the Avatar, who had come to bring about the changes in society that seemed to be so desperately needed, and this awaited his Word.

> All this world confusion and chaos was inevitable, and no one is to blame. What had to happen has happened, and what has to happen will happen. There was and is no way out except through my coming in your midst. I had to come, and I have come.[6]

Then another Family Letter arrived. Baba had fooled me, so to speak. I wanted to be in Myrtle Beach to hear news of darshan, but after the disappointment of the last letter, I had moved away. Now I received a call that another letter had just arrived. I drove to a Baba gathering in New York for the reading, although by the time I left, I knew the contents. Here is how Mani began:

> This unexpected letter following on the heels of the last one, is a momentous messenger carrying momentous tidings: the announcement from Beloved Baba for which His lovers have been waiting, waiting, waiting. That which seemed so far away such a short while ago, is now so close and large that the years of waiting appear small beside it. The first hint Baba gave us of it, was scarcely a month before His announcement was finalized and formulated in a Circular to reach all His lovers. . . .

Baba said: "No doubt . . . my lovers everywhere have been wondering why, when my period of intense Work in seclusion has finished, I have still not allowed my lovers to see me. The strain of that 18 months Work was tremendous. I used to sit alone in my room for some hours each day while complete silence was imposed on the mandali and no one of them was permitted to enter the room, during those hours every day. The strain was not in the work itself although I was working on all planes of consciousness, but in keeping my link with the gross plane. To keep this link I had to continuously hammer my right thigh with my fist. Now, although my health is good, and I would like to fulfill immediately the longing of my lovers to come to me—many to see me for the first time—it will yet take some time for all traces of the strain to disappear and for me to be 100% fit to see them all; and so because of this, and for practical considerations also, I have decided to give my darshan only to my lovers but not to the general public.

This is the time for my lovers. The time for the world's crowds to come to me will be when I break my Silence and Manifest my Divinity. The 1962 East–West Gathering was nothing compared with what this Gathering will be....[7]

The specifics were that darshan was to be given from April 10 to June 10, 1969, in Poona, India. Groups from different parts of the West and the East would have designated times to arrive, and for the Western Baba lovers the darshan period would last one week during that two-month period. Everything was spelled out in precise detail in the circular—the main body of the Family Letter. Visiting periods were set up for thirty-five groups from India alone.

So this seemed to be it. I would get a chance to see Meher Baba after all. Or at least I hoped so. I already knew that Baba would often change plans, and I had experienced the disappointment of that last Family Letter. But here was the incredible announcement of the long-awaited darshan, incredible especially for those who had come to Baba after he went into seclusion in the early 1960s.

The need to get a real job to raise money for the trip was paramount—and so out from the counterculture and into the culture itself.

I heard of an opening in the Department of Justice for a social scientist in the newly created Law Enforcement Assistance Administration. I cut my hair, interviewed, and got the job. It involved prison reform research—monitoring grants that the Justice Department had bestowed for this research.

It seemed strange to go from campus radical to perhaps one of the most conservative areas of government. But I already knew from Baba that embodied life consisted of the duality of opposites. That when we align with a Master, our spiritual life course (or *karma*) speeds up. So here I was, already feeling the quickening of my passage through the opposites. But that was just the beginning.

Dropping the Body

*I am come as Time,
the waster of the peoples, ready for the
hour that ripens to their ruin.*

BHAGAVAD GITA

I settled into my work area on an upper floor of one of the innumerable government office buildings in downtown Washington, commuting to it from the commune where I lived. Mountains of reading quickly came to my desk; I needed to catch up with the research grants that were already approved as well as the numerous applications for new grants.

Richard Nixon had been elected President in November, and there were rumors that all new appointees under the previous administration would be let go when the new administration took office. Because new staff in any branch of the Justice Department underwent a FBI security clearance that often took several months, an employee was hired only as a "consultant." When interviewed, I told the department head about my antiwar background and participation in Students for Democratic Society (SDS). It seems that he, too, was antiwar—as were others, at least in the lower levels of the government—and he didn't think my background would be a security check problem. In any event, I had my job until the check was complete, and I told the department head that I would be going to India for a week in April.

Near the end of January 1969, I was given a two-fold assignment to the Bay area in California. The first purpose of my trip was to meet with several grant recipients to see how their research was proceeding, but this was more or less tacked on to the second purpose, at least in terms of the timing of the trip. The student strike against San Francisco State University was in full force. Student demonstrators were attempting to shut down the school and the president of the school, S.I. Hayakawa, along with a large phalanx of mounted and unmounted police, were trying to keep the demonstrators out of the way and the school open. The strike was highly confrontational and featured regularly in the national news.

The Justice Department wanted an investigation of the demonstration and a representative report on the nature of these students as well as information on campus unrest throughout the country. It was proposed that I—who had a personal background in these matters and in that sense was an "expert"—be one of a group of three people to go to San Francisco. A military security specialist was also assigned to the group. To take this assignment certainly seemed strange, but I knew that my life was taking a new direction and this was a part of it.

A THOUGHTFUL BABA.
JABULPUR, JANUARY, 1939.

When we arrived in San Francisco, we met with the local TV station, KQED, to view recent videotapes of the confrontation. Watching the tapes of the students, with whom I easily identified, while my government associates made less-than-sympathetic comments felt like the "twilight zone." This feeling of ambiguity increased later when we went to the campus to meet with Hayakawa and other school administrators. There I was, dressed in a dark suit and part of the government team, being escorted by police through student demonstrators with armed police on the roof and students shouting epithets at us as we made the long walk from our vehicle, down a path, and up the steps into the administration building. Once inside, we all breathed a sigh of relief, but for me it was all quite strange—psychologically I felt both on the outside and inside at the same time.

When I walked into the vestibule of Hayakawa's office, I was amazed to see a poster of Meher Baba on the wall! What was this? Incredible. The improbable appearance of a picture of Baba appearing during this strange, threatening, and wrenching circumstance was as if he was saying, "See, here I am. I am always with you." After the meeting, I was told that an office assistant was a Baba lover and had been allowed to hang the poster.

The meeting with Hayakawa was brief and mostly ceremonial after which we collected background information from his deputies. When we finished, I steeled myself for the agonizing walk through the demonstrators to our car. Later, there were meetings with teachers, some of whom were sympathetic to the strike. All the while, I was busily writing notes for the report.

During my time off, I visited the Sufi Center on Sutter Street, where I had gone to that first Meher Baba meeting a year and a half before. Much had changed in my life since that meeting—from atheist to believer, from one who saw the world in mechanical and materially causal scientific terms to one who began to see all things as directed and happening for a purpose. From one who made his own way in the world—whatever that was and in whatever direction—to one who now had a "master" and accepted that master to be the long-awaited Savior. This time I went to the Sufi Center as a Baba lover, feeling very much a part of the group—a distinct contrast to how I felt about my role as a government agent.

One evening, I met with one of the research grant recipients. We planned dinner out and to look over her research in her office. The most convenient place to meet was her apartment. As she ushered me into her living room she said she'd like me to read an interesting essay while I was waiting for her to get ready for our meeting. She was intrigued by a writer that she thought was special, an Argentinean named Jorge Luis Borges. As she handed me a book of his essays she asked, "Do you know what an Avatar is?" I almost fell off the couch.

My immediate, impulsive response was, "Do *you* know what an Avatar is?"

"Of course," she answered. "It's a reincarnation of a Hindu god." Close enough, I thought.

The reason for her remarkable question was that the Borges essay she wanted me to read was called *Avatars of the Tortoise*. I didn't get a chance to read all of it then, but I've since read it numerous times. I revealed how remarkable her question was to me and told her something of Meher Baba. She, too, was struck by the coincidence.

This was my introduction to Borges, who, a few years later, received the Nobel Prize in literature. He was truly a great writer who, in both fiction and nonfiction, wrote of the strangeness of life, the ironic and seemingly symbolic twists and turns of fate, of paradox lurking everywhere, of the intriguing but just-out-of-reach sense that there may be a guiding purpose behind the otherwise seemingly random and purposeless play of events. In this particular essay, the tortoise refers to the Greek philosopher Zeno of Elea's paradox of the race between the swift Achilles and a tortoise.

If the race is analyzed a certain way, Achilles will never overtake the tortoise. That is to say, suppose the race begins, and the tortoise is given a head start of fifty yards. Let us also say that Achilles is ten times faster than the tortoise. When Achilles arrives where the tortoise was when the race started (the fifty-yard line), the tortoise has moved five yards ahead. But when Achilles gets to that point, the tortoise is still a half a yard ahead. The same thing happens at every point in the race. Achilles gets closer and closer to the tortoise but can never catch it. When he arrives at a spot where the tortoise was, the tortoise has moved a little bit ahead. Achilles' approach to the tortoise becomes an infinitely declining series of distances, but the gap between them is never eliminated.

Borges recounts how this same paradox, in one form or another, has been presented by writers throughout history along with various attempts to explain it; that is his meaning of "avatars of the tortoise." Each appearance of the paradox, which he defines as a regression ad infinitum, is another "avatar" of it. Although there are various ways to resolve the paradox, it gives us a fundamental understanding of the limitations of the intellect.

That evening's experience with avatars of the tortoise was another striking event in a week that seemed to have an intense energy.

As my work and visit to the Bay area was coming to an end, I decided to pay a last visit to the Sufi Center before leaving for Washington. Hanging on to the pole of the cable car on my way up the hill to the center, I recalled that Baba had repeatedly said that he was everywhere, and I felt that I had experienced that most pointedly during the week. I had been wondering whether I wanted to live in Washington, D.C. after the darshan or to move back to Myrtle Beach to be in close proximity to Baba's home in the West. Now I strongly sensed that because Baba was everywhere, I really didn't have to live in Myrtle Beach, but it seemed clear to me that any decision should be on hold until after I had seen Baba.

Although I was going to the Sufi Center on a weekend, I was still surprised to find so many people there. I was more surprised when I saw the looks of sadness and dejection on their faces. I gave a wary, but cheerful hello, and then someone took me aside and asked if I knew what had happened? I said no and was told that the news had just arrived that Meher Baba had died in India at 12:15 P.M. on January 31, 1969!

I was fortunate to be at the Sufi Center when I got this news; it would have been much more difficult for me if I had been traveling or alone. Rick Chapman and Lud Dimpfl, a longtime Sufi teacher who had been with Baba on numerous occasions, came to the Sufi Center and talked to the group about this incomprehensible event. Lud pointed out that Baba had said that "a dark cloud" had been over his head and was going to burst and that his "humiliation" would precede his "glorification." This was it, Lud said. Baba died and had not broken his silence. Then Lud drew our attention to something interesting. A family letter from Mani, dated January 26, had come from India just a few days ago. In it she said she was surprised to be writing so soon after her letter announcing darshan. It contained a message that Baba had dictated for his birthday, which was not for another month, February 25. The message was:

> To love me for what I may give you is not loving me at all. To sacrifice anything in my cause to gain something for yourself is like a blind man sacrificing his eyes for sight. I am the divine beloved worthy of being loved because I am love. He who loves me because of this will be blessed with unlimited sight and will see me as I am.[1]

The news was numbing, at least initially. I had returned to Washington thinking that Baba would break his silence any minute now, or any day, or any week. It was as if the drama of his life had reached its denouement and Baba would now have to produce. I began to feel a curious sense of freedom. No tension now. There was great disappointment concerning the darshan, but if Baba broke his silence, the fact of not seeing him would hardly matter.

I had been told by some of my closest friends that the FBI had been to visit them to ask about me. We felt this was amusing because logically, given the counterculture background of some of my friends, this would set up an infinite regress of the FBI asking my friends' friends about them and so on ad infinitum ad absurdum. More avatars of the tortoise. Yet, I had an uncomfortable feeling of being under suspicion or accused of a crime when, in reality, I was an American citizen working for my government. Typical of many in the antiwar movement, I never felt that my opposition to the Vietnam War was an opposition to America—rather that America was acting in opposition to its own best principles and that the actions of opposing the war were actions of true patriotism.

It was a surprise to my boss, my coworkers, and by this time even to me, when the FBI informed my department that they had concluded that I was a security risk and had to leave my job. This had never happened to anyone else in the department and my colleagues looked at me with a mixture of regret, curiosity, and even some apprehension. My boss came to me and said, "My God, Ken, what did you do?" I thought I had already told him. Well, whatever I did, it was enough. I had to pack up and leave immediately—and wasn't able to hand in my part of the report on the San Francisco State University strike.

I went to the American Civil Liberties Union (ACLU), but found that there was no legal recourse to confront the decision. The experience certainly did not serve to endear "the system" to me. A year later, I discovered just how nasty the system could be.

In Washington there was massive discontent toward the government and ever-mounting opposition to the Vietnam War. After I came to Baba in 1968 during the demonstration in South Bend, I began to feel differently about politics. I had entered politics as an atheist, believing that whatever did or didn't happen in the world was entirely up to us. There was no guiding force behind the universe nor the affairs of human beings. There was no benevolent God overlooking and directing things so that all would turn out well in the end—even if that end was not on Earth but in an afterlife. For me there was no such thing as an afterlife anyway.

After coming to believe in Baba, all that slowly began to change. I say slowly because the implications of the existence of God (versus the lack of that existence) run so deep that this change in outlook must take time to slowly work its way through the totality of one's mind and being. The question of God, of course, is the ultimate question of existence and all else rests upon it. In fact, the completion of this transformation from atheism to full oneness with the divine is the completion of spiritual realization.

After accepting Baba, I found that I lost some of the desperation that was a part of my political activism. It wasn't just up to me or us—there *was* something greater behind all of creation and it was moving in its own omniscient way to bring the world to where it needed to be. Baba had specifically described this state and said that he had come to bring about this transformation. He referred to it as a "New Humanity" in which "cooperation will replace competition; certainty will replace fear; generosity will replace greed. Exploitation will disappear."

So I knew, or at least felt I knew, that even in the midst of the tragedy of the Vietnam War and the tragedy of all other human inequities and injustice there existed a plan and a purpose, and the carrier of that plan and purpose had come to Earth once again to "true the standard of human values" and restore a golden age. All of this was to come into being when Baba broke his silence.

But now Meher Baba was dead and he had not yet broken his silence. Around me were desperate and frantic opponents of the war. Before

Baba died, I had taken hope and sustenance in the newfound security that God existed and that this was a special time in human history when he made a direct appearance on Earth in human form to give us this assurance and hope. I was aware that when Baba was alive this knowledge didn't easily communicate; I had learned to more or less keep my belief to myself. It would be nice to give this news to others and to help them realize the same sense of inner assurance that I now had, but I found that this was not easy to do. However, this didn't matter so much—Baba had to and would break his silence soon and then all would know anyway. Meher Baba had said, "When I speak, I shall manifest the Divine Will, and a world-wide transformation of consciousness will take place."

Meher Baba was dead. I expected the silence to be broken imminently. As the days stretched into weeks, I began to lose some of my confidence. The antiwar movement was working hard to end the war, and I was still involved, but with a certain sense of detachment that I had never had before. Now where was I? What was going on? In one corner of my mind the skeptic arose or, should I say, arose again. I had been a typical modern scientific materialist, which is also to say atheist.

The atheist is the inheritor of the skeptical stance first and most powerfully introduced into our history by René Descartes who felt impelled to confront medieval Christian mentality with what was to become known as *radical doubt*. This doubt set off a train of historical development in which science, not only as a method but as a particular metaphysic belief system, gradually replaced religion as a source of knowledge and as the basis of truth. By the late nineteenth century, the metaphysic of materialism replaced the spiritual as the dominant conception of what is real. Given a push by what can be referred to as the "doctors of modernity" (replacing the "doctors of the Church" of the Middle Ages)—Marx, Darwin, Nietzsche, and Freud—God, and all that God implied was pronounced dead.

This, of course, did not mean that there was a God that actually died, but that the false idea of God, inherited from humankind's ancient past, could now be replaced by true knowledge—that is, the only reality is physical reality. Anything not material, such as the mind, and by implication the spirit, was a byproduct of matter (that is, the brain). Darwin said that the mind is just a secretion of the brain. This metaphysical concept not only defines the modern mind, but is what makes that mind modern.

The skeptic, therefore, is an important person in our world, and a part of myself as well. Skepticism had played a vital role in my life and my coming to Baba. Because Meher Baba died and did not break his silence as he had repeatedly said he would, doubt naturally arose. Were the materialists right after all? Was this notion of an Avatar, a God in human form, of God at all, a fantastical belief formed from human weakness, credulity, and wishfulness?

Suddenly, surprising news arrived from India: the darshan was still on. How was this to be?

The reason that Mani wrote that surprise letter of January 26 was not to send Baba's birthday message in advance, although she did that as well, but rather to send a circular that Baba's secretary, Adi, wrote in regard to the upcoming darshan. At the age of 74, after the strain of the arduous work during his lifetime and two severe car accidents, Meher Baba's health had inevitably deteriorated.

Beginning by a reference to the last three years of Baba's seclusion work, Adi wrote:

> Beloved Avatar Meher Baba wishes all His lovers to know that His three years of intense work has shattered his health.
>
> In spite of this He has invited His lovers from all over the world to come to Him for His darshan next summer, for it is the time for them to come to Him and receive His Love.
>
> It is the time; and the place, Guruprasad, Poona has been fixed.
>
> But with the present condition of His health, how beloved Baba will give His darshan to the thousands who will come, yet remains to be determined; but it will be. He will give His darshan.
>
> This darshan, Baba says, will be the last given in Silence—the last before He speaks His world-renewing Word of Words.[2]

When the mandali approached Baba about how difficult it would be in his fragile state of health to undergo the strain of such an extensive darshan program, more extensive than he had ever given before, and then he was younger, Baba reassured them:

> It will be easy for me to give my lovers my darshan, so you are not to feel concerned about it. I will give darshan reclining and that will be no strain on my body. It will be different from all previous darshans and it will be the last in silence. Although I will be reclining I will be very strong. My physical condition now is because of my work, but by then my work will be complete and my exultation will be great.[3]

Mani's next letter in March 1969 announced that darshan would be held as planned. In her letter, she gave an account of Meher Baba's death and said that because of this statement, the mandali knew that Baba intended the darshan to take place.

Almost all of Meher Baba's time in seclusion had been spent in his home quarters at Meherazad, nine miles north of the city of Ahmednagar. In early December 1968, he began having muscle spasms and after January 12, 1969, he never left his room. Around that time, Padri, one of the mandali, in a conversation with Meher Baba, casually remarked, "Baba, the mandali have become old and it is better to close the shop." Baba replied, "No, the shop will now be opened." The spasms increased. Baba said to some of the mandali, "This is my crucifixion." Even Baba gesturing with his fingers would bring on a spasm. A doctor was called on January 30 to see him, and there were no spasms. As soon as the doctor left, the spasms increased. On the morning of January 31, Meher Baba gestured to the mandali to bring in a board on which were written three couplets by the Persian poet Hafiz, whom Baba said was a Perfect Master. The couplets stressed complete surrender to the will of the Perfect Master and his omniscience, even if not understood by others. The couplets were:

BEFITTING A FORTUNATE SLAVE, CARRY OUT EVERY COMMAND OF THE MASTER WITHOUT ANY QUESTION OF WHY AND WHAT.

ABOUT WHAT YOU HEAR FROM THE MASTER NEVER SAY IT IS WRONG BECAUSE MY DEAR THE FAULT LIES IN YOUR OWN INCAPACITY TO UNDERSTAND HIM.

I AM THE SLAVE OF MY MASTER WHO HAS RELEASED ME FROM IGNORANCE; WHATEVER MY MASTER DOES IS FOR THE HIGHEST BENEFIT TO ALL CONCERNED.[4]

At 12:15 P.M., Baba had an extremely strong spasm. He was sitting on his surgical bed with his back and head raised. Baba flexed his arms and closed his mouth tightly. His respiration stopped. There were vigorous efforts to revive him, but they did not work. Previously Baba had said, "The dropping of the physical body of the Avatar or by the Sadguru [Perfect Master] is not death, for even while he uses the body he is in no way attached to it and has no sanskaric link with it." When Adi sent out a telegram that day to various Baba centers around the world to inform them of this event, it read,

AVATAR MEHER BABA DROPPED HIS PHYSICAL BODY AT TWELVE NOON 31 JANUARY AT MEHERAZAD TO LIVE ETERNALLY IN THE HEARTS OF ALL HIS LOVERS. BELOVED BABA'S BODY WILL BE INTERRED AT MEHERABAD ARANGAON ON 1 FEBRUARY AT 10 A.M. IN THE TOMB HE HAD ORDERED TO BE BUILT LONG AGO.[5]

From that point on, the term "dropping the body" was generally used to refer to Baba's physical departure to indicate the intentional aspect of the Avatar's death, as compared to other deaths. A number of years previously Baba had relayed another message for his birthday, in which he said, "I am never born, I never die. Yet every moment I take birth and undergo death. . . . Although I am present everywhere eternally in My formless Infinite State, from time to time I take form, and taking of the form and leaving it is termed My physical birth and death. In this sense I was born sixty years ago and will die when My universal work is finished."[6]

Baba's words made it clear to the mandali that Baba had meant for the darshan to proceed as planned, even without his physical presence. What that would be like, no one had any idea, but I was determined to go. Some Baba lovers in the West, including Don Stevens, Alan Cohen, and Rick Chapman, flew to India to try to be there for Baba's interment at Meherabad on February 1. Because of the Indian heat, it was expected that the interment could not be delayed for more than one day even with blocks of ice arranged around Baba's body. He was placed in the open crypt in his tomb. His face was peaceful and serene, as if he were asleep. Besides the handful of Westerners, thousands from India came to pay their last respects to the physical form of the Avatar. There was a definite and intense awareness of Baba's presence; no one wanted to leave. At the end of the first day, many followers were just arriving to have a last contact with Baba. Singing and music were spontaneously struck up by various groups of Easterners, which continued into the night. No deterioration in Baba's body was observed, and with people constantly arriving, the mandali decided not to close the crypt that day. These same conditions continued into the next day and the day after that. Baba's body remained "fresh and lovely" as Mani described it. This went on for seven days from January 31. This time was later described as the

MEHERA AND MANI HAVING TEA.
MEHERA'S BIRTHDAY, 1987.

"Last Sahavas"—the last intimate stay and visit with the Avatar. Finally, on February 7 (coincidentally Baba's birthday on the Zoroastrian calendar), with still no deterioration, the decision was made to enclose Baba's body in his crypt.

Although it was not reported in the Western press, an extraordinary event occurred during this time. The Kaaba is the holy shrine of pilgrimage for Muslims throughout the world and every Muslim expects to make a *Haj* or journey to the Kaaba in Mecca, Saudi Arabia, at least once. It was front-page news in Eastern newspapers, especially in Muslim countries, that flooding had submerged the Kaaba in nearly six feet of water making it inaccessible to pilgrims. The Kaaba area is desert and flooding had not happened in the fourteen hundred years since the time of Mohammed, whom Baba said was his previous incarnation as the Avatar. The flooding lasted seven days, from January 31 to February 7, 1969, the period of Meher Baba's lying in state—his "Last Sahavas." This seemed a powerful sign that Baba's tomb in Meherabad had become the Kaaba of the new age. Clippings of these newspaper reports have been archived in Meherazad.

In Washington, I was far removed from the interment and did not know anything about it until Mani's letter arrived in March. I was without a job and had little money saved, which would not be enough to go to darshan in April. I applied for jobs in psychology in the Northeast, but it was apparent that I probably would not find anything or certainly not save enough before it was time to leave for India. Fortunately, I belonged to a teacher's credit union in South Bend, and I was able to get a loan to cover the expenses that I needed for the trip.

THE LAST DARSHAN

Is it true there is a God?
If it be true, can I see Him?
Can I realize the truth?
The Western mind may think
all this very impracticable, but
to us it is intensely practical.

VIVEKANANDA

I went to India with the second of three groups from America, which was referred to as the "Myrtle Beach group." The West Coast group, which included members of Sufism Reoriented, left first, and we were followed by a group from New York and New England.

We were flying on an Air India charter flight, and as the day for my departure from Kennedy International Airport approached, I could feel the excitement building. The excitement could be attributed to this being my first trip to the exotic land of India, but I knew that it was related more to the unknown of going to "meet" Meher Baba even though he was no longer in the body.

At the airport, James Ivory, a writer from *The New Yorker*, approached several members of the group. He was interested in India and had heard about the trip. (Years later, he directed with Ismail Merchant, producer, a series of elegant films based on classic novels—among them *Heat and Dust, Room with a View,* and *Howard's End*) Ivory hoped to interview us before and after our trip and compare our expectations with our actual experiences. Several of the group said that they had no, or were at least trying not to have any, expectations. Other than the excitement of the unknown darshan, what else was there for us to expect?

When I landed in Bombay, after 24 hours and several touchdowns, I had traveled halfway around the world. Disembarking from the plane directly onto the airport tarmac, I collided with India; a combination of humid heat unlike anything I had ever felt before and a pungent, fetid smell surrounded me. The East, the Orient, lay directly against my face and skin. In the old dilapidated terminal, Indian faces were all around us pressed up against the screens that served as barriers between the outside world and the customs area. When we were through customs and walked into the Indian populace, we were met by a group of Bombay Baba lovers who greeted us with a vigorous and glad shout of "Jai Baba!" (victory to Baba). My heart opened. Here, in this foreign place was a most intimate welcome. I began to feel that I was coming home.

MANI WELCOMES BABA'S LOVERS TO THE LAST DARSHAN. APRIL, 1969.

On the ride from the airport to our Bombay hotel, I began to experience a feeling of ecstasy. At the hotel, we were fed lavishly even though we had been served appealing Indian food many times on the plane. I was uncomfortable with so much food. In the street in front of the hotel, we had been approached by adults and children begging for pennies who pointed to their open mouths and said, "Uncle, uncle, I am hungry," but somehow even this could not dint my mood of exhilaration.

As we rode to Victoria Terminus, the huge, ornate train station built by the British during India's colonial period, I began to sense the meaning of India. It was as if scales had been removed from my eyes, and I could see into the core of Indian life—perhaps all life. What I saw was bliss. This feeling stayed with me during our kaleidoscopic train ride on the *Deccan Queen* through the *ghats* (mountains), fields, and hills of the Deccan plateau to

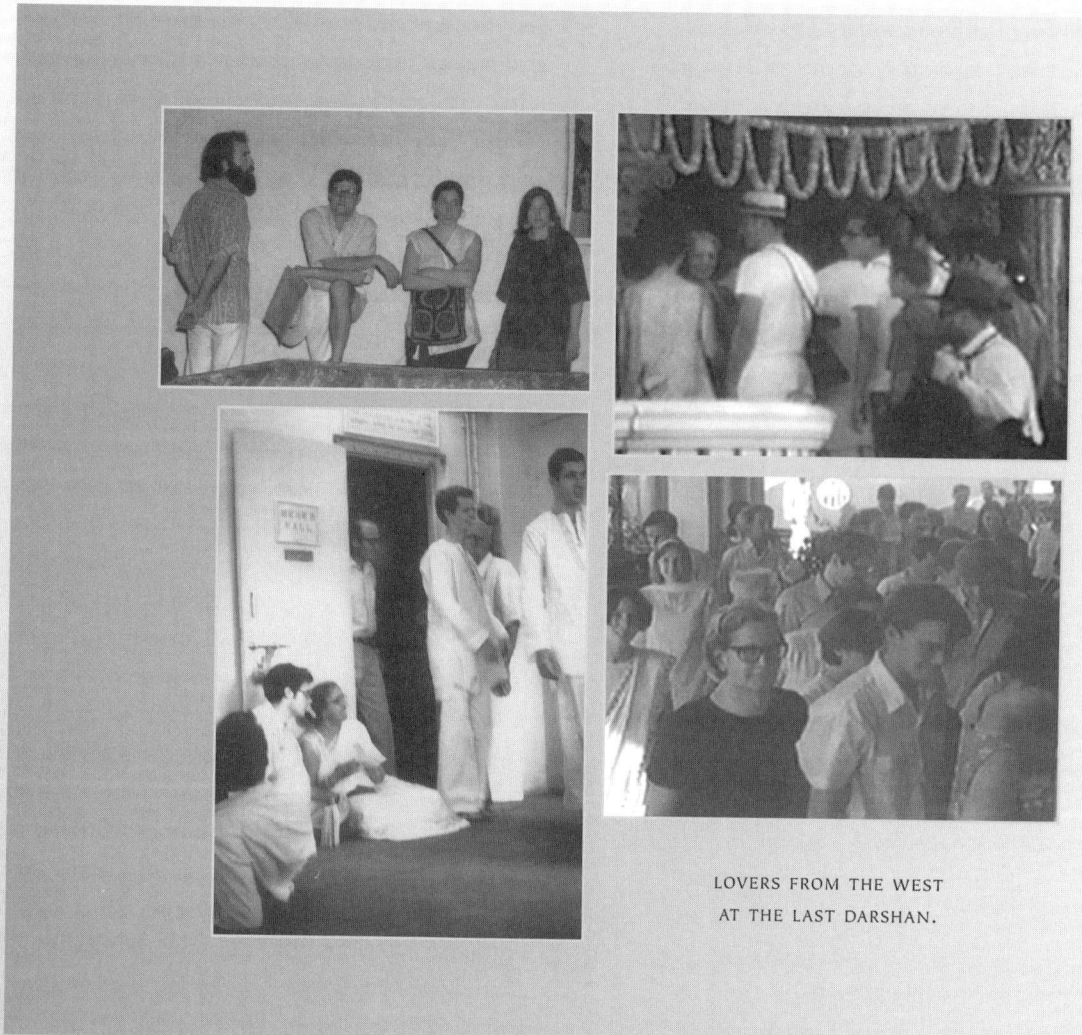

LOVERS FROM THE WEST
AT THE LAST DARSHAN.

the city of Poona where the darshan was to be held. As we passed through the railway stations along the way, the teeming crowds were remarkably still and quiet with little of the rush that is commonplace in the United States. Even in the late afternoon when the stations are most busy, the crowds were peaceful—like a vast human still life suspended in contented waiting.

In the countryside, the people seemed close to nature. They appeared organic, conscious of the earth and sun, living on the brink of pure naked being. As the sun set and the train moved across the land, I saw family groups gathered on the ground in quiet circles. Twice I saw a solitary figure with legs crossed, sitting on a hillside or outside a hut meditating or contemplating the setting sun. I realized that nowhere else had I seen people engaged in meditating as a natural part of the passing of the day. How many high-rise buildings is this worth? How many factories? I visualized these people coming face-to-face with their existence—no false covering between. It is this, I thought, that must be measured against their "poverty."

The darshan program was scheduled to begin the next day at 9:00 A.M. in Guruprasad, where Meher Baba would have met with us. Guruprasad is a large Indian residence owned by a Maharani, but given to Meher Baba for his use. It is an ornate structure with statuary in a front garden, and a large tiled porch extending around three sides of the building. The main room was a small hall and where we gathered. Some of the mandali, including Mani, were already there, greeted us warmly when we arrived, and asked us to sit on carpets on the floor. We faced a large armchair where Baba would have been sitting. A large framed photograph of Meher Baba was placed in the chair encircled with a heart-shaped garland of flowers, and Baba's sandals were at the foot of the chair. I felt a twinge of disappointment when I saw the chair with Baba's picture. We had traveled halfway around the world to see a picture of Baba? For me he seemed painfully absent. I felt a sense of make-believe; let us pretend that Meher Baba is here.

The mandali were gathered near Meher Baba's chair, and as the large wall clock chimed nine times, Eruch Jessawalla stood up in front of us and announced, "We have kept an appointment with God." That statement touched my heart and eased my feeling of Baba's absence. One by one, the mandali spoke. Like Eruch, each of the mandali, in their own way, conveyed the absolute sense and conviction of Meher Baba's reality as God—and as the ever-present God. This, of course, was the first time that I had seen them, but I recognized most of them from biographical material I had read. They spoke in an easy natural way and expressed the feeling that "we were all in the same boat" when it came to Meher Baba. They didn't have inside knowledge or special secrets that the rest of us were not privy to. I was surprised, and when I left the gathering, a bit confused. I had unconsciously expected that the mandali would reveal secret information to us. But this was not the case. What *did* they know, I wondered? Surely they must know something.

After a while, Eruch announced that we would now take darshan from Baba. He said that

Mehera, who is esteemed as Baba's closest mandali, would begin. I watched her go to Baba's chair and bow down, placing her head at the base of the chair as if at Baba's feet. Then she stepped aside. There was a pause, an expectancy, and it became clear that each of us was to follow her lead. I had no idea that this was to be a part of our gathering. One by one our group went to the chair and bowed as Mehera had done. My mind was caught in a frozen position; I didn't know what to think.

Some went to the chair and stayed longer than Mehera had. Some laid down in a *pranam* (flat) position in front of the chair. A deep, solemn atmosphere filled the hall. I saw a number of people weeping as they came away. Those who had bowed down spontaneously hugged others as they finished. As the rows of people dwindled, my time to take darshan was quickly approaching. My heart beat stronger and stronger. Was it fear? I didn't know what it was. I felt that my beating heart was a hand knocking to gain entrance through a door within me.

When I returned to the States, I wrote an account of my first darshan with Meher Baba:

> I walked up to the chair and kneeled down, and I was overwhelmed. There were several strong physical sensations, one was the knocking supplanted by a fire that rose within my chest and spread to my mind, my consciousness. Baba was in the chair! No visions, I did not see him, but I knew he was there . . . I felt it was the apex of the feelings that had been building in me since landing in India. Here at the base of a seemingly empty chair, Baba showed me Who He was. I wanted to call it supernatural, but in a deep sense it was the most natural thing that ever happened to me. A Sufi-type phrase came into my mind: "When the oil of mind is touched by the fire of love, there is consuming heat and light."
>
> At some point the physical became purely mental, or spiritual, and I keenly felt the relationship of the lover to the beloved. Someone said that he felt like a son at the foot of a loving father. Another Sufi-like phrase came to me, "The lover assumes many forms in order to catch the eye of the beloved."
>
> One of the group very cogently noted that it was particularly important for Baba to have this darshan without His physical body so that we could realize the darshan is given to us by ourselves. For me, Baba's presence in the chair was uncanny, but it was none other than my true Self. Baba, in the body, is an externalization of what is within each of us. He is pure love, the ultimate distillation of what we are.[1]

The trip to India lasted a week. The week's schedule included a one-day trip to Meherazad and Meherabad, which are about a hundred miles from Poona, and another darshan at Baba's chair in Guruprasad on the last day. In Meherazad, we saw where Baba spent his last years in seclusion, where he died, and where most of the Mandali live and would return to after the darshan in Poona was over. Meher Baba's tomb is located at Meherabad. Although I felt awe going to where Baba's body was buried, I did not experience the power and presence of the darshan. It felt like a visit of historical importance rather than spiritual. Taking darshan again in Guruprasad on the last day was not like the first day. It merely felt "normal," perhaps devotional, but I felt nothing unusual within.

After that first darshan I was in heaven. Meher Baba's divinity, for me, was confirmed beyond measure. Even though Baba was not there outwardly, I knew that my inner experi-

BABA AT AN EARLY DARSHAN IN THE 1930S.

ence was exactly what it would have been had Baba been physically present. That is what Meher Baba showed me. He did not need to be physically present to give darshan.

Many others had a similar experience, but it is important to note that not all did. Some in the group felt much less—maybe even nothing. It wasn't automatic. This was similar to when people met Meher Baba physically. Some had a strong, emotional inner reaction and some had little or no reaction. The evidential meaning of these differences in personal reactions is difficult to grasp and contains some of the essence of the mystery of spirituality—and a fundamental challenge to the questioning intellect.

By the end of the week, India began to lose some of its initial incredible charm. More and more I noticed the dust and the heat. The beggars and the crowds began to wear me down and remove me from the serene reaches of the heaven that I was in for a while. I became disturbed by Meher Baba's brother selling Baba buttons and other memorabilia (even though I liked having my Baba buttons and the pendant picture of Baba that I bought to wear). In that skeptic's corner of my mind, which I found had not totally vanished despite the darshan, I questioned: Why are they selling us this stuff? Is this whole thing just a gambit for a group of Indians to make some money off the Westerners? Faint though these questions were, they were there.

When we landed at Kennedy International, sure enough there was James Ivory waiting to get the follow-up story. His article entitled "Jai Baba!" appeared, unsigned as per usual, in the Talk of the Town section of the June 21, 1969, issue of *The New Yorker*. I was surprised to find it beautiful and sympathetic. He was evidently open and responsive to the joy and energy our group shared when we returned. In my growing penchant for sensitivity to coincidences, I noted that June 21 was the day after my birthday as well as the Summer Solstice—the day of most sunlight.

Baba lovers who had met Meher Baba and been with him for a time did not waver as I and others did. Their experience of the darshan remained steady, strong, and profound. Darwin and Jeanne Shaw of Schenectady, New York, first met Meher Baba in 1932 and were among the longest-term American/Western Baba lovers. The article in *The New Yorker* ended with Ivory interviewing Darwin about the darshan:

> Between the Indian Baba disciples and our group there was a heart-to-heart exchange of pure love reminiscent of the love feasts of the early Christians. Everyone felt that the barriers had been broken down. There was a sense of newly experienced oneness . . . Throughout our stay, there was the

BOMBAY DARSHAN. DECEMBER, 1957.

quality of a timeless experience, which became intensified as each day passed. We feel that that will remain with us, even when we are back in the Western world and we return to our everyday lives. And we also feel that Baba's work will now expand very greatly, because he is no longer encumbered by the gross body but can operate from the level of the spirit as infinite consciousness, which he has always said he really was. And *is*. "He restoreth my soul"—this is what everyone feels.[2]

I spent a week in New York visiting parents, family, and old friends. One night, driving along the New Jersey Turnpike outside New York City, I passed the oil refineries that line the turnpike. Smoke and oil fumes poured into the air. At night, with a multitude of gas jet flames and the smoke, this looked like a scene from hell. To me, it seemed evident that because of the pollution and ugliness this was a world that could not continue and must pass away. In 1969, this was my first explicit thought of the environmental problem. I had not yet heard the word *ecology*.

Later that week as I walked in downtown New York City, I heard the faint sound of live music. The music got louder. I heard drums and brass, and then a marching band turned the corner and came my way. The music was stirring and uplifting, and I began to cry. As ordinary as it was, this event had the sense of an act of God. It was sheer spontaneity; its coming right my way a gift. It seemed to exemplify that all of the world is brought to us—given to us, if even in the most seemingly mundane ways.

∞ ∞ ∞

Before I left for India, I had applied for a job in Albany, New York. When I returned, I received a letter asking for an interview. Darwin and Jeanne Shaw held a weekly Baba meeting at their house in Schenectady, a neighboring city to Albany. If I got the job in Albany, I would be in close proximity to their home. The Baba meetings at the Shaws were the longest running in the United States or indeed anywhere in the West. This made the job in Albany much more attractive to me. Fortunately, I was hired as a psychologist on the acute inpatient unit of Albany Medical Center and as an associate faculty member at Albany Medical College.

During the time I was in Albany, and certainly in retrospect, I was aware of Meher Baba's special care and guidance in placing me in an environment that gave me the grounding in his reality, specially and uniquely supplied by regular contact with disciples as close to him as the Shaws. Often out-of-town visitors would come to the Shaws' just for this contact and experience. Shortly after I arrived in Albany, several people moved into the area specifically to live near them.

When I write about Meher Baba placing me in Albany and Baba's guidance in the events of my life, it is from the perspective of believing that Meher Baba is God and that God guides all the events of the universe. For he says, as it has been classically revealed, "not a leaf falls without my will." Saying this about God's control of all phenomena raises questions about human free will and where it fits into the whole picture. But the bigger issue raised by this perspective is the question of whether God exists as well as the claim that Meher Baba is God.

I am well aware that the skeptic will see my beliefs that Meher Baba is God and that Baba places me in such and such a situation as a fictitious belief system that seeks to ascribe a directed purpose to events to satisfy a need for order, security, and meaning. As such, it is fundamentally divorced from reality. For the skeptic, the *scientific materialist*, there is no purpose behind anything in the universe but the natural order that exists. Scientific materialists certainly admire and wonder at that order, and their research and theory building is based on it. Although, in the past, spiritual and scientific perspectives were at loggerheads, today there is development afoot to reconcile the two or to see the scientific materialistic view and the spiritual one as existing in two different spheres of knowledge—one need not exclude the other.

This development is an interesting one and relates to the grand question of whether God exists or is a figment of one's mind.[3] When I write about Meher Baba doing this or that, I know that I am adopting a stance that is either absurd or pathological to the traditional scientific mind.

As to the question of God's guiding hand, I relate an experience I had when I first moved to Albany. Earlier that summer of 1969, I had driven to Albany and put down a deposit on an apartment before my job began in September. When it was time to move, I packed all my belongings in the old Nash Rambler I had bought with borrowed money and headed to the city. I arrived at twilight and had a little trouble locating the street where I had rented the apartment. Not quite sure where it was, I pulled into an open parking spot. Someone was walking down the street, and by the time I parked and got out of my car, he had advanced to where I stood on the sidewalk. I decided to ask him for directions. As I approached him, I saw the face of Meher Baba. He was wearing a Baba button on his shirt—a picture of Meher Baba! The stranger was as surprised as I was when I said Meher Baba's name in recognition and equally amazed when I pointed to a large photograph of Baba laying on top of my things piled in the rear seat. For me, this was Baba's way of appearing and saying "welcome to Albany"—again letting me know that he was always with me.

The man I met on the sidewalk that night had been a student at State University of New York–Albany and was returning to the area to visit some friends. Indeed, he had come to tell them about Meher Baba. Our meeting was incredible because it was a coincidence of spectacularly low probability. At that time, Baba lovers were scattered throughout the world, but their relative number was infinitesimally small. To arrive in Albany at dusk, pull into an open parking space because I'm lost and need directions, get out of my car, and at that moment (with a picture of Meher Baba visible in my car), come face to face with someone wearing a Baba button seemed beyond normal to me.

No matter how spectacular or unlikely a coincidence may seem, the skeptic invokes the concept of *event space* or *probability space*. For the believer who experiences the event, it seems unlikely to have happened by chance but rather reveals the presence of God's guiding hand. The skeptic might then say, "Ah, but you have misunderstood the probability space, a typical human failing—compounded by the human desire to have a father figure controlling the world and providing security."

For the skeptic, probability-space reasoning properly compares thousands of encounters with people when nothing special happened versus when a "special" event occurs. Rather than believe that the experience could not happen by chance, the so-called specialness is not surprising at all, but likely given the number of times the dice is tossed.

Not surprisingly (probability space or no probability space), a rich Meher Baba community developed in the Albany–Schenectady area over the next two years.

One notable event during this period was a visit by my former boss from the Law Enforcement Assistance Administration. We had hit it off during my short reign of employment and stayed in touch after my return from India and move to Albany. He was interested in my trip to India, but thought of me as "this good guy who has this odd thing about following an Eastern guru. Oh well, everybody has their thing." He was a somewhat serious practitioner of tarot cards, however, and could not, in good conscience, dismiss another's involvement in something he believed to be esoteric.

During his visit, a Baba meeting was scheduled at the Shaws'. He asked me what occurred at a Baba meeting, and I told him that it was quite a natural and straightforward event—that we gathered informally and chatted, mostly about our lives with Meher Baba. After our discussion, Darwin would read a Meher Baba Discourse and we would have a short, silent meditation. Sometimes, if someone brought a guitar, we sang. Then Jeanne would serve light refreshments in the kitchen where there would be more informal chatting. When it got much too late, Darwin and Jeanne would sweep us out of the house.

Because that seemed safe enough, my friend decided to go. During the more formal part of the meeting, he appeared to be paying rapt attention to the Discourse reading and the discussion. Later, I saw him in animated discussion with Darwin and Jeanne. On the way home, he told me that he heard Baba's voice during the meeting—actually a little dialogue back and forth with Baba. He felt Baba's presence and reality (reminiscent of my inner exchange with Baba at his chair in India). After he returned to Washington, he contacted the Sufis and eventually became a member of Sufism Reoriented.

The next year, 1970, The Who performed their rock opera *Tommy*, which became a popular contemporary classic on stage and in film. Pete Townshend, the composer and leader of the group, was drawn to Meher Baba in 1968 and accepted him as the Avatar. In *Behind Blue Eyes*, a Townshend biography, he is quoted as saying, "Never will I be able to stand back from myself and pretend anymore that God is a myth. That Christ was just another man. That Baba was simply a hypnotic personality. The facts are coming home to me like sledgehammers, not through the words I read in books about Baba, not through even his own words. But through my ordinary daily existence. Meher Baba is the *Avatar*, God incarnate on our planet. The Awakener."[4]

Although it is not common knowledge, *Tommy* was inspired by and dedicated to Meher Baba, and Baba's name is listed in the credits as the Avatar. In one of The Who's anthem songs, "Go to the Mirror Boy," is a reference to Meher Baba, "Right behind you I see the millions," and a 1970 issue of *Rolling Stone* featured an article by Townshend entitled "In love with Meher Baba" with Baba's picture on the cover.[5]

Another singer, Melanie Safka, became nationally known with the launching of her album, *Candles in the Rain*. The cover of the album featured Melanie wearing a Baba button and the words "Meher Baba lives again, candles in the rain" from the title song.

And then there was "Woodstock." Because Albany is relatively close to Bethel, New York, several of us planned to go. Bruce Hoffman, an English professor and Baba lover from down state, printed two-sided cardboard flyers with quotes from Baba and his picture and widely distributed them at the festival. In the Woodstock documentary opening scenes, as the camera pans around the festival, it briefly stops at a tree showing a poster of Meher Baba. The August 29, 1969, *Time* magazine story of the event pictured a thatched shelter at the festival with a Meher Baba poster at the entrance.

One appearance in the media soon after Meher Baba dropped his body was a *Time* cover story in the June 21, 1971, issue entitled, "The Jesus Revolution." The story discussed the renewed interest by young adults in the life of Jesus. *Time* titled its essay, "The New Rebel Cry: Jesus Is Coming." The article's author wrote of the Jesus movement with its mass baptisms in rivers, Christian coffee houses, and two popular musicals, *Jesus Christ Superstar* and *Godspell*. The date of the issue, June 21, was interestingly synchronistic to me: It was the solstice as well as the same date that *The New Yorker* had printed its Meher Baba article two years previously.

The 1971 *Time* article did not mention Meher Baba nor the claim that Meher Baba is Jesus come again because that claim had not then, any more than now, risen above the threshold of recognition within our culture. As for me, however, there was a telling sign in the article. The four-page centerfold section of the article was a layout of color photographs of various happenings within the Jesus movement. The section ends with a full-page image of Jesus Christ in *Godspell* "crucified" on a chain-link fence. The caption was, "Unlike *Jesus Christ Superstar*, *Godspell* has a hopeful ending suggesting resurrection." If you looked closely, the photograph of star Stephen Nathan, who portrayed Jesus in the musical, showed Meher Baba's face printed on a button pinned to Nathan's red suspenders—right over his heart.

∞ ∞ ∞

My work at the Albany Medical Center was intense. I led a therapy group and managed a psychodrama program in the acute inpatient unit, met with and evaluated individual patients, and occasionally taught at the medical school. The hospital's psychiatric program was excellent, well run, and relatively progressive. I have fond memories of my colleagues.

The Albany Medical Center was not far from the Upstate Medical Center in Syracuse, where the famous, or infamous, dissident psychiatrist Thomas Szasz taught. Szasz wrote *The Myth of Mental Illness*. Some of the doctors associated with the program in Albany had been his students. At times, these doctors presented a questioning, critical attitude toward traditional psychiatric procedures. Although the "old" was still present, the age of biological psychiatry was beginning, eventually gathering steam to become the dominant point of view today. This movement has swept away almost all alternative approaches to psychiatric disturbance and largely rejected Szasz's critique of the "illness model." Clinical psychology, with its less biological underpinning than traditional medicine, has fared somewhat better but not much.

At that time, I was very much the young radical with energy, enthusiasm, and an optimistic desire to change the world. The Avatar had come, and he was about to break his silence. It was the job of his disciples, like myself, to be the avant garde of this coming revolution in consciousness—Baba's "New Humanity."

My office at the Albany Medical Center was next to that of a well-known doctor who was a cystic fibrosis expert. Because he was in general medicine, and I was a psychologist many years his junior, we did not appear to have much in common and seldom talked at any length. Yet, he seemed friendly toward me and went out of his way to make me feel welcome at the hospital.

About a year after my arrival, the doctor approached me and confided that before my move to Albany, he had been questioned by the FBI, who implied nefariousness and asked if he had any knowledge of my previous activities. He told them he knew nothing about me because we had never met. It was an astounding revelation for me. It seems that after the FBI performed the security check and told my department to let me go, they then proceeded with this action, which could have no other purpose than to taint my future employment. Fortunately, when they spoke to this doctor he was offended by the government harassment and so bided his time, got to know me, and then told me.

In spite of the hospital's progressive psychiatry program, I felt it was still out of tune with the times. Although it was a medical institution and not part of the general profit-oriented economy, it still seemed to function under the "industrial" system. Patients were shuffled in and out assembly-line fashion and the staff was pressured to keep them moving through the system. Early psychiatric drugs such as Thorazine and Mellaril were used, as was electric shock. This was long before the days of managed care, which explicitly places medicine within the corporate-for-profit care framework.

So, after nearly three years at the Medical Center, this young, impatient, naive radical was burned out. In 1971, a couple I knew, good friends from graduate school, joined forces with two other families and moved to Maine. They bought wooded land on the coast in Hancock County not far from where Scott and Helen Nearing had their homestead. The Nearings practiced back-to-the-land living and wrote the book *Living the Good Life*. The three families planned to build homes, begin gardening and farming, and build an alternative community. After their move, I visited several times and found their life and their plans appealing.

I considered changing the direction of my career and my life. A big decision: What should I do? Should I stay in Albany where I had a well-paying job and a strong Meher Baba group even though my work was increasingly unsatisfying? Or should I move back to Myrtle Beach to be near the Meher Baba Spiritual Center? I even considered "dropping out" altogether and moving to India.

After considerable deliberation and meditation, I decided to leave the Medical Center and move to Maine. The final clincher was that land adjacent to my friends' acreage became available for purchase. I could buy the land and eventually, with the help of the others, build my own house. Meher Baba said that after all due consideration, once a decision is made one should let go of all second-guessing and move ahead wholeheartedly. No matter what one decides to do, Baba is always there to help and guide, which gives one confidence to take risks and approach life with a sense of adventure.

Not that careful and practical matters are to be overlooked. Not at all. Meher Baba cautioned us to be practical, but to make decisions and live life with a full sense of confidence. As for making mistakes, because of his influence, I now believe that there is no such thing as a mistake. God requires only that we are careful and thoughtful in considering our options (using reason) while listening to the voice of our heart (intuition, not our emotions). Once we make our decision, we are to go with it and do our very best.

In the summer of 1972, I moved to Maine. I didn't have a job—actually I didn't want one. I had some money saved and friends. I would soon own my first piece of property. This time when I moved, I pulled a rental trailer. As I drove up the winding dirt road to the old farmhouse where my friends lived while building their new home, the back wheels of the trailer went off the road and into a ditch. I was stuck and had to walk the rest of the way. Welcome to Maine!

Over twenty-five years later, I am still here. And, I did get the trailer out of the ditch.

·7·7·7·7·7·7·7·7·7·7·7·7·7·7·

WHEN I BREAK MY SILENCE

And your ears shall hear a Word behind you saying, this is the Way, walk you in it, when you turn to the right hand, and when you turn to the left.

ISAIAH

It had been three years since Baba dropped his body and he had still not broken his silence. In one sense, my move to the Maine woods in 1972 was an attempt to hole up and wait it out. I realized that some Baba lovers believed either that Baba had already broken his silence in some way or that he was gradually breaking his silence. Not every Baba lover was still waiting for Baba to give the "one Word." Communication with the mandali indicated that, again, they had no inside track, and, themselves, held varying opinions as to whether Baba had broken his silence. To a large extent it didn't matter to the mandali. It wasn't that way with me. It mattered a lot to me.

The world that Baba came to redeem seemed utterly unredeemed to me. The destructive, negative trends of the past decades, nay, the whole century, continued unabated. Added to the threat of nuclear destruction were the ominous trends of environmental pollution and devastation. Baba said that his advent and the breaking of his silence with the Word would end the destructive slide of humanity and initiate a new age of peace, fulfillment, and harmony:

> I veil myself from man by his own curtain of ignorance, and manifest my Glory to a few. My present avatãric Form is the last Incarnation of this

cycle of time, hence my Manifestation will be the greatest. When I break my Silence, the impact of my Love will be universal and all life in creation will know, feel and receive of it. It will help every individual to break himself free from his bondage in his own way. I am the Divine Beloved who loves you more than you can ever love yourself. The breaking of my Silence will help you to help yourself in knowing your real Self.

All this world confusion and chaos was inevitable and no one is to blame. What had to happen has happened; and what has to happen will happen. There was and is no way out except through my coming in your midst. I had to come, and I have come. I am the Ancient One.[1]

Throughout the years, Baba often said he would break his silence—that was the purpose of keeping his silence, to break with "just one Word." The Word would not be the word or words of a philosopher, but the original word of God, which would penetrate to the heart of all humankind and awaken a love that would lead to the solution of all problems.

I intend, when I speak, to reveal the ONE Supreme Self which is in all. This accomplished, the idea of the self as a limited, separate entity will disappear, and with it will vanish self-interest. Co-operation will replace competition, certainty will replace fear, generosity will replace greed. Exploitation will disappear.

When the God-man speaks, Truth is more powerfully manifested than when He uses either sight or touch to convey it. For that reason, Avatars usually observe a period of silence lasting for several years, breaking it to speak only when they wish to manifest the Divine Will and world-wide transformation of consciousness then takes place.

Time, implying a beginning and an end, like space, has no existence in the eternity of God. For us here, time does exist, and the present is fast approaching a junction that is the end of an old and the beginning of a new cycle. The time is thus almost ripe for a fresh Universal Divine Manifestation that will infuse new vitality in the body of the old and time-worn truths.[2]

When I speak there will be many proofs of my spiritual power and of my ability to bestow Illumination. People will then realize that Truth, which is the

UNSPOKEN "SSSHH." MAHABALESHWAR, OCTOBER 1950.

Source of All Love and Existence, rules supreme in all departments of life.[3]

Ages and ages ago, I did perform one great miracle and the whole of this illusion of creation came from Me. I will perform another such miracle at the time when I break My silence. That will be My first and last miracle in my present incarnation. Expect no other miracle from Me.[4]

The breaking of My Silence will reveal to man the universal oneness of God, which will bring about the universal brotherhood of man. My Silence had to be. The breaking of My Silence has to be—soon.[5]

All confusion and despair are your own shadow which will banish when I speak the Word.[6]

Not only had Baba made these and other statements about the breaking of his silence, but he had repeatedly over the years given out dates when he would break his silence— "My silence will be broken by March of this year" and so forth. The Hollywood Bowl incident is one of the most famous examples. The setting of dates and the dates passing continued to the end of Baba's life, as is seen from the statements announcing the Last Darshan. In fact, the intensity and urgency of these statements seemed to increase as Baba neared the end of his physical life.

It is amazing how his followers retained interest and belief in Baba breaking his silence despite his numerous failures to do so. In fact, his humor often dispelled his lovers' anguish and consternation over not breaking his silence by his self-appointed dates. Once he said, "Instead of breaking My Silence, I am breaking My promises," or he might say something like, "But next year I will definitely do it. The time of my putting off the breaking of My Silence is over."

Sometimes he compared not breaking his silence to a doctor who tells a patient in the hospital that he will be better and able to leave in seven days. At the end of seven days, the patient finds he has still not recovered and will not be discharged. The doctor then tells the patient that it will be another few days, and this continues again and again. Baba explained that the doctor knows that the thought of being in the hospital for a long time will be depressing for the patient. So, to keep the patient's hopes and morale high, the doctor strings him along with promises of a short-term release. Typically after Baba gave such an illustration, he would say something like, "But now I know the patient is ready to recover, and so when I say I will break My Silence soon, it is definitely so."

He might even set another date, and yet that date too would pass. Other times he might say something like, "I have been continually putting off breaking my silence, but that cannot continue. I must break my silence before June 20." At times he would emphasize that humanity was not ready to receive his Word, and that's why he had not released it. Sometimes he emphasized his compassion, stressing the upheaval that would attend his silence breaking and saying that out of compassion he waits.

He gave an analogy of a soldier who is shot on the battlefield. As he begins to fall, he notices some ants on the ground in front of him. Not wanting to crush the ants, he averts his body when he falls. Then again Baba would add that time has passed and now he will "definitely" break his silence. When confronted by skeptical questions of not breaking his silence despite repeated promises to do so, he might say something like, "Of course I will break My Silence; otherwise why would I have observed it?"

The issue of Baba breaking his silence continued throughout his life—a constant drama and tension that gave vital energy to all his plans, actions, and every word dictated about doing so. For me and many other Baba lovers, the question of *when* did not vanish when he dropped his body. As the world continued on in its wayward and unrenewed course, there certainly could be reason to doubt him. For some, it formed the basis to reject him and his claim of being the Avatar. For me there was undeniable anguish; I continued to believe, but the doubt remained in the periphery of my mind.

∞ ∞ ∞

I married in the summer of 1974; however, the happiness of the event was tempered by my agony about Baba and the world. The Maine community that we had joined was coming apart. Eventually two of the couples split up and moved away. The new-life community became just my wife and I, in our rustic, small, self-built cabin, and our neighbors, my friends from Indiana University.

I profoundly struggled during this time with what Baba was, or rather seemingly was not,

EXPRESSIVE GESTURES, BANGALORE, CIRCA 1939–1940.

doing in the world. Any expectation of a "Baba movement," which had seemed inevitable with the energy surrounding the Last Darshan, was disappointed. Baba groups formed throughout the United States and in other countries, as ours did in Maine, but new people "coming to Baba" progressed on a relatively small scale. Other spiritual movements led by various gurus and teachers formed and quickly gained large numbers of followers and substantial media attention. From a sociological perspective, Baba seemed to be another one of these and not a very successful one at that.

In the early 1970s, I wrote a detailed and intricately reasoned essay on the point of Baba breaking his silence. Part of the impetus was my chagrin as well as my inability to accept what some Baba lovers were saying: that Baba had broken his silence, or that the breaking of his silence was symbolic, or some variation of this assumption. I just could not accept this point of view, although I envied the serenity that these Baba lovers portrayed. For me, to believe in Baba was to believe that he would break his silence as he said he would, to take him literally and not rely on fancy mental footwork—a symbolic interpretation of what Baba meant. Moreover, for me, it was a matter of the world. What about the world? I would ask, both of myself and others. My feelings at the time are revealed in an extract from that essay:

Now it is only death; let us come to recognize that. The dying do not go down easy, it is an instinct of nature. One of the primary reactions of the dying is anger and resistance to their condition. So I find myself getting angry at Baba.

I think the tendencies toward these fallacies are greater if we do not face up to the realities of our present condition, no matter how grim it appears at the moment.

Why Baba has led me to expect something to happen in the future, only to have me eventually struggle and wrench myself back again to trying to find the Reality in the present is something that I really don't understand.

So life was difficult—socially and culturally, the breakup of the community and the fading bloom of the back-to-the-land movement; politically, Nixon had trounced McGovern in the 1972 election; economically, our family struggling to make ends meet; personally, my marriage was under increasing strain; and spiritually.

The marital issues revealed deep, problematic parts of myself. From within the faith I was holding on to, I caught glimpses of how Baba was working. At our wedding ceremony on a coastal beach, my vow was inspired by Baba's words. I said that in our day and age marriage may seem to be impossible, but that it is still a worthwhile undertaking to strive for "because only the impossible has any meaning." For all its existential intensity, my statement could not be seen as a ringing endorsement of our future.

Both of our parents came to the wedding—mine from the East Coast and my wife's from the West Coast. Although, in my eyes, my parents had a terrible relationship, they stayed together. My father had a drinking problem (something I did not know until after he died in 1984). He was often irritable, angry, or yelling—mostly at my mother, but often at my brother and me.

I never understood why their marriage endured. Although it was an unconscious thought until my own marriage, I vowed to never live that way. Because of my leftist political background, I referred to their marriage as a "bourgeoisie marriage" and no doubt felt that marriage itself was a bourgeoisie institution, in spite of Baba's describing it in the highest terms as a spiritual path that presents itself as a "disguised opportunity."

Despite the frustration and disappointment, I somehow managed to sustain my faith in Baba. Accepting that Baba is God, it would seem that *he* sustained the link. Baba often said to his lovers, "Hold on to My daaman." *Daaman* is a Persian word meaning the hem of a garment. As Baba said this, he would hold up the hem of his *sadra* (white Indian tunic). He explained the phrase with the image of a mother moving through a marketplace as her child, at her side, holds onto her skirt so as not to get lost. Following the master is like holding onto him as he takes you through the world's marketplace of allurements and challenges, safely and most directly. Holding on, he said, would be difficult.

Baba repeatedly warned that events would conspire to make people lose their faith in him and let go of his daaman. These events were not specified, but surely among them were the two car accidents in which he and those riding with him were badly injured and one of the mandali died. Who is this Avatar, this world savior, who cannot save himself and his close ones from a car accident? Other such issues were his unpredictability, which suggested he didn't know what he was doing, and his broken promises in the matter of his silence. Who is this capricious God in human form who breaks his promises? Undoubtedly, the most supreme challenge to faith in Baba was his death without breaking his silence and his seemingly nil effect upon the world.

∞ ∞ ∞

The get-togethers of the Baba lovers in Maine *were* sustaining. Somehow, amidst the general bleakness of the world situation, these gatherings were a light and a joy that gave us a sense of Baba's presence and guiding hand in our lives. When I spoke with a friend, who was not a follower of Baba, about these meetings and how wonderful Baba was, he tactfully suggested that perhaps the joyfulness was just the usual phenomenon of social support. Nevertheless, I thought it remarkable, almost miraculous, that somehow in an out-of-the-way corner of the United States, there were a handful who followed Baba and gathered together to feel his natural presence.

For me, trips every year or so to the Meher Spiritual Center in Myrtle Beach were also sustaining. To arrive there at the end of a long Maine winter was like coming into a paradisiacal oasis of Baba's beauty and love. It was a splendid experience; no matter what was happening in our cynical, stressful, negative world, visiting the Center was like coming home. The Center's natural beauty is part of its charm; Baba's having been there and establishing it as his "home in the West" contributes to its grace. The places where he stayed and lived (the Lagoon Cabin and his house and bedroom); the presence of his devoted and loving caretakers, Elizabeth, Kitty, and Jane; and visiting Baba friends and lovers invigorated, renewed, and inspired. There were special visits from some of the India mandali—Adi, Meherjee, Bhau—people who had spent a good part of their adult lives with Baba. Their faith and conviction in Baba was 100 percent and was communicated to us in every way. Adi had a favorite statement: "Conviction in Meher Baba is God Realization in disguise." The reason that he said "in disguise," is because our lives entailed little or no "spiritual experiences" that are often associated with the occult; we were very much rooted in the everyday. That was, by all means, the description of my life at the time.

To be sure, there *were* some specific and personal ways that I experienced Baba's workings. A good example of this happened during a Baba festival that we organized in the summer of 1975 and held on land belonging to a family of Baba lovers in western Maine. One of them, Alan, had recently attended a Baba *mela* (the Indian word for festival) that was held in Hamirpur, a very poor region of India. Hamirpur has a great many people who follow Baba with enthusiasm and the fire of love. A well-known disciple of

BABA WITH LOVERS AT DARSHAN.

Meher Baba, named Pukar, was one of the central figures at that mela in India.

I had met Pukar at the Last Darshan in Poona. *Pukar*, an adopted name, is the word for "call" and was also the name of a broadside that he formerly published in the Hamirpur district years before he came to Baba. During those publishing years, Pukar was an active revolutionary against British rule in India, an atheist, and a Communist. He became aware of an increasing interest in the district for a spiritual figure named Meher Baba, whom people referred to as the Avatar.

Pukar disliked what he perceived as the typical gullibility of the masses, particularly in India, toward these spiritual gurus. He saw them as phonies who led the people of India to believe in otherworldly fantasies of salvation and away from the real and necessary task of liberation from Britain.

Pukar felt that it was his duty to expose Meher Baba as a fraud and a hypocrite and to put an end to his growing popularity in the district. His opportunity came when Baba made a trip through Hamirpur. Pukar planned to meet Baba, challenge him to a debate—probably disrupt Baba's fake silence—and show Baba to be a spiritual deceiver.

As Baba's procession was traveling through one of the villages, Pukar, a husky and imposing figure, moved in front of Baba. In a vision unlike anything Pukar ever had before, he saw Baba as Krishna—the God-man's appearance as Avatar in the *Bhagavad Gita*. At the same time, Pukar became aware that he was reliving an actual scene in Krishna's time when he had been a disciple of Krishna. In this rare visionary experience with Meher Baba, Pukar was suddenly aware of the reality of reincarnation and thus the soul—that God, the Avatar, and Baba were one. Pukar had found his revolution, but it was a revolution of his consciousness. Other experiences bolstered this one, and soon Pukar's *Call* became a publication devoted to Meher Baba.

Pukar later also became known as Baba's horse because he liked to get down on his hands and knees and have Baba sit on him so that he could carry him around the way Arjuna's chariot carried Krishna.

So, when we organized the 1975 Maine Mela, Alan wrote to Pukar to ask if he could come to the United States to be a special guest. Alan also contacted other groups across the country. Money was raised and pooled to fund the trip for Pukar and Sitaram, another Baba lover from Hamirpur, who would travel with Pukar if he could come. We received a provisional yes from Pukar, but there were visa problems as well as some health issues for the elderly Pukar. Although there was a cloud of uncertainty over whether Pukar and Sitaram would make the trip, we decided to go ahead with the plans for the Mela. A date was set and announcements sent out to the Center and

Baba groups throughout the country. Before this festival, the largest Baba gathering that we had ever had in Maine was maybe fifteen people. This gathering involved building suitable structures on the land to accommodate what could be well over a hundred people. The centerpiece of the construction was a dome-covered building about four feet above the ground and open at the sides, which would serve as the central meeting place and where the main programs would be held.

The arrangements for Pukar and Sitaram were handled by others within our group. It was presumed that they would arrive for the opening date of our three-day event, but there was uncertainty. I knew that several people in Boston planned to meet them at the airport when they arrived from India and bring them to Maine, but we were unsure if they would actually arrive as planned. In the afternoon of opening day, I was sitting under the dome shortly after the Mela had begun when I saw two pair of sandaled feet peeking out beneath Indian dress move into view. Pukar and Sitaram walked toward the entrance. They were there! They had made it! As Pukar entered, with his white hair and beard and flowing sadra, he reminded me of Sri Aurobindo, an inspiring Indian mystic and yogi.

Over the next several days of the mela, Pukar told his story in vivid detail. To me it seemed like an Indian epic—the *Gita*, the *Ramayana*—come to life. I wished for a chance to spend some time alone with him. I wanted to ask him my usual questions about Baba breaking his silence and inquire as to his politics at this point in his life. But Pukar was busy and because of his age, tired easily and rested frequently. So many wanted his attention. Suddenly, almost magically, I was alone with him sitting off to the side of the field under a tree. As I told him about myself and asked my questions, he lovingly stroked my arm. Something opened inside of me as I felt a warm, tender love emanate from him. At that moment, I realized that I was experiencing a gentleness and love that I had never received from my father.

I also realized that I had unconsciously been uncomfortable with the meaning of Meher Baba's name—"Compassionate Father" and with Baba's urging that we make him our "loving father." Intellectually, of course, I accepted it, but in that brief encounter I realized that deep down it did not make sense to me. Within my emotional unconscious, the concept of a father as someone who was gentle and loving was impossible to comprehend. I had a sudden glimpse into this part of myself as I felt love from Pukar, an unambiguously loving father figure. This was the beginning of my being able to see myself as a father, which had been impossible until then.

Even though I eventually moved toward intentionally having a child, my wife and I first entered a period of marriage counseling that lasted four years and involved three different therapists. In 1979, on my fortieth birthday, our first and only child was born.

∞ ∞ ∞

Despite the active presence of Baba in my life, I continued to struggle on all fronts, philosophically, politically, and even spiritually. I wondered whether it was worth it or even made sense to stay active in any work for social change. After all, wasn't it just a downhill slide until Baba broke his silence and manifested to the world? And was he going to do that? Was I a fanatical cult member waiting for the world to end? Through my work, I was very familiar with psychological and sociological literature categorized as "cognitive dissonance"—titles such as the classic study, *When Prophecy Fails: A Social and Psychological Study* by Leon Festinger.

I wrote another, longer essay concerning the question of Baba breaking his silence. Again, in a detailed, logical deliberation, I reasoned through all the issues I could come up with. As God, Baba said that he is "infinite honesty" and truth personified, and yet, he was apparently the most dishonest. Almost maddeningly, he spoke of this apparent dishonesty from time to time, saying, "I am consistent in inconsistency,"[7] and "My only plan is to let you know there is no plan."[8] And yet he often spoke of "God's plan of a fresh dispensation of love and truth to the weary world."[9]

Whether this brought me close to a breaking point or not, one effect of this intense reasoning was that I noticeably sharpened my analytical abilities. It was a curious development. Baba often said that spiritual realization was beyond the mind and that at the end of the New Life phase of his work he had, as the perfect aspirant, gone through the period known as "the annihilation of the mind"—a process that humanity would eventually follow. I don't know if my mind was being annihilated, but at times it felt like that. I did know that the intellect that Baba was to take us past, for me, actually seemed to become more effective.

My interest in Zen—a Japanese sect of Mahayana Buddhism—helped me with the silence-breaking puzzle. Or, shall I say, Meher Baba through his previous appearance as the Buddha, helped me work through the Zen expression. I realized that with the silence breaking puzzle, Baba had created a giant *koan*—a paradoxical riddle used to help Zen Buddhists attain enlightenment. One day I read that an effective koan is not just an imaginative riddle or strange enigma but—more vividly described—a hot ball of wax taken into the mouth. You can neither swallow it, because it will burn your throat, nor spit it out, because it will burn your tongue. So you have to keep rolling it around inside your mouth. I saw this image as a perfect description of the effect of Baba's apparently not breaking his silence—at least for me.

Thus, within a relatively short period of time in the mid-1970s, I experienced Meher Baba both as the incarnation of love (with Pukar's help) and as the stern and demanding Zen master. I tried to capture this many-sided nature of Baba, in his seventh appearance as the Avatar, in this poem.

On being asked, "Who is Meher Baba?"

The guidebooks may describe
his path as Bakhti,
but between ourselves, we never took
that word seriously.
For yoga, it's "you go,"
and not a mention of asana,
an answer that will disappoint the readers
of the *Gita* and the *Ramayana*.
What about mantra, meditation, and kundalini?
No, nothing going for this one,
who is neither saint, swami, or genie.
Some say that love comes closest
to naming his way,
but who really knows what
is meant by that today?
The standard categories won't do,
and we are pressed to extremes.
It's either silence for us
or foolish hyperbole in streams.

But he didn't shrink from the extremes
as the Alpha and the Omega,
and as Gautama there was the silence
of the one hand clapping and the flower.
From time immemorial it's been only told
in paradox,
and I do it once again.
For Christians he is more heaven than heaven,
for Buddhists, more Zen than Zen.

Is Baba God?, I would ask myself. Well, I really couldn't know. He said he was God, but he also said that we really could not know this until we ourselves were God. I did know that Meher Baba was a man, that there really was such a person who said that he was Christ come again, who was silent for forty-four years, and who lived a life that was unparalleled in the history of lives that are not shrouded in the mists of time and myth.

Now if this man was a liar and a deceiver, that would be a terrible thing. It would be another monstrous deception in the vast history of human perfidy. So, I did not know if Meher Baba was God, because I could not really know. The issue then was whether I could have faith in him as a man. Could I put my faith in this man? And I decided that the answer was yes. My faith in God then, was also my faith in the human.

THE MIRACLE WORKER

The whole course of time is subject to eternity in one simple glance.

AQUINAS

I was hired for the position of director for the acute admission unit of the state mental hospital in Bangor, which helped our tenuous economic situation as well as our equally tenuous marriage. Despite the financial benefits, the job was a strain. I was employed by the community mental health center, which was contracted by the state to run the acute admission unit. Whenever there was a budget conflict between the state and the mental health center, the state would consider ending the contract, suggesting that it could manage the unit less expensively. My stance against the increasing dominance of the biological model in mental health created an uneasy relationship between myself and the unit psychiatrist, which was aggravated by the ambiguity in authority as to unit policies. I was the director, and the psychiatrist was the clinical director.

It was now the fall of 1980. I was aware that since I had gone to India in 1969, many other Baba lovers, who had also gone about that time, had returned again and again. It was a bit mystifying to me why they did so. I had read a book by Bernard Gunther on relaxation massage and yoga exercises developed at the Esalen Center in California entitled, *Sense Relaxation Below Your Mind*, a takeoff on the expression, "blow the mind."[1] One of the chapters was entitled, "What to Do Until the Messiah Comes." This chapter title resonated with me in a way that had nothing to do with the purpose of the book.

I believed that the Messiah had already come, even though the world in general had no knowledge of it happening. Furthermore, the state of the world seemed ever-increasingly uncertain to me and gave no indication that the World Redeemer had returned. My understanding of this state of affairs was that the Messiah,

Meher Baba, had not yet broken his silence and released the world-redeeming Word. Therefore, I translated the expression "What to do until the Messiah comes," to "What to do until Meher Baba breaks his silence." So it seemed to me that having nothing better to do while waiting for Meher Baba to break his silence, his lovers returned to India.

By this time, I had accumulated two weeks vacation, and a colleague at the hospital, a psychiatrist with similar mental health views, spoke to me about traveling to India together. He was not a follower of Baba, but he was interested in Indian spirituality, particularly the teacher, Rajneesh, who had a center in Poona—Meher Baba's birthplace. The Last Darshan in 1969 had been held at Poona, which was only a few hours from Baba's tomb in Meherabad near Ahmednagar.

My wife and I discussed the possibility of my traveling to India. Because our child was only a little over a year old, my wife was not thrilled about my going and leaving her alone with the baby, but she would not stand in my way either. I felt, and she may have sensed it too, that a break from each other might be a positive move.

So, I went back to India. As luck would have it, several people from Myrtle Beach were accompanying Kitty Davy to India at the same time. Kitty was then almost ninety years old and welcomed our joining their group. So we planned to travel with them.

About a week before our scheduled departure, I began to have second thoughts about going. One evening, my colleague came to our home to see slides taken during my wife's trip to India and to Baba's tomb in the early 1970s. Other than some nice shots of India scenery, most of the slides were of people standing around, holding teacups, and smiling into the camera; it seemed static and boring. What was I going to do for almost two weeks in India? After mulling it over, I reasoned that it would be a much-needed break from my job at the hospital—an opportunity for me to read and rest. I decided to pursue a meditative outlook on the trip—not to formally meditate (I had stopped doing that long ago), but to be an observer and use this time to practice a detached attitude, which I had trouble maintaining in my everyday life.

Once on the plane, I remembered how long and grueling the 24-hour trip to India was. One of the women accompanying Kitty said that the trip to India was like childbirth—you forget how bad it is or else you would never do it again.

When the plane finally landed in Bombay, and I walked out onto the tarmac, an intense wall of heat and smell put me in touch once more with exotic India. I sensed that on this visit I needed to separate Baba from India. After a struggle with the various taxi *wallas* who competed with each other and pressed in upon us to take their vehicle, we four finally fit into

MEHER BABA CIRCA 1941.

a small, prearranged Italian Fiat. With our luggage piled and tied down on the roof, we began the harrowing, final leg of the journey from Poona to Meherabad. I say *harrowing* because the driver, a Baba lover who had known Kitty for years, went at breakneck speed, Indian fashion, with the apparent mission of getting Kitty to Baba's tomb as quickly as possible. Perhaps he felt that at ninety years of age, she might pass away before we got there. I felt that his driving might be the very event that would bring on her demise—along with the rest of us.

As we wove in and out of traffic on a barely two-lane winding road and darted back into our lane just before an oncoming bus smashed into us head-on, I could hardly bear to look out the window. I glanced over at Kitty. She clearly knew that danger was whisking down the road with us, but there was a detached serenity on her face. She had long ago surrendered to Baba; whatever happened was in his hands. I thought, "To go to Baba, you have to risk death." I resumed *trying* to maintain my detached observer stance that I had intended to bring with me to India.

Finally, many long and dusty hours later, there was the tomb—a gleaming white dome on the top of upper Meherabad Hill. Although it was unusual, our driver drove up the hill in respect for Kitty. As the car moved slowly ahead, I looked over at Kitty and saw something I had not noticed before. On her lap was a bouquet of flowers wrapped in an Indian newspaper. She evidently had bought them in Poona or at one of the stops on the way. I was surprised that I had not noticed the flowers earlier. Of course, Kitty had brought them to lay down with respect and love at the tomb. I felt terrible. What did I bring? Nothing. Self-centered me brought nothing to lay at Baba's tomb—except my nothingness. When we got out of the car, Kitty turned to me and said, "Would you mind carrying these flowers for me up to the tomb?" and held out the package for me to take.

KITTY DAVY ON HER 89TH BIRTHDAY. MYRTLE BEACH, 1980.

Kitty, of course, had no idea what I had been thinking and probably asked me to do this so that it would be easier for her to walk to the tomb, but this simple gesture stirred something inside me. It was as if Baba had heard me and brought about this response to my anguish. At the threshold of the *samadhi* (tomb), I handed the flowers back to Kitty and watched as she laid them on the white marble tomb.

Then it was my turn to approach and the stirring within me broke through to another level. I immediately knew that the emotion I was feeling was more than something brought about by flowers—they had only been a catalyst. There was an energy for me in that little tomb that had an incredible solidity—an overwhelming reality and force. I felt Baba's power—something I had not felt for years.

At the time, I did not and could not have expressed what happened to me. Ultimately, words are insufficient to cover the depth and meaning of such experiences. In retrospect, I would say that the wall that I had erected between my inner and outer self collapsed. On reflection, I understood that until that experience in the tomb, I had unconsciously placed Baba's existence *within* me. This internal understanding of God was more in keeping with an Eastern belief system as opposed to a more Western stance that God is *without*.

My coming to God through Eastern-influenced channels led me to place God on one side of a wall that we naturally construct to divide our inner being from the outer world. An Eastern cultural view of God as an inner presence made more sense to me than the Western culture's placing of God outside—such as the classical placement of God in the sky. In that crashing moment in the tomb, I understood that if God was infinite, then it was absurd to believe that infinity could be limited to one half of a totality. With this knowledge came an understanding that Baba was indeed God—the Ancient One, the Christ, the Avatar—come once again to renew the world. Whatever doubts I had since first coming to Baba were instantly swept away, and I recognized that the previous ten years had been in preparation for this moment. I had been suffering a darkness and spiritual isolation the depths of which were only revealed by the contrast with that moment of breakthrough and light.

When I walked out, Nana Kher, who faithfully kept watch at the tomb, gave me a hug and spoke his well-known phrase, "Welcome home." Although Nana said these words to each person who arrived, this welcome home was truly given in love—he knew. For days, I remained on the verge of tears. Again Baba had opened up my heart giving me insight into what he meant when he said that he was infinite—that he was both within *and* without.

I had known that a Pilgrim Center was being built nearby, which was intended to be a restful, convenient lodging for pilgrims while visiting Meher Baba's tomb. In fact, it had opened just a few months before our trip. It was a magnificent brick and stone structure designed to house fifty-six visitors in various-sized rooms and featured several interior gardens and a marvelous common room that served as a dining hall. Now, I was struck by its significance. It was obviously a work of love. How did it get built? Where did the money come from? While I was sleeping in the Maine woods, this, in all its spiritual grandeur, was being prepared for pilgrims who came to Meherabad. I had thought that, in terms of Baba, nothing was happening in the world, but here was this new center near Baba's tomb, perhaps insignificant by world standards, but for me, a miracle.

When I saw the mandali again, I had a similar reaction. When I had met them at the Last Darshan in 1969, I thought they were loving and kind, but beyond that I felt no special connection with them. At that time, I had gone to India for Baba's darshan—at his invitation, and the mandali were a backdrop as they had been for Baba's work while he was in the body. Now it was so very different. I felt Baba's love pouring forth from the mandali. They were living beacons and fountains of love. Though ordinary people, neither God-realized nor Perfect Masters, they were magnificent human beings—instruments of Meher Baba's love and service. Over a decade later, it was evidently time for me to see them as the wonderful, loving disciples of Baba that they truly are.

∞ ∞ ∞

I also became more aware of the significance of Amartithi day in India, January 31—the day Baba dropped his body. Our group in Maine sometimes commemorated that day together, and I had at least always noted it by myself. Now, in India, I learned that many thousands were coming each year to Meher Baba's tomb at Meherabad to observe Amartithi, and these numbers were increasing. Although most of those who came were Baba lovers from India, a substantial number of followers were from other countries. I was told that throughout Amartithi day, the line outside Baba's tomb stretched so long that it required a wait of several hours to enter the tomb for only a few moments alone with Baba. On a platform outside the tomb, music and singing went on from morning into the night.

Eruch Jessawala, a close mandali with Baba for over forty years, had been the prime communicator for Meher Baba. He read the alphabet board and Baba's hand gestures, transcribed the words into written messages to be read at gatherings, and transcribed the manuscript for *God Speaks*. Three days before I was to leave India, I joined a group of visitors in mandali hall where Eruch was talking about his life with Baba.

Aloba, a fiery, passionate Iranian mandali—who, as a boy in the 1920s, had come to Meher Baba at the children's school—was also in the hall. In about two hours, Aloba was to take us to Seclusion Hill where Baba had worked in seclusion. At this time, the Meherabad area was experiencing one of its frequent dry spells, which was verging on drought. Aloba was going to the hill to pray to Baba for rain as he had done once before and his prayers had been answered.

Meanwhile, Eruch was telling one of his moving stories when someone asked him about the breaking of Baba's silence. In response, he asked one of his helpers to retrieve a letter from the files that Eruch had transcribed in answer to this same question. He then turned to me and asked, "Can you read this out?" I was jarred by the coincidence. I had not spoken to anyone about my absorption with this question.

My reading of the letter led to further discussion about the silence breaking and to Eruch being asked about "spiritual desperation." Baba once gave out a statement called "Twelve Ways of Realizing Me" that illustrated qualities such as faith, humility, peace of mind, and desperation, with a short phrase for each. For example, for peace of mind he said, "If you have the peace of mind of a frozen lake, then you will realize

THE TOMB, OR SAMADHI, WITH BABA'S LOVERS WAITING TO GO IN FOR THEIR DARSHAN.

me." For desperation, "If you experience the desperation that causes a person to commit suicide and you feel that you cannot live without seeing me, then you will see me."

Baba had also spoken of "divine desperation" in which the potential power of desperateness is harnessed and used creatively. Someone asked Eruch, "Is it important to be desperate?" It was not Eruch's answer to this question that startled me, but the image he used. He said, "No. Desperation is ultimately no good. It is like having a sweet ball of candy in your mouth. You don't want to swallow it, and you don't want to spit it out, so it is stuck in your throat."

"My God," I thought, "This is nearly the same image [the hot ball of wax in your mouth] I used to contemplate the riddle of Baba's breaking or not breaking his silence. I had never heard anyone else use that image and here Eruch was saying that this desperation was not good. I could not help but sense that this message was specifically meant for me. My mind was in a whirl. Was I to drop the riddle and accept that Baba had broken or was now breaking his silence?

Almost at that moment, Aloba rang the bell to call us for the climb to Seclusion Hill. Because Aloba had long believed that Baba was yet to break his silence, I was struggling with opposing suppositions that seemed to be pulling me in two directions.

With Aloba in the lead and our procession joined by about a hundred local villagers and farmers, we solemnly and resolutely marched up the hill. On the way, I was moved by Aloba's statement: "It is very easy for Baba to bring rain; it is very hard for us to pray to Baba from the bottom of our hearts." I prayed fiercely for a miracle of rain, but it did not rain, then or within the next two days before I left. I was disappointed and sorry for the people of the area, but this prayerful event was a deeply moving spiritual experience prompted by the marvelous love, energy, and faith of Aloba, and I appreciated him for that.

As I bounced along during the twelve-mile bus ride from the mandali's residence to Meherabad, I felt lulled into an altered state of mind and wrote this verse:

> From here on all rains
> will be His rain,
> all suns bursting through the clouds
> will be His sunburst.
>
> For He has inscribed His name
> on the pageant of nature,
> and its script
> will constantly reveal Him.

∞ ∞ ∞

The first rain I saw was as the plane landed in Bangor, Maine. The next day, my wife and I had tickets to a play. Our neighbor's daughter was starring in *The Miracle Worker* as the young Helen Keller. In the climactic scene, Helen feels a splash of water as her teacher, Annie Sullivan, inscribes the word water on her palm, and, in a flash of understanding, she not only learns her first word, but the existence of language as well. A new world suddenly opens to her. Again: miracle worker, water, the Avatar—who works miracles without seemingly working them.

The miraculous and the difficult continued to coexist upon my return. Soon after my arrival, the state finally took over the acute admissions unit, and, except for some part-time work at the mental health center, I was out of a job. Marital counseling seemed more and more unproductive, and after Christmas, my wife and I separated. My life was turned upside down. It was a good thing I had been "initiated in the life of eternity," because "life in time" was getting tough.

This period seemed perfectly described by Baba in *Discourses* with words that had great resonance for me: ". . . evolution from the standpoint of the creature, with its limited knowledge, limited power, limited capacity for enjoying bliss, is an epic of alternating rest and struggle, joy and sorrow, love and hate—until in the perfected person, God balances the pairs of opposites, and duality is transcended."[2]

Earlier that fall, the first Northeast Gathering was held in upper New York state. It was modeled after the Silence Day Sahavas, a July multiday gathering of Baba lovers that had been occurring for several years in the Los Angeles area. A similar gathering had also been held in Georgia for the Southeast Baba lovers. These were sleep-over events with speakers, music, perhaps a Baba art display, panels, discussions, and a chance to meet and be with others followers of Baba.

Filis Frederick, who was one of the first Baba lovers that I had met, was instrumental in establishing the Los Angeles Sahavas. She wrote that in 1974 a small group of Los Angeles Baba lovers went to a cabin in the San Bernardino mountains for a weekend. Filis, as I indicated previously, was known to be psychic. On the way to the cabin, they stopped at a fork in the road, where suddenly Filis saw Baba standing. The group had so much fun camping out that they decided to do it again and to find a larger place so that more people could join them. They found a perfect site and their first sahavas drew about a hundred people. The sahavas site was reached from the same fork where she had seen Baba.[3]

I don't think I realized at that first Northeast Gathering in 1981, that these get-togethers really are spiritual darshans or sahavases. When people gather for Baba or "in Baba's love," as it's put, his loving presence *is* there. On the surface, these events may seem like social occasions, but I believe something more is going on. These gatherings, as well as Baba meetings, are a way of being together in his presence. They are natural, casual gatherings where what happens within each of us cannot be seen, but a sense of Baba's presence and love can surely be felt.

∞ ∞ ∞

The biggest darshan may be Amartithi in India. After having not returned to India for eleven years (from 1969 until 1980), I soon longed to go again. As soon as possible I did just that—a year and a half later, in 1982, I returned again in time for Amartithi.

For months before going—living alone in a small apartment, working part time, with our cold Maine winter, and my old car not starting—my mental picture of being on the Hill and seeing Eruch again was the beacon that drew me forward. It was sometimes touch and go whether I would make it back to India again.

Thus, it was magical when in 1982 I stood on Meherabad Hill with Eruch right in front of me. I was there again and it was real! I wanted to pinch myself. I had remained intensely focused on returning and I had made it—face to face with Eruch again on the night of January 30 on the top of the Hill—it was as if I had awakened from a trance.

For several days around Amartithi, it was Eruch's practice to stay on the hill all night and to stay awake. When someone asked him why he did this, he said, "It's a darshan program and I always stayed up all night during a darshan program," which for me confirmed that all Baba gatherings are darshans.

Even though it was the night before Amartithi, there was a long line outside the tomb of those waiting to take their brief darshan. I left Eruch and the group gathered around him and went over to the tomb to sit outside and watch people go in to take their darshan. As I sat there watching people go into the tomb, stand in front of Baba's picture with palms together in a prayerful gesture, or bow down and place their head on the marble slab, a feeling of being exactly where I wanted to be filled me with joy. It was a contentment that I had never known before. There *was* absolutely no other place to go and nothing else to do. This was it. I felt like I could be there forever.

The Magic Flute

We do not chart and measure the vast field of nature
or express her wonders in terms of science; on the contrary,
we see miracles on every hand—the miracle of life in seed and egg,
the miracle of death in a lightening flash and in the swelling deep.

OHIYESA (CHARLES EASTMAN)

For a child, love needs to be visible and felt. That was lacking in my childhood. I had grown up in an unhappy home with an alcohol-abusing father and parents who were often arguing. I never had a sense that there was love between my parents. The subtle, underlying meaning of two people arguing while working out thorny problems completely escapes a child's mind, or at least it did in my case. As a young adolescent, I saw marriage as a curious institution. When I experienced anger and conflict in my own marriage, it felt like a repeat of my parents' relationship, and I could not accept that. Even though, almost twenty years later, I see my divorce as a failure, I am still convinced that we made the right decision.

In 1982, my wife and I divorced. I knew at the time that I did not have the spiritual strength to continue in the relationship. We probably could have "stayed married" some way or another, but by then I had come to believe that it would not be a good marriage or a happy one. It seemed that we were prolonging the inevitable, and if we remained together, we would most likely end up divorcing when our son was at a more impressionable age. Because we separated before our son was three years old, I felt that a divorce would be less harmful to him at that point in time rather than later in his childhood.

When I say I lacked the spiritual strength for my marriage, I mean the strength to turn the relationship around, to make it into a good marriage despite the obstacles and problems. I did not have it then, and I don't know if I have it now despite any relationship skills I may have gained since then. Sometimes the better part of wisdom is to know one's limitations.

In the course of time, I came to realize that having a good relationship with my son was more important to me than continuing the marriage and struggling and arguing. Although at the time of our divorce, I was not conscious of that choice, in retrospect, I saw that if I had stayed married, the stress and conflict of our relationship would have eroded my ability to be the parent that I wanted to be. Outside of marriage, I had the strength to be that parent, and my relationship with my son has always been positive and fulfilling.

It was obvious that following Meher Baba did not promise a charmed life; everything was not going to be an easy success. Other couples that followed Meher Baba also divorced—certainly less than the fifty percent average seen in the United States during the 1970s and 1980s, but still to a notable degree.

There *is* a difference between life with Meher Baba and life in a secular sense, but the life of one who believes in Baba does not fall into the category of what can be called an "ideal life." Baba made a profound distinction between a so-called ideal life and life with him. The former suppresses the negative, thereby rendering life dormant, and the individual falls into a false, ego-enhancing sense

AJMER, 1939.

of self-satisfaction and superficial "perfection" that is ultimately stilted, falsely pious, and unnatural. Meher Baba is the divine ego surgeon, who brings one's bad as well as good qualities to the surface. It is only in this way that the whole self, which contains both good and bad elements, can eventually be eliminated.

Bhau Kalchuri in *Lord Meher* illustrates this point in a story about himself. Two boys were brought into the Baba community to work in the kitchen. Bhau observed that Aloba, who was in charge of the boys, treated them harshly. One day, Aloba and Bhau were traveling with Meher Baba, and Baba asked Bhau, "What are you thinking?" Bhau answered that he was thinking about the severe way that Aloba treated the boys. With that, Baba began scolding Bhau, telling him that he could leave and go to any of the many ashrams in India where people seemed to live according to the principles of virtue. Bhau was taken aback and confused. Wasn't life with Meher Baba supposed to be a life of virtue?

Then Baba explained that life with him was not bound by any principles. Life with him was a "spiritual life," not a moral life. A spiritual life is only lived under the guidance of the Avatar or Perfect Master "who knows the pulse of everyone and treats everyone according to his particular malady." After the explanation, Baba smiled and asked Bhau to which of the ashrams he would like to go. "None," Bhau replied.[1]

While living in Penobscot, I met Mark Lutz. Mark had received his doctorate from the University of California at Berkeley and was a new professor of economics at the University of Maine. At the time of our meeting, I had been pondering the dilemma of some of my low-income clients. I was being paid by the state (through Medicaid) to provide counseling and psychotherapy for presumed psychological problems. Yet, I was becoming more and more aware that many of my clients' major problems stemmed from the lack of money. Either they did not have jobs or, if they did, what they earned was too low to adequately meet their basic needs. I knew little about academic economics, and I was interested in talking with Mark and perhaps learning something about these issues through him. When I approached him, I was surprised to find that he, in turn, wanted to know more about psychology. Thus, an instant friendship developed.

One of the first books Mark gave to me to read was by the British economist, E. F. Schumacher entitled, *Small Is Beautiful: Economics As If People Mattered*.[2] The provocative title was an obvious takeoff on the civil rights phrase, "Black is Beautiful." When I began reading the book, I recalled that I had recently seen an essay with the intriguing title "Buddhist Economics," by E. F. Schumacher.

I found Schumacher's *Small Is Beautiful* to be an exciting, informative economics book, and with Mark's tutelage, I was off to a good start. For my part, I introduced Mark to humanistic psychology, which differs from the traditional behaviorism and Freudian psychoanalysis. The main premise of humanistic psychology is that human beings have a hierarchy of needs, from basic physical needs such as food and shelter to a higher spiritual need termed *self-actualization*.

One night I woke up from a dream with the words *humanistic economics* turning over in my mind. My unconscious had combined humanistic psychology and Schumacher's economics and given this combination a name. I told Mark about the term and suggested that we write a book with this title. Wondering what humanistic economics would be, we jokingly said that we should write the book to find out. Mark proposed we contact Schumacher and ask if he would read our manuscript and write a foreword for the book.

Shortly after we sent the letter, it was Mark's turn to have a dream and he was shaken by it. He dreamed that Schumacher had died. I, in my knowing psychologist's way, assured him that it was merely an anxiety dream and, of course, had nothing to do with Schumacher. Not long after, we read that during a trip away from his home in Switzerland, Schumacher had suddenly died. A few days later, Mark called me to say that we had just gotten a letter from "a dead man." Schumacher had received the preliminary material that we sent to him and replied that he was looking forward to reading it when he returned from his trip. In 1979, Mark and I published our book, *The Challenge of Humanistic Economics*, and dedicated it to "E. F. Schumacher, the gentle giant of humanistic economics."[3]

Much later, I discovered what influenced Schumacher's economic writing and thought that I saw the hand of the Avatar at work. This reinforced my belief that what was happening to me in connection with Baba was also part of a much larger pattern of the Avatar's unrecognized action.

Schumacher was an economist member of the British Coal Board, an important, but no doubt conventional organization. He had been a promising economist who studied with the historically eminent English economist, John Maynard Keynes. Keynes wrote primarily in the 1930s and 1940s and is credited with developing ideas that helped to lead the world out of the Great Depression. In the 1940s, Keynes is quoted as saying, "If my mantle is to fall on anyone, it could be Otto Clarke or Fritz Schumacher. Otto Clarke can do anything with figures, but Schumacher can make them sing."

How did someone like Schumacher come to write a book as economically radical as *Small Is Beautiful*, which had little to do with statistics and more to do with philosophy and metaphysics? Obviously, there had been some transformation that turned this heir to mainstream economics into something quite different.

During his tenure on the Coal Board, from 1950 to 1970 while commuting between Caterham and Victoria Station, Schumacher began reading books by the Eastern philosophers and mystics who seemed to answer a question that had been uppermost in his mind after World War II: What had caused humankind to fail despite its high level of expertise? The writers of the books he was now reading all gave a similar answer. For example, Schumacher quotes Sir Sarvepalli Radhakrishnan, the first President of India and an outstanding Vedantic scholar, who wrote in 1939: "The present crisis in human affairs is due to a profound crisis in human consciousness, a lapse from the organic wholeness of life. There is a tendency to overlook the spiritual and exalt the intellectual."[4] During this same period, Schumacher became friendly with John G. Bennett, a member of the Coal Utilization Board and a disciple of the mystic, G. I. Gurdjieff, and Schumacher began the practice of yoga.

On February 1, 1951, during his daily meditation, Schumacher had a profound experience:

> But suddenly all sorts of things that I had not understood became completely clear—and in the most simple manner . . . Sentences and scripture that had been a mystery to me up to now and which I have since re-read suddenly became completely unambiguous and true. It became clear what Buddhists and Taoists understood by "emptiness," "nothingness," "Nirvana" or "Tao," and how it is possible that "Plenum," "abundance," "All," or "Life," can be used just as well. Since the 1st February I have not had any more doubts about the "truth. . . ."[5]

Near the end of his life, Schumacher wrote, "The modern experiment to live without religion has failed."[6] By "religion," he did not mean institutions, but the transcendental.

∞ ∞ ∞

In 1988, Mark and I published a revised version of our book because the first edition had sold out and was out of print. Even though our book was far from a bestseller and had not transformed the field of economics, we were pleased and surprised by the effect it did have: To some degree, the concept of humanistic economics became established in the field as an alternative. We presented at economic seminars, at universities, were asked to do a chapter for an anthology, and saw the start-up of a newsletter from Mankato State University in Minnesota entitled, *The Human Economy Newsletter: Economics As If People Mattered*.

After Mark and I finished our revised edition, I began to work on a book that I had been mulling over for several years. As the new work took shape, I was amazed at how long it had taken me to get to the root point.

The foundational idea for the field of economics, begun in the late 1700s with Adam Smith, was the value or even virtue of self-interest. The opening chapter of any economics textbook usually begins by describing how the economic system makes productive use of selfishness: "Economic rationality refers to a basic assumption made by economists about the economic behavior of human beings: that is, they are motivated by self-interest and therefore want as much of 'good things' as they can get."[7]

I knew that this position ran counter to what Meher Baba had said. He didn't describe self-interest as a virtue. For instance, he said: "The root of all our difficulties, individual and social, is self-interest"[8]—one of the many messages Meher Baba gave on this theme. Meher Baba's statement was diametrically opposite that of standard economic philosophy. When I first began to study economics, I minimized this opposition in my mind. I believed that somehow the self-interest that economics lauded was different from the self-interest that Baba said was our "root" problem. How I overlooked the unmistakable meaning of Baba's statement, "Exclusiveness is parading as nationalism; self-interest is known as economics. . ."[9] I do not know. Perhaps I needed a lot of preparation before I could really see just how off-course much of modern thinking, particularly economics, is.

After several years of criticizing economic thinking, the significance of Meher Baba's incisive statement about economics was validating. When all the voluminous economic theorizing is said and done, both pro and con, Baba puts it in just six words: "self-interest is known as economics." I decided that my next task would be to translate these six words into many more without directly connecting Meher Baba's name to my work. In 1990, I wrote, and Shambhala published, *Adam Smith's Mistake: How a Moral Philosopher Invented Economics and Ended Morality*.[10] Meher Baba is not mentioned in the book, but it is dedicated to A.M.B. The book was moderately successful, and I was frustrated when it went out of print in the mid-1990s.

I was intellectually charged by this work in economics. My experience in India and the realization that the infinite cannot be on either side of duality but must encompass both, brought about a change in the way I thought. My analytical abilities seemed to take a subtle jump forward, and I sensed that the proper place of intellect is grounded in spiritual life. Meher Baba had commented on this theme in several ways, such as when he spoke about the presumed controversy between science and spirituality:

RAHURI, OCTOBER 1936.

The *New Humanity* that emerges from the travail of the present struggle and suffering will not ignore science or its practical attainments. It is a mistake to look upon science as antispiritual. Science is a help or hindrance to spirituality according to the use to which it is put. Just as true art expresses spirituality, science, when properly handled, can be the expression and fulfillment of the spirit. Scientific truths concerning the physical body and its life in the gross world can become mediums for the soul to know itself; but to serve this purpose they must be properly fitted into larger spiritual understanding. This includes a steady perception of true and lasting values. In the absence of such spiritual understanding, scientific truths and attainments are liable to be used for mutual destruction and for a life that will tend to strengthen the chains that bind the spirit. All-sided progress of humanity can be assured only if science and religion proceed hand in hand.[11]

The Christian writer and scholar C. S. Lewis spoke of the Christian writer of spiritual fantasy, Charles Williams, as having "baptized" Lewis's imagination, thus enabling him to embark on his writing of spiritually metaphorical books, such as the space trilogy[12] and Narnia chronicles. I, myself, felt that Meher Baba had baptized *my intellect* with my experience in India. I needed this baptism. As a modern academic, I had always been an over-baked intellectual. Now, perhaps, the "bread" would come out right.

Whether it was this intellectual propensity or not, I found that I could not shake my concern for troubling events around the world and the awesome problems of our time. In India in 1980, I felt that Baba had indeed broken his silence and, until that experience, I just had not heard it. After the meeting with Eruch and the climb up Seclusion Hill with Aloba, I was convinced that was the case. That sense stayed with me for the next two years and during my trip to India for Amartithi in 1982. Certainly something inside me had changed. Some twenty years later, it still seems to me that I have never been the same. Evidently, I needed those years between 1969 and 1980 as a difficult and painful incubation period that then bore exquisite fruit on my return trip to India. This was a long process, and not everyone has to go through something like that. I needed to. A Baba friend of mine, Ann, heard about Meher Baba just a few years ago and came to believe in him in her own way through a series of her own experiences. She gently chides me when I talk about Baba still needing to break his silence, because for her, from her first coming to

Meher Baba, he has. Her coming to Baba *was* his breaking his silence.

In saying this, I am revealing that after 1982 I could not hold on to the conviction that Meher Baba had broken his silence. Because of the "me" and the "greed" decade that followed and the world's weak and inadequate attempts to deal with intensifying environmental crisis, my uncertainty became palpable again. Nevertheless, my anguish between 1969 and 1980 mercifully eased and Baba gave me sustaining insights.

One of these came out of a fortuitous combination of my relationship with my son and my continuing chagrin at the materialism of our time, both in terms of scientific philosophy as well as modern consumerism. A week before my son left for college, I had the opportunity to stay with him at the house we built in the woods. I rarely stayed there with him, but his mother was away for the weekend and my schedule was open. It was a very special time for me. My son was embarking on a special period in his adult life and moving away from home for the first time. It was great fun helping with things he needed for college, the preparation and packing, and then taking time out for a movie or concert.

I had been reading *The Waking Dream: Unlocking the Symbolic Language of Our Lives* by Ray Grasse,[13] and I brought it with me that weekend. It was a beautiful late-summer day when I awoke on Sunday morning. The past few days had been glorious and emotionally perfect, and I felt uplifted. I picked up the book by my bedside and began to read before getting out of bed. A blurb on the back cover caught my eye: "Wake up to a world of meaning."

Suddenly it hit me—all of it coming together. All of it? What was all of it? Many different strands and themes of my life, emotionally and intellectually. I, literally, just then, woke up to a world of meaning. Like Archimedes, I had my Eureka!—though not in a bathtub, but in bed. My insight: "Meaning is primary; matter is secondary." What this meant (or *I* meant; who knows at a time like that?) is that *matter*, rather than being the primary stuff of reality, is only the conveyance, the carrier, of the actual primary stuff of reality, which is *meaning*. Immediately following this insight, I knew I understood the answer to the classic question, "What is the meaning of life?" I saw that the question hid the answer. It did this by deflecting the one who asks away from the question to look for the answer outside of it. The question is like an arm throwing a ball; the person looks away from the question toward the trajectory of the ball. The ironic answer is that the meaning of life is *meaning*, meaning itself.

Life is a structure, a play of meaning or meanings. All of matter, in its infinite forms, including our bodies, all bodies, and the interactions of these bodies (events), is for the purpose of conveying meaning, or significance. What meaning? It could be any meaning, but the ultimate meaning was God, the divine. Meher Baba put this beautifully when he said that the master "has entered into the sanctuary of Truth, which is the abode of that eternal significance which is only partially and faintly reflected in the fleeting values of ever-changing creation."[14]

Life brings us to that point despite the "fleeting values of ever-changing creation." That is how it works out. Meher Baba said, "My will works to awaken you to this." And that morning was a time of awakening for me. To look at the world in this way is radically different from the conventional secular view that has scientific naturalism as its underpinning. This secular viewpoint proclaims that there is no purpose to anything; that any purpose we perceive is one that we mentally impose on a random universe.

To live with God was to "re-enchant the world," to quote a phrase from the late-nineteenth-century German sociologist, Max Weber.[15] Weber said that it was the nature of modern rationality to *enzaubert* the world—to take the "magic" out of it. (The German word *zaub* means magic or enchantment, as in the Mozart opera, *Die Zauberflote*, "The Magic Flute.") Weber wrote about modern bureaucracy and the cult of efficiency. I realized that morning that a view of the world as devoid of intrinsic purpose sucked the magic out of it. Science, with its false metaphysics, had bequeathed to us a world that was inert—in essence—dead. Where there is no purpose, there is no life— only the pseudolife of complicated machines. If *meaning* is fundamental and the purpose of life, then the world is active and dynamic on its own and that activity speaks to us. *It* is Meher Baba's book, *God Speaks*.

Meher Baba also said, "The book I want you to read is the book of the heart which holds the key to the mystery of life." I was starting to read that book and to rediscover the magic and meaning in life.

Karma Sensitive Psychotherapy

We assume that spiritual is its own unique domain and cannot be subsumed by other domains such as cognitions, emotions, social systems, and so on.[1]

P. SCOTT RICHARDS and ALLEN E. BERGIN

My insight that meaning comes first in the universe and matter is secondary paralleled what was happening to me in my work as a psychologist. Despite my work in economics, it has always been as a psychologist that I earned my bread and butter. As mentioned earlier, the field of psychology has become dominated by the idea that genetics and the brain, and what goes wrong with them, are the fundamental causes of psychological disorders. From this standpoint, the use of drugs to treat psychological problems is viewed not just as a chemical blanket to cover them, or even as a "straight jacket," but also as an actual *cure* of the fundamental problems of human misery. Essentially, this position is the reverse of my insight.

I increasingly came to see this development in psychiatry as yet one further expression and extension of the materialism that had become the driving force of our age. Scientists and philosophers who give voice to this biological materialism are always at pains to distinguish it from the materialism of consumer culture. So, a textbook in philosophy tries to caution us against equating the two: "In fairness to the materialist it should be added that materialism in none of its [philosophical meanings] need carry with it the implication that only what are usually called material values (roughly, those that can be bought by money) are worth seeking."[1] But is it a sheer accident that the two different meanings of materialism, the philosophical and the cultural, happen to exist in prominent fashion alongside each other in the same society? That is greatly to be doubted.

The principles of philosophical materialism have gotten so extreme that a psychiatrist invited to a White House conference on the problem of youth violence said that the answer to such violence is to put ever more youth on psychiatric drugs. He ridiculed what to him was the outmoded idea that someone's parents or cultural environment had anything significant to do with their psychological condition:

> It is hard to believe that until 20 years ago we still believed that inadequate parenting and bad childhood trauma were the cause of psychiatric illnesses. And in fact, even though we know better today, that antiquated way of thinking is out there, so that people who wouldn't dream of blaming parents for other types of diseases, like their child's diabetes or asthma, still embrace the notion that somehow absent fathers, working mothers, over-permissive parents are the cause of psychiatric illness in children.[2]

Fortunately, as a psychologist in private practice since 1984 and not part of the organizational mental health system, I was able to go my own way. In a very natural way, I was guided by Meher Baba's teaching that we all share the same real Self, and fundamentally, beyond the differences in the ego self, we are all one. This encouraged me to try to solve my clients' problems by putting myself in their place (while, of course, still being me). In effect, I would ask myself what I would do in their place to solve their problem. This led me to the somewhat unusual practice of "thinking out loud" with my clients about their problems. This approach dovetailed quite nicely, it turned out, with an approach in the field that was becoming popular in the 1980s called "Problem Solving Psychotherapy," although I approached it in my own way.

This approach led me to something else, the significance of rationality. When I engaged in problem solving with my clients, I realized that the basic human tool for solving problems was the use of reason. As obvious as this might be, it is strangely blocked by the usual social science education. I remember sitting in a meeting of therapists and talking about developing an employee assistance program to present to businesses. One of the group spoke laughingly about the naive beliefs of a particular business manager about services like ours. In a derisive tone, the therapist quoted the manager as saying that he understood that our work was to help people dominated or swayed by their emotions become more rational. The group members, except me, chuckled at this.

There is a curious paradox, a contradiction even, that besets the modern world. Although that world was conceived in what was called "The Age of Reason," which replaced the debacle that had become "The Age of Faith," or the Middle Ages, it eventually devolved to reject the very principle of reason that was its supposed foundation. This occurred through the combined work of major philosophers and scientists such as David Hume, Frederich Nietzsche, Charles Darwin, Karl Marx, and Sigmund Freud. There is no denying the intellectual brilliance of these great lights of modernity, as they shaped the mental structure of a whole cultural era. All of them were materialists and naturalists, in that they saw the human being as the product of material nature, such as that studied by the natural sciences. In this regard, Hume declared that "reason was the slave of the passions." Reason had no independent standing in its own right, and could not claim true objectivity. All of the others sounded a similar theme, each in their own way. For Nietzsche, morality was not something that derived from God, since "God was dead," but through social conventions. All was relative to culture. For Darwin, human reason was an extension of animal nature and served the survival instinct. For Marx, reason served self-interested economic motives. And for Freud, the forces of the irrational unconscious made reason not more than a socially acceptable subterfuge for instinctual urges. So, the modern mind, getting its start in presumably sovereign reason, eventually came to undermine and delegitimize reason's own foundations.

In rediscovering the value and what seemed to me the true legitimacy of reason, I appreciated the significance of what critics of the modern mind have pointed out. By radically undermining the foundations of reason, these thinkers actually undermined their own arguments. In making their case against reason, they had no other way to do it than through the practice of reason itself! All intellectual argument uses reason to make a case. If you use reason to say that, in the final analysis, there is really no such thing as reason, you unwittingly contradict yourself. This is a modern form of the ancient fallacy known as "the liar's paradox." If I say, "I am a liar," if it's true, it's false, and the reverse. So such a statement really makes no sense. Since all sense is based on the independent existence of truth, to deny such truth is to deny sense itself.

This awareness helped me to have increasing confidence in the powerful "weapon" that I now realized I, as a human being, had at my disposal—reason. As in so many other things in my life with Baba, the natural unfolding and progression of my everyday experiences was reinforced and given confirmation by Meher Baba's statements. Things that I had read before would suddenly flash to mind, imbued with a new, deeper meaning, and so with reason as well. Baba, in a Discourse on "Perfection," described the meaning of this state in the divine being, and how the Perfect Master or Avatar is the embodiment of Perfection. Baba says that the Perfect One is not devoid of humanity, but rather the only one who is fully human—"not inhuman but superhuman." He goes on to make the statement that was utterly significant for me, describing the state of perfection as "the full development of that rationality which is implicit in humanity."[3]

Meher Baba's words validated my essential tool of rationality in working with my clients, and encouraged me to help them develop their own gift of reason, which is their birthright, so curiously undermined by modern beliefs. It seemed to me that the refutation of the dominant biological model in psychiatry could be couched in the classic phrase of "mind over matter." For the modern, this was impossible because mind *was* matter. But it can be seen, with perhaps some thought, that the doctrine of mind is matter is yet another form of the liar's paradox.

In a more general sense, applying spiritual principles to psychotherapy became part of my practice, and I was seeing the effective results on an ongoing basis with my clients. Baba's teachings in myriad ways gave me a foundation for helping troubled people find answers to their dilemmas and, from time to time, genuine breakthroughs. My practice became the practical context for me to develop my intuition—a faculty, in addition to and even beyond reason, that Baba said would emerge in its own right in the "New Humanity" to come. My intuition began to speak (or I began to listen). Even without the necessity of "thinking out loud," I would find myself spouting words that applied to the situation, but were other than what I thought I knew. After some of these spontaneous utterances, I asked myself with some sense of wonder, "Now where did that come from?" It was not as if someone was whispering things in my ear for me to say, but rather these statements seemed to come from my most confident inner self. It seemed to be the actual experience of Baba's promise that he would teach us how to live in the world and yet be in touch with him at all times, with him being nothing other than our real Self.

Therefore, we can say that Baba takes the Freudian concept of the ego, so important for our age, and puts it in a spiritual context. For Freud, the ego was the balancing element within a tripartite structure consisting of the ego, the id (urges and drives), and the superego (the socially derived conscious) as an individual (the self) interacts with the world. In this sense, Freud referred to the ego as embodying the "reality principle," but it was far from being a source of true and independent reason. It had no real "interests" in its own right, but mostly served those of the id and superego.

Baba dictated three beautiful and enlightening Discourses on the ego. The ego was critically important, he said, and carried one's sense of "I" or self. In that regard it *was* the center of conflict of all the urges or forces in the individual. If the ego wasn't functioning properly, we could not help but be mentally unbalanced. However, the ego could never really do this job on its own. For the ego was only a reflection in the natural world, which is the world of duality, of the higher Self, or the divine within, which was the true Self. So the ego, then, is not the real Self. It is only the "provisional" self, until the real Self could be realized. Without this relationship between the provisional self and the real Self, one would not have a sense of the real meaning and significance of one's life. Life as a journey to the real Self would ultimately become confused in a world of conflicting values, as is so much the case with the rootless and ungrounded ego in the modern world.

At one point, I was having a discussion with a therapist friend who, while not a Baba lover, is a spiritually oriented person. She asked how I would describe or define the kind of therapy I did or the approach that I took. In my response, I found myself not talking about the use of reason and so forth, but instead saying that in doing therapy I tried to make myself sensitive to a person's "karma." I had been practicing this intuitively for a while, but I had never put it in those words before. They struck me. "Hmm, karma sensitive psychotherapy." And thus, a special name for my practice was born.

Meher Baba said much about karma, although usually in terms of sanskaras, the minute mental impressions that make up karma. From the standpoint of reincarnation, we come into this life with a multitudinous background of all our past lives and their sanskaras. This background determines the conditions of our birth as well as making up the bulk of our unconscious. From this perspective, the growing interest in "past life therapy" makes sense. While I can see the value in such an approach, which usually involves the use of hypnosis, I generally prefer to work in a more natural way. Baba makes it clear that the reason that we don't ordinarily have conscious recall of our past lives is that the circumstances of this life are an adequate way of dealing with our karma, or material that forms the structure of our ego. Eventually, when I developed a firmer intellectual grasp of what I was doing in my work as a therapist, I wrote a brochure called "Karma Sensitive Psychotherapy," and used that name to advertise in Maine's holistic, *New Age* newspaper. The themes that I have been discussing in this chapter come together in what was written in that brochure:

> In many ways Karma Sensitive Psychotherapy appears to be no different from most other psychotherapy. That is, it uses the common psychotherapeutic methods of conversation and dialogue and does not involve any practices that might be considered esoteric or unusual, such as meditation, visualization, hypnosis, or extensive dream interpretation.
>
> Where Karma Sensitive Psychotherapy does differ from conventional psychotherapy is in its interpretation of the meaning of life situations and problems.
>
> Conventional psychotherapy typically relies—as does the conventional approach to life—on the assumption that this life that we are now living is the only life that we have lived and the only life that we will live. The question of what happens at death or afterward is left to religion to interpret or explain and is not brought into the framework of psychotherapy. By ignoring the issue of death and afterward, conventional psychotherapy wittingly or unwittingly adopts the philosophical position that is held by science that material existence is all there is.
>
> However, as the prominence and pervasiveness of religion in human affairs gives ample evidence, the question of death and afterward is fundamental to the issue of the meaning of life. By relying on the scientific assumption of materialism, which ignores the questions of death, psychotherapy accepts the position that the meaning of life is, at best, limited.
>
> ### A Different Fundamental Assumption
>
> It is here where Karma Sensitive Psychotherapy offers a distinct and radical departure from conventional psychotherapy. Karma Sensitive Psychotherapy involves an assumption that differs from the conventional Western religious assumptions and certainly from the conventional scientific assumptions. It assumes that this life we are now leading is only one of a succession of many lives that we have led and will lead.
>
> In this assumption it shares the beliefs held by millions of Hindus, Buddhists, and other religious faiths, though it is not affiliated with any one of these faiths specifically. Its most

specific influence is that of the spiritual teacher of India, Meher Baba, who himself was not affiliated with any specific faith. Meher Baba said, "I am not come to establish any cult, society or organization; nor even to establish a new religion. The religion I shall give teaches the Knowledge of the One behind many."

The fundamental assumption is that our existence began with the beginning of the universe. As the life forms gradually evolved, consciousness also evolved until both life and consciousness reached the human stage, as the thrust of evolution is always forward.

When we are born into a particular life we are unconscious of the experiences of our past lives and have no memory of them. However, all the conditions of our birth, including our race, nationality, sex, and the nature and makeup of our family, are determined by our past lives. This also includes our particular instincts and the kinds of tendencies we have to respond to the conditions we find ourselves in.

Thus our genetic and family makeup is a result of our past lives. As we go through life we deal with all of these issues, and the purpose of life itself is the same as the purpose of evolution. All of this can be referred to as karma.

Your Karmic Situation

When you enter psychotherapy with a problem, that problem involves what can be called your karmic situation. This situation encompasses your environment, yourself, and the interaction between the two. Your karmic situation presents you with certain tasks at this point in your life that you need to engage in and master in order to resolve the karmic impasse you find yourself in, and move on with your personal evolution.

Karma Sensitive Psychotherapy endeavors to assess the nature and dimensions of your current problems in terms of the larger picture of your karmic situation and karmic tasks. It does this through the development and use of intuition and rational analysis. This therapy is not past-life regression, and does not involve hypnosis or the attempt to remember past lives. All the issues, problems, and tasks accumulated over past lives are present in some form in this life, and can be addressed in this life, as we are meant naturally to do.

The Deeper Meaning of Intuition

As has been explained in classical reincarnation doctrine and by Meher Baba, the beginning and end of the individual soul are coexistent with the beginning and end of the finite universe itself. Beyond or outside of this there is nothing less than Infinite Being—the foundation or Source from which the soul derives its individual existence. Therefore, at the root of our own individual being is Infinite Being. It is this Infinite Being that we need to learn to draw on in order to get guidance, find answers, and solve our problems. The process of doing this is the deeper meaning of intuition. Karma Sensitive Psychotherapy helps you develop this ability in order to actively find ongoing guidance from this Source within.

Through deepened intuition, and the practice of looking at your life from a larger karmic perspective, you become more easily able to make meaningful and helpful choices, both internally and externally, in responding to your problems and life situations.

There are exceptions to my general practice of not using "unusual" methods. From time to time, certain clients come to me who have psychic or meditative abilities. It is natural for them to put these abilities into practice in the course of therapy. While doing so, some spontaneously have memories of past lives. It has been a wonder for me to witness and be a part of this. I have seen living proof of a part, at least, of what Meher Baba and others have described as the deeper, usually hidden structure of our lives. These memories that have emerged in my office directly connect to issues, tendencies, and problematic feelings in the client's present life. I consider it my privilege to have seen this, and also my privilege to pass this on to you.

But, we may ask, giving vent to our skeptical side, isn't this just imagination of some kind? Are these clients responding in some subtle, unconscious way to my own belief system, and creating past-life memories to fit the situation and satisfy my interests as a therapist? Perhaps. But the matter does not and should not stop there. As discussed in this chapter, we have two great tools in our reason and our intuition, whose prime functions are to help us discern what is true. It is these tools that we must use in addressing the central issue of this book—Is Meher Baba God? This issue is much more vital, and of insurmountable metaphysical as well as historical importance, than the limited and even curious matter of psychotherapy and reincarnation.

· 11 · 11 · 11 · 11 · 11 · 11 · 11 · 11 · 11 ·

EXAMINING THE POSSIBILITIES

Man is made by his beliefs.
As he believes, so he is.

BHAGAVAD GITA

By giving this account of the major events in my life since I learned of Meher Baba, I hope to illustrate how Baba becomes an active guiding force in one's life. I believe that divine guidance exists and that one can avail oneself of it.

One's relationship with God is personal, and each relationship is unique. My life with Baba is not a prototype, but rather reflects my particular biography—my interests, proclivities, weaknesses, and strengths. Meher Baba, being universal, the Soul of souls, works with each individual in an intimate, individual way. Even though the details of my story are specific, however, there are generalities relevant to anyone dealing with God, apart from whether one accepts Meher Baba to be the Avatar or God in human form. I've used my life to illustrate the premise that all happenings are a result of divine will. Nothing is an accident or without purpose. The intent of divine will is to bring one closer—ultimately to merge with it and discover that one is nothing other than that will itself.

To speak of divine will is to give an anthropomorphic cast to God. We know that humans have will—that we resolve to do things and then proceed on our intentions, sometimes succeeding and sometimes failing. I believe it is foolish to literally think of divine will in these terms. God doesn't entertain an idea and then *try* to carry it out. God's purpose and fulfillment are one and the same. God says, "Let there be light." So be it, and it is done. Meher Baba described the shortcoming of the idea of purpose in relation to God in the following simple, yet profound message.

> Purpose presumes a direction, and since Existence, being everything and everywhere, cannot have any direction, directions must always be in nothing and lead nowhere. Hence to have a purpose is to create a false goal.
>
> Love alone is devoid of all purpose and a spark of Divine Love sets fire to all purposes. The Goal of Life in Creation is to arrive at purposelessness, which is the state of Reality.[1]

Therefore, when we talk about God's purpose or God's will we are speaking metaphorically, as we usually do when we talk about God. For the skeptic this might lead to the question, "Then why talk about God at all?" If we believe that God exists, we must discuss that existence. To believe that God exists and remain silent is to consign that existence to nonsignificance. When great issues of human life and existence are taken up without reference to God, by implication, God's existence is irrelevant to these issues. If it is irrelevant to these issues, then what is it relevant to? This irrelevance of the divine has been the achievement of modern secularism. In its capitalist expression, it is perfectly all right to believe in God, as long as that belief does not extend outside the church, synagogue, mosque, or the Sabbath. In its communist expression, which turned out to be much less successful than its capitalist counterpart, one was not even allowed the Sabbath.

So, in proper metaphorical terms, if there is a God, all events in the universe, including the creation of the universe, are purposive and intrinsically meaningful, even if, as Baba stated, the paradoxical goal of this purposiveness is to lead us to purposelessness. In our modern age, we use the term *synchronicity* to refer to this principle in a specific way. Synchronicity refers to the coincidental occurrence of events, especially between things of the mind and external events. From a spiritual perspective, these synchronicities are emphasized moments in the flow of time. And events are, in a larger sense, *all* synchronistic. Meher Baba puts this so well:

> Perfect timing is a mysterious process which becomes obvious to you only at its fructification. In fact, every moment is the culmination of a perfectly timed sequence that you are not aware of; there is no such thing as "imperfect timing." Try to live the truth of this in your relationship with Me.[2]

To live in this awareness as a follower of Meher Baba effects a marvelous transformation of life. Meher Baba is always present, "behind" all things, and, more pointedly from time to time, revealed within those special coincidences or synchronicities. Because of his constant presence, one always can be in conversation with God—inwardly as well as outwardly. Meher Baba said the "inner approach" is the true meaning of prayer——not the outward codified group recitations often identified as prayer. Through inner communication—a training of the spiritual vision—one learns the ways in which God responds. Eventually, Baba assures us, one comes to see God everywhere and more plainly than one sees the material things of this world.

For the skeptical mind, all of this is self-deception—as I have said before, a fantasy creation that believers construct for comfort. I want to acknowledge this point of view but not attempt at this point to counter it. Instead, I return to two points that are implied in my account of God as a guiding force: (1) God exists, and (2) Meher Baba is God in human form, the Avatar.

When I first heard of Meher Baba, I did not believe in God but did believe in enlightenment, which I took to be the most desirable state of mind and worthy of pursuit. After coming to Meher Baba, I came to believe in God—"coming to Baba" means coming to the belief that Meher Baba is God in human form. So it was through Baba that I came to believe in God. Those who believe in God but reject the idea that Meher Baba is God, have to question one such as I: How did I come to something true—God—through means that are false? I believe there is an answer to this, but first let's examine the question of what Baba could be if he is not God.

Was Baba Only a Spiritual Authority?

There are a number of people who know Meher Baba and respect him as a spiritual authority, but do not accept Baba as God. As reasonable as such a position may seem, it is a weak one. Meher Baba emphatically and explicitly said that he is not a spiritual authority. He is either God in human form or just an ordinary person (perhaps a deluded one at that), but he should not be classified as an advanced soul, one on the spiritual path, or even a saint. In "The Highest of the High," he said:

> In the world there are countless *sadhus*, *mahatmas*, *mahapurushas*, saints, yogis and *walis*, though the number of genuine ones is very, very limited. The few genuine ones are, according to their spiritual status, in a category of their own, which is neither on a level with the ordinary human being nor on a level with the state of the Highest of the High [the Avatar].
>
> I am neither a *mahatma* nor a *mahapurush*, neither a *sadhu* nor a saint, nei-

ther a yogi nor a *wali*. Those who approach me with the desire to gain wealth or to retain their possessions, those who seek through me relief from distress and suffering, those who ask my help to fulfill and satisfy mundane desires, to them I once again declare that, as I am not a *sadhu*, a saint, or a *mahatma*, *mahapurush* or yogi, to seek these things through me is but to court utter disappointment, though only apparently; for eventually the disappointment is itself instrumental in bringing about the complete transformation of mundane wants and desires.

The *sadhus*, saints, yogis, *walis*, and such others who are on the *via media* [in the middle places between the origin and the end of creation], can and do perform miracles and satisfy the transient material needs of individuals who approach them for help and relief.

The question therefore arises that if I am not a *sadhu*, not a saint, not a yogi, not a *mahapurush*, nor a *wali*, then what am I? The natural assumption would be that I am either just an ordinary human being, or I am the Highest of the High. But one thing I say definitely, and that is that I can never be included amongst those having the intermediary status of the real *sadhus*, saints, yogis and such others.[3]

Baba made it clear that he is not in the middle between an ordinary person and God. Those who accept Meher Baba as a spiritual authority, but not as God, may not be aware of his clarification or may have dismissed it without worthy consideration.

In such a dismissal (if it is not intellectually lackadaisical) may be the position that Meher Baba is a legitimate spiritual authority, or master who claims divinity to further his purpose of

BABA, SO ACTIVE, SHOWS PERFECT REPOSE.
POONA, MAY 1957

being a spiritual teacher. This position may be based on the assumption that part of the purpose of *legitimate* spiritual authority is to claim total adherence of the disciples and that Baba's means of doing this is to claim to be God.

Such an argument does not hold up. If a *legitimate* (and that is the key word here) authority needs to have total adherence, why would he need to deceive his followers in order to achieve it? If total adherence is spiritually necessary, why deception? Don't the concepts of "spiritual," "God," and "truth" go hand in hand? How can a claim for truth be made that needs falsity to establish its point? I find this an outright contradiction; it makes no sense to me. I reject the idea that Meher Baba can be a legitimate spiritual master and at the same time essentially lie about being God in human form.

Was Baba Deluded?

A more realistic position would be that Meher Baba is deluded. This position was adopted by Paul Brunton, the author of *A Search in Secret India*. Brunton accepted all of Meher Baba's own "masters"—Hazrat Babajan, Narayan Maharaj, Tajuddin Baba, Sai Baba, and Upasni Maharaj—as legitimate, but he speculated that when Babajan "kissed" Meher Baba on the forehead and transmitted some type of spiritual energy to him, his mind could not handle it and he became delusional. This theory is lent credence because of the six-month period when Meher Baba was in a strange state, detached from the world, and certainly not functioning normally.

This explanation based on delusion or derangement is faulty on several grounds. One is that these Perfect Masters never repudiated Meher Baba, but rather spoke of him as the Avatar and world Savior until the end of their lives. Key disciples of each of these masters affirmed Meher Baba and had cordial, loving relations with him and the mandali. Godavri Mai, the leading successor of Upasni Maharaj, continued the spiritual tradition of Upasni (and it continues to this day in Sakori), but there are numerous accounts of her meetings with Meher Baba and her affirmation of him as the Avatar despite her position as the leader of Upasni's ashram.

What evidence is there that Meher Baba was deranged or deluded apart from the prima facie grounds of his claim? The question of delusion cannot be and, I believe, should not be readily dismissed. It goes to the heart of what Meher Baba said is his mission on Earth. The delusion question cannot be brushed aside, because in many ways Baba's behavior can be described as "enigmatic." That word and a few of its near-synonyms, such as *puzzling* and *unpredictable*, are common descriptions by some of those close to Meher Baba as well as in accounts of his life (such as that in Chapter 3). In all of these accounts, the enigmatic quality of Meher Baba's behavior comes through loud and clear.

There is no question that Baba was enigmatic. The next question then is, what does this mean? Is it a sign of his mental unbalance or the attribute of the God-realized being—one who is not "out of his mind," but beyond the mind?

The attempt to answer such a huge question should be set in the context of God in general. Believers often say that the ways of God are indeed unfathomable. "The Lord works in mysterious ways" is an often-used phrase. Non-believers take this to be a sure sign that God does not exist and this "mysterious ways" is the justification believers use to uphold and support that which makes no sense and cannot be logically justified.

So, the first thing we can say about Baba's being enigmatic is that this may be consistent with what has traditionally been the believer's account of the way God is. Second, Baba was well aware of this quality of his, and continually throughout his life would make remarks such as: "My ways are unfathomable. Do not try to understand me. Just love me." He then would go further and explain why this was so—"To ask for a purely intellectual proof for the existence of God is like asking for the privilege of being able to see with your ears!" Mind cannot understand that which is beyond mind. Baba's "Manonash Statement" further explains this idea. *Manonash* is an Indian word meaning "annihilation of the mind." Meher Baba made this statement in 1952, some forty years after the initiatory kiss from Babajan, and after his extensive world work as the Avatar had been undertaken. In it he talked explicitly about the paradoxical nature of spiritual reality. He said:

> Unless and until ignorance is removed and Knowledge is gained—the Knowledge whereby the Divine Life is experienced and lived—everything pertaining to the Spiritual is paradoxical.
>
> God, whom we do not see, we say is real; and the world, which we do see, we say is false. In experience, what exists for us does not really exist; and what does not exist for us, really exists.
>
> We must lose ourselves in order to find ourselves; thus loss itself is gain.
>
> We must die to self to live in God: thus death means Life.
>
> We must become completely void inside to be completely possessed by God: thus complete emptiness means absolute Fullness.
>
> We must become naked of selfhood by possessing nothing, so as to be absorbed in the infinity of God: thus nothing means Everything.[4]

Regarding his unpredictable way of changing, making, and breaking plans—a part of his enigmatic being—Baba once said: "I never make plans, never change plans. It is all one endless plan of making people know that there is no plan."[5] This is compatible with what Baba said about purpose and purposelessness and is another expression of that theme.

The principle of holding fast to the *daaman* (hem) of the master despite his unfathomable ways was emphasized by Baba on the last day of his life. Unbeknownst to the mandali, Meher Baba was about an hour away from dropping his body when he had the mandali read his printed board with the three couplets from Hafiz (see Chapter 5). The essence of the three couplets is that one should adhere to the Master despite not being able to understand his ways. This, in effect, constituted his last message.

To answer the question of whether Meher Baba was mentally disturbed in some way, one must look at his level of functioning. Baba led an active life over a long range of years—a life of intricate, multilevel activity on many fronts and on a global scale. A deluded person may appear to be normal or even gifted, but is almost never able to maintain this appearance and self-organization over long periods of time. If they are deluded, a breakdown almost inevitably occurs in which their mental illness comes dramatically to light. This was never the case with Baba. His pattern of working, despite its phases and often hard-to-understand nature, continued consistently throughout the duration of his spiritual career—some forty-seven years.

Baba's messages themselves argue against insanity. During the course of his work, often without any special emphasis or a seemingly adequate amount of time, Meher Baba, gave out a multitude of messages that were eventually gathered into a book entitled *Discourses* and later *God Speaks* and several others. On objective criteria—such as apparent knowledge and profundity—these "writings" have to be seen as being on the highest level of expression. They are also some of the most striking spiritual statements ever recorded. This has been attested to not only by tens of thousands of Baba lovers but also by authorities who were not followers. Included in this group is the renowned scholar of Tibetan Buddhism, W. Y. Evans-Wentz, who wrote a foreword to a collection of Meher Baba's messages and stated that "No wiser definition of the term God has ever been formulated." In regard to *God Speaks*, Eric Schroeder, curator of Islamic art at the Fogg Museum at Harvard, said, "Meher Baba's dictation of this work may be called a systematic metaphysic of consciousness; and since the consciousness of so notable a mystic transcends that of us, he speaks as one having authority." So again, it is very hard to see how a mentally disturbed person, even with great abilities, could produce "writings" or books that are recognized as being on the highest level of organization and of articulate and unique expression.

A final piece of evidence, weighing against insanity, is Meher Baba's sense of humor, which was known by most who had contact with him. This humor was never at another's expense, but often enough at his own. It was interwoven with profound moments and used at times to lend to the atmosphere around him a special quality of lightness and buoyancy. His humor seemed to be uniquely his, and all who knew him for an extended period came to identify it with him. Among the examples of Baba's humor is the one that I related in Chapter 1—"All Quiet on the Western Front." Another happened during a visit by Meher Baba to the West. Some American disciples got some soda to pass around, and one asked Baba if he wanted some Seven Up? Without skipping a beat, Baba replied (through gestures), "I am seven up," referring to the seven planes of consciousness.

About humor and God or Perfection incarnate, Baba said, "Human activities are limited by the opposites, and Perfection is beyond them. It should not be imagined, however, that Perfection has no human element about it. When human beings are unhappy, they laugh to make themselves and others happy. But even a Perfect One, who is eternally happy, is not without a sense of humor. In other words, Perfection does not consist in being inhuman but superhuman." Meher Baba goes on to add that Perfection "is the full development of that rationality which is implicit in humanity."[6]

I examine Baba's sense of humor because it is a characteristic that the deluded or mentally ill generally lack. A sense of humor is one of the traits of the well-integrated, balanced, and flexible personality. It signals one who is able to take themselves and life lightly—a trait lacking in the deluded. In this regard, there is also Meher Baba's pithy comment that ties in with several related themes: "most people take God lightly and life seriously, whereas it should be the reverse."

In arguing for Baba's sanity, I am well aware that some Baba lovers (and perhaps others who are not) will think it inappropriate and arrogant for me to do so. After all, who am I to pass judgment on the mental soundness of this majestic being? Meher Baba, whom they believe to be God, Jesus, Buddha, Krishna . . . being examined, pondered, measured, and summed up by an ordinary, very fallible human being (and a psychologist to boot)—unthinkable.

On the contrary, the purpose of reflecting on this issue is not to pass judgment on Meher Baba, but rather to present Baba publicly. Meher Baba's claim that he is God in human form—the Redeemer come to save the modern world—is the most outrageous claim that it is possible to make. The reader who does not already follow Baba is confronted with one of the greatest challenges to the human belief system or the human heart. Touching the heart is up to Baba and beyond the capabilities of anyone else.

What I *can* deal with are the intellectual issues in this challenge. I don't think that this task should be eschewed. While it is impossible to "prove" anything about Meher Baba or about God, there is value in speaking to the issues surrounding Baba's claim. It is the reader's right to challenge this claim and I strongly encourage the reader to do so. Pertinent facts about Baba and the reasoning used in any evaluation need to be presented to the reader who is seriously weighing this issue. At the very least, I feel I should make the best case I can that Meher Baba cannot be easily dismissed.

Therefore, I contend that the assertion that Meher Baba was deluded in his claim is a difficult one to sustain in light of the evidence. Does this mean that it is impossible? No, it's not impossible. Meher Baba may have been deluded, but one can reasonably say that based on the history of all false claimants to Messiahship, his would have been a unique form of delusion.

Was Baba a Charlatan?

Was he a charlatan? The world has witnessed a legion of false claimants—ordinary people with perhaps occult, charismatic, or hypnotic abilities. In fact, Meher Baba stated in "The Highest of the High" that if he was not the Avatar—God in human form—then he was just an ordinary person, but nothing in between. The larger context of this message addressed the question of whether Baba would or could perform miracles, especially to help individuals, either to advance in life or to overcome situations of unhappiness or suffering. Meher Baba said:

> If I am the Highest of the High my Will is Law, my wish governs the Law, and my Love sustains the Universe. Whatever your apparent calamities and transient sufferings, they are but the outcome of my Love for the ultimate good. Therefore, to approach me for deliverance from your predicaments, to expect me to satisfy your worldly desires, would be asking me to undo what I have already ordained.[7]

Furthermore, throughout his life Meher Baba spoke out against hypocrisy and those claiming to be what they were not. He said that hypocrisy is the one thing that God cannot forgive, and it is the greatest of all spiritual and personal errors. He said that honesty is one of the key attributes in spirituality. Regarding the greatest of all hypocrisies, the claim to be God, he noted that at that time there were seventy-three persons claiming to be the Avatar.

A false claim to be the Messiah is often grounded in personal gain. One motive is adoration. The ego can find no greater glory than grandiosity. From this standpoint, Meher Baba's life is most curious. From time to time, tens of thousands came to pay homage to Baba as the Avatar at darshan. The mandali were astounded by the numbers and questioned how so many came to know Baba and heard of these gatherings. Even though these public events were announced, there were no widespread publicity campaigns. Meher Baba never allowed ongoing publicity, so how the word spread and so many were drawn to him seemed miraculous.

One incident took place in 1956 in the town of Sangamner, India, about fifty-five miles from Baba's residence in Meherazad. A devoted Baba lover, Waman Subnis, came to Meher Baba imploring him to give darshan in the Sangamner area. Baba responded to his love and agreed.

A tent large enough to accommodate four to five thousand people was erected for the event. At first, a couple hundred came. Then Baba began giving a small token *prasad* (gift of God—usually a piece of fruit or candy) to each of them as they came before him. More and more people came, until some ten thousand poured into the area. This multitude was a surprise to Subnis and other devotees in the area. Meher Baba gave out prasad with both hands and the crowd pressed forward until there was almost a stampede. Baba had originally allowed two hours for the darshan, but even after four hours there seemed to be no end to this sea of humanity that continued to pour in to see him. People from neighboring villages and towns were coming, so Meher Baba touched the remaining prasad to be distributed later. At the sight of this crowd, Subnis cried out to those nearby, "See Baba's miracle; look at the miracle of Baba! This is nothing but a miracle! Otherwise, it could never have happened! How could so many have come?"[8]

For most of Meher Baba's life, he worked privately, not in the public eye. When he traveled, sometimes extensively, he was usually incognito, and the mandali were not to say who he was. During these tours, when asked about this curious party with Baba as the obvious center, the mandali referred to him as their "elder brother."

In the 1920s before Meher Baba was known outside his local district in Maharastra province and before he traveled for the first time to the West, there were upwards of ten thousand that came to his public appearances in Poona. Baba allowed these events for only a short time before stopping them and continued his work with a relatively small number of mandali and people close to him.

There were two decades separating the earliest darshans from the later ones of the 1950s and early 1960s. During that twenty-year period, Meher Baba's main activity consisted of traveling incognito throughout India with a small group of mandali, searching for masts. He found them in alleys, near or even *in* sewers, and living in cemeteries. For two decades, Baba's life was not a glamorous one of being adored by multitudes. Furthermore, when Meher Baba did have a large-scale public appearance, it was clear that he was there to work. As at Sangamner, while giving out prasad hour after hour to an endless line of people, the mandali described how the sweat poured from Baba's body. He seemed to be giving himself to those whom he loved from a depth known only to Baba.

Most of Meher Baba's trips to the West took place without publicity or public notice and he never used these visits to gather large groups of followers. For the most part, Baba met individually with small groups of people who wanted to know him and maintained intimate contact with those relative few of "his lovers."

ERUCH JESSAWALA READS OUT BABA'S WORDS FROM THE ALPHABET BOARD AT DARSHAN. SEPTEMBER 1954.

Meher Baba had the power to gather the multitudes. In this day of the publicity-seeking guru, his reluctance to use this power may seem strange. Yet, as we have seen in Chapter 3, this pattern seems to have been set by Baba with his 1932 appearance in Hollywood. A public reception was held at Pickfair, the home of Mary Pickford and Douglas Fairbanks, and many were entranced by Meher Baba. There were also many personal contacts with movie stars. By most accounts, Meher Baba had the film world in the palm of his hand. He quickly ended that phase of public recognition with a deliberate announcement that he would break his silence in the Hollywood Bowl. Then he canceled it. All of those drawn to him in Hollywood and the Los Angeles area, except for a very few who became close followers, instantly dropped away. If Meher Baba had wanted to build a large following and be idolized by many, the Hollywood Bowl incident was not the way to do it.

Was Baba an Ordinary Man?

Finally, we contemplate the question of whether Meher Baba was an ordinary man seeking adulation and fame. First, in arguing against this possibility, is the issue of Meher Baba not explicitly announcing that he was the Avatar until the early 1950s, some fifteen years before the end of his life. At that time he was around sixty and had been seriously injured from two auto accidents. Physically, he was far from the stereotypical handsome, graceful Messiah. (Interestingly, for many years after Meher Baba began his work in 1922, and during his visits to the West in the 1930s, he physically fit the classical picture of a charismatic savior, but he did not proclaim himself as the Avatar.)

During his early work, Meher Baba was only known as a *master* or a *Perfect Master*, which were the terms used in the first biographical account of him written in the 1930s by Charles Purdom. As many of the mandali noted, in time it became difficult for Meher Baba to hide his divinity, although that was his intent until the 1950s. From the earliest days of his advent, many who were in contact with him or who became his disciples believed him to be the Avatar. An American follower, Jean Adriel, gave her 1947 biography of Meher Baba the title, *Avatar*.

Nevertheless, Meher Baba himself did not announce his divinity and avoided confirming this distinction until a night in February 1954 in a tiny village in India. The irony of Meher Baba making this announcement at that point in his life was most keenly felt by Eruch, the mandali who most often read out Baba's messages at public gatherings and darshans. When Eruch had to read out Baba's messages revealing himself as the Avatar, he wondered why Baba was doing this when he was old and disabled rather than when he had been young and vibrant. In that sense, Eruch's job as "the proclaimer" could have been much easier in the early days of Meher Baba's work. Eruch knew as well as anyone could that Meher Baba's ways were not the usual ways of the world and could not be understood by normal standards.

To all who knew Meher Baba, his ways were that of an ordinary man; that is, there were no miracles or demonstrations of supernatural powers. Meher Baba said that he came to awaken all to his Divine Love and wanted nothing but love in return. He explained that miracles would not bring forth this love from his lovers, only awe and wonder. The Messiah Jesus most specifically performed miracles, which Meher Baba said was central to Christ's advent and crucifixion. But in this advent, it was neither necessary nor spiritually appropriate for the Avatar to do so because miracles alone are not a sign of divinity. He explained that an advanced being on the fourth plane of consciousness can perform the complete panoply of *sidhis*, an Indian word for control of the forces of the world of phenomena. However, it is critical to again emphasize that Meher Baba said that in his advent he would perform one miracle—and one miracle only—when he broke his silence.

Is Baba the Avatar?

Now on to the other aspect of this reflection—the *positive* case that can rationally be made for Meher Baba being the Avatar. After examining the negative possibilities—Baba is deluded, Baba is a charlatan (or some combination of the two), Baba is an ordinary man seeking fame and recognition—none of which hold up, it is fitting then to ask, "What are the positive indications for Baba being not an ordinary man but the Avatar? Meher Baba's mandali repeatedly said that it was impossible for Baba to hide his divinity. Despite the issue of Baba breaking his silence, there were indications that he was something other than an ordinary person. When one examines Meher Baba's life, the range and extent of these indications is not bound by any finite catalog and occurred continually. The most explicit proof of this, of course, was Meher Baba's radiation of love, compassion, and wisdom that drew countless thousands to him in recognition of God in human form. Although this cannot be tangibly conveyed in print, it was experienced by those in Meher Baba's presence and now in the lives of those who follow him.

What can be conveyed in print are *facts* about Meher Baba's life that demonstrate that he was not an ordinary person. All of these facts are verifiable. Which of these facts one chooses as significant is just that, a matter of choice, and not necessarily *the* facts.

Money, power, and sex: Together and individually, these issues compose the most common stumbling blocks for the false sage, guru, yogi, master, prophet, messiah, or hierophant.

Meher Baba literally never touched money except to make a symbolic gift of it to the poor. Throughout his life, he lived in relative poverty or material simplicity even though, for his work, relatively large sums of money passed through his offices. A meticulous accounting was handled by his mandali secretary and did, in fact, only *pass through* to his work. Extensive accounting records show that there is no question of material gain.

Now this, in itself, is certainly not superhuman. There are, fortunately, many people who have no interest in accumulating wealth, but that fact does not remove them from the category of an ordinary human. Even so, Meher Baba definitely

MEHERA, BABA, AND MANI.
MEHERAZAD, 1944.

cannot be placed in the all-too-familiar category of the guru or so-called master who revels in his accumulated wealth.

What about power? Meher Baba did not seek power and had no power in any worldly sense. It is true that Baba had close followers who obeyed him implicitly as their master and that Baba stressed the importance of obedience to the master who is the God-man, as with Christ's admonition "Leave all and follow me." Baba was clear that he did *not* mean that one should forgo his or her worldly responsibilities, but rather that low desires, selfishness, and dishonesty were to be rejected and replaced with the pursuit of Truth and Love. The request from Meher Baba for obedience to the values of the Avatar was and is an essential part of his mission.

It would be a hard case to make that Meher Baba was an ordinary man who professed to be God in order to gain power over the lives of a few people who become his mandali and even less influence over his followers dispersed throughout the world. This does not make sense, especially in the context of Meher Baba's life of hardship and incredible service to humanity with no recognition for this work. As stated earlier, most of Baba's work was done incognito and the utmost effort was made to ensure that none should recognize him. If someone seeks power in a pathological sense, it would be odd to find this seeking confined to a small sphere of influence and to the matter of spirtual direction. Pathology, at least in the form of imposture, is not an orderly, restrained, and unchanging behavior. In fact, megalomania is by its very nature expansive—eventually voraciously so and, over time, inevitably shows itself as the aberration it is.

We find no such pathology over the course of Meher Baba's life. Indeed, after Meher Baba formally declared late in his life that he was the Avatar and this "Call" touched the hearts of an increasing number of people, Baba withdrew into seclusion for his "inner" work, limiting his public contact. The last major phases of Meher Baba's life, the Avatar's Call and seclusion, directly preceded his physical departure from this world. For a scheming master who wants to be recognized and followed as God and who dedicates his life to this nefarious end, Meher Baba's timing and mode of behavior would seem to have been wasted and the opportunity for ever- greater adulation lost.

The great stumbling block, and the chink in the armor of many male spiritual leaders who present themselves to the world as beyond the range of mundane desires, is sex. As we have seen time after time, many of them preach sexual chastity and are later found to have secret sexual liaisons—often with their closest, most trusting disciples. This is so often the case that if we find a supposed spiritual master who is truly celibate, this *may* be a sign that the person

MEHERA AND BABA. BENARES, 1939.

is above and beyond the ordinary human. I say *may*, because there are celibate individuals who are not spiritual masters. My point is that charismatic pretenders often use their influence and power over others to obtain sexual favors.

With this in mind, we need to be aware of the *fact* that Meher Baba never engaged in sexual relations or contact of any kind. Baba said that "sex for me does not exist," and his life was a verifiable demonstration of this. Especially noteworthy is that Baba, as we know, emphasized love above all else and had intimate and loving relationships with numerous individuals of both sexes. Meher Baba's life was a living embodiment of the possibility that love can exist in the most intimate form and be complete without sex. Although this way of life is not necessarily attainable or even a goal for most of us, to know that it was so for Meher Baba is to recognize something that seems to approach the superhuman. At the very least, it shows a life of one whose integrity must be recognized.

The greatest expression of this was Baba's relationship with Mehera, his closest female disciple. Mehera was a beautiful woman, who embodied the role with Baba that Sita had with Ram, Radha with Krishna, and by implication, Mary Magdelan with Jesus. Meher Baba said that each Avatar has a female counterpart, his closest Beloved, who loves him "as he should be loved." In Eastern traditions this person is often described as the Avatar's consort. For Baba, this consort was Mehera. The pictures and films that we have of Baba and Mehera together show them looking at each other with eyes of love. One could easily think that these

MEHERA AND BABA WORKING TOGETHER BUILDING MEHERA'S GARDEN AT MEHERAZAD.

two were lovers in the usual human sense. For anyone acquainted with Meher Baba, however, it would be impossible to think so. Baba's sister,

Mani, who was as close to Meher Baba and to Mehera as it is possible for anyone to be, gives us this testimony.

> This love between Baba and Mehera is in an inner realm which has nothing to do with "love" as defined in the world's dictionary. In these times, when the outer has become the altar of worship, when the wrapping of a gift often receives more attention than its contents, it is natural that everything concerning "love" should be translated into the external, the physical. But do not make that mistake about Mehera's relationship with Baba; or for that matter, about any of us living with Baba. The keynote of our life with Baba was purity, and Baba was very, very particular and strict about it. He never allowed the slightest compromise in this regard, so our relationship with Baba and with each other was always totally innocent of physical involvement.[9]

Was Meher Baba only a spiritual authority, but not the Avatar? Or was he deluded or a charlatan? In this chapter, I believe I have made the case that there is scant evidence of Meher Baba being any of these. Was Baba just an ordinary man? If Meher Baba was an ordinary person, he was an ordinary person the likes of which we have not encountered in modern times. But this is only the starting point for an intellectual or "objective" examination of the question, "Who *is* Meher Baba?"

·12·12·12·12·12·12·12·12·12·

ONCE IN A THOUSAND YEARS

*I was a hidden treasure, and I longed to be known;
so I created the world, in order to be known.*

HADITH SAYINGS

Who was he after all? The question then turns to an examination of Meher Baba as someone beyond the ordinary human. Many had earlier suspected or believed that Baba was who he eventually announced himself to be in messages such as "The Avatar's Call."

Age after age, when the wick of Righteousness burns low, the Avatar comes yet once again to rekindle the torch of Love and Truth. Age after age, amidst the clamor of disruptions, wars, fear and chaos, rings the Avatar's call:

"COME ALL UNTO ME."

Although, because of the veil of illusion, this Call of the Ancient One may appear as a voice in the wilderness, its echo and re-echo nevertheless pervades through time and space to rouse at first a few, and eventually millions, from their deep slumber of ignorance. And in the midst of illusion, as the Voice behind all voices, it awakens humanity to bear witness to the Manifestation of God amidst mankind.

The time is come. I repeat the Call, and bid all come unto me....[1]

From July 10, 1925, until he dropped his body on January 31, 1969, Meher Baba was silent. During those forty-four years, he led a worldwide and often whirlwind life as one who is said to be God in human form. His life in seclusion was not lived cut off from the world—quite the opposite. Baba's periods of seclusion can hardly be seen as a chance to maintain his silence; he was never alone, was constantly active, and interacted with countless people during those periods. Baba said that his silence was not a spiritual exercise for him, but rather part of his work.

For me, Meher Baba's silence was a sure sign of the superhuman. Other individuals have maintained long periods of silence; in Indian spirituality, the term *Muni* means "the one who is silent." Baba's disciple, Gustadji, with Baba's guidance, was silent for more than twenty-five years. However, I have found no case on record of anyone's silence lasting as long or with as full and vigorous interaction with the world as Meher Baba's. His silence is perhaps the perfect expression of an attribute that, while not miraculous, is hard to compare with that of ordinary men and women.

MEHER BABA AT DARSHAN.
WADIA PARK, AHMEDNAGAR, 1954

In connection with looking at Meher Baba's work in seclusion, one must also consider his fasts. Baba fasted from all food, taking only liquids, for frequent periods throughout his life, saying that this also was not an exercise or discipline for him, but was connected with his work. The fasts were incredible; they rarely lasted less than a week and the longest was forty days. While some fasts correlated with the seclusions, the majority of them did not. Often during his fasts, Meher Baba was intensely active and carried out his work with no apparent change. As with his silence, the fasts were a humanly possible activity, but at the outer limit of that capability.

Meher Baba's sleep, however, transcended that of an ordinary person. He said that the state of the fully realized or God-conscious being was equivalent to conscious (dreamless) sleep. On the surface, this expression is a contradiction; dreamless sleep is the very definition of unconsciousness, but according to Baba, God

BHAU KALCHURI, MANDALI, NIGHT WATCHMAN,
AND LATER NOTED BABA BIOGRAPHER AND SPEAKER,
WITH HIS BELOVED, MEHER BABA.

Realization is a totally impressionless consciousness or full consciousness without content.

The Perfect One has no unconscious; unconsciousness has been absorbed into consciousness by the attainment of Self-realization and is what we refer to as the state of superconsciousness. Meher Baba said,

> The waxing and waning of consciousness is applicable only to the limited individual. In the case of the Perfect Master, the conquest of the unconscious by the conscious is final and permanent; and therefore his state of Self-knowledge is continuous and unbroken, and remains the same at all times without any diminution. From this you can see that the Perfect Master never sleeps in the ordinary sense of the word. When he rests his body he experiences no gap in his consciousness.[2]

That this was Meher Baba's sleep state was confirmed by those closest to him. Bhau Kalchuri, who for many years served as Baba's night watchman (along with countless other duties), wrote about this in a beautiful, slim volume with the ironic title, *While the World Slept*.

> Whenever I went for nightwatch, Baba always stated three instructions. They were: "Don't make any noise. Don't move. And keep awake." One night in Satara, Baba repeated these injunctions about four or five times. Then he told me to go and sit outside. I went out, closed the door behind me, and sat like a statue on the chair.
>
> Usually, throughout the night, Baba would clap every fifteen or twenty minutes, and the night watchman would open the door, go inside and attend to him. But that night Baba did not clap. Not after fifteen minutes, not after half an hour, not after one hour, and not even after two hours! And there were plenty of mosquitoes furiously pestering me! I became stiff from sitting rigidly in one position, but I kept comforting myself with the thought that Baba would clap and I would get some relief.
>
> Finally I heard Baba snoring loudly. I thought, "Ah, at last, here is my chance. I must at least change my position. He is sleeping soundly and won't hear me."
>
> Very gently, without making the slightest sound, I started to lift my leg. The instant I began lifting it, Baba clapped and I went inside. Baba asked, "Why did you move?" I was wonderstruck. I hadn't made any noise. The

door and windows were tightly shut. He was snoring. How could he have known?

Baba gazed at me and explained: "You moved thinking I was asleep. But remember, my eyes roam the entire universe even in sleep! When I can see so far, can I not see you who are so near to me? My sleep is conscious sleep. I am always awake."[3]

Meher Baba did not *conspicuously* display his omniscience—his All Knowingness. He seemed to be ignorant of what an ordinary person would be expected to know. Baba said that "ignorance is one of my greatest weapons." On the other hand, in the everyday course of events, many times Baba would do something in a natural way that revealed that he knew all. One of the most dramatic occasions is when he gave a wildflower to Elizabeth as they were walking through a woods in 1932 as I described in Chapter 3. He told her to keep it and mark the date, May 24. Twenty years later to the exact date, Elizabeth was driving when Meher Baba experienced his first car accident.

While this is a spectacular coincidence, it should not be seen as Meher Baba demonstrating omniscience. Rather, its meaning lies within the context of Baba's compassion and love. The act of giving Elizabeth the flower on that day was essentially Baba's way of giving assurance to Elizabeth who would naturally feel deeply guilty about an accident in which there was so much severe injury. It was Baba's unique way of letting Elizabeth know twenty years later that it was planned long in advance, part of his work, and not her fault.

Meher Baba's superhuman capabilities are also seen in other events surrounding the 1952 accident. Baba, Mehera, Meheru, and Elizabeth were badly hurt in the accident—broken bones for all and Mehera's skull was fractured. Baba

BABA, FOLLOWING DARSHAN ASSISTED BY MEHERJEE KARKARIA AND ERUCH JESSAWALA. BOMBAY, DECEMBER 1957.

had facial lacerations, a broken leg, and a broken arm. Only Mani was not injured. In *Love Alone Prevails*, Delia DeLeon, who was in a second car following, describes Baba as they came upon the accident:

> With lightening speed we jumped out of the car and rushed forward. The anguish of that moment is unforgettable . . . . Baba's face with blood pouring from His head, the extraordinary expression on Baba's face, His eyes just staring straight ahead as if into unfathomable distances. He made no sound or sign . . . just lay there motionless. . . . Elizabeth was in the car doubled over the wheel. Her first question had been "Is He alive?"[4]

The first car to arrive at the scene was a man driving his wife, who was in labor, to a clinic seven miles away. The man continued on and when he reached the clinic, two ambulances were dispatched to the accident site. The clinic had been founded two years earlier by Dr. Ned Burleson who describes his first encounter with Meher Baba as a patient in the clinic:

> When finally I got around to attending to Baba, I was surprised to see an individual who was injured as badly as he was still smiling. I was also astounded to find that he did not speak a word, or make any sound denoting discomfort. I assumed that he could not, but was informed soon by Dr. Goher Irani that he did not speak because of a willful act. I knew that we were going to have to give him a general anesthetic (Pentothal) to set his fractures and suspected that he would say something at that time, but he didn't.[5]

Whether this description of Meher Baba during the accident is superhuman or not, I leave to the reader to judge. Of further interest is this quote from Dr. Burleson's written account:

> The most attractive quality of his personality that first day was the way he looked at me with those big brown eyes as if he were reading my mind. Later, I determined that the most astounding quality was that something which made it possible for him to receive such profound devotion and loyalty from so many fine and educated people. That quality cannot be forced. Such devotion can only be possible because he deserved it or earned it.[6]

The final area in which we can find positive evidence for the belief that Meher Baba was well beyond the ordinary human—to the extent, even, of being who he said he was—is the experience that thousands (like Dr. Burleson) had in his presence. I have already referred to and quoted from some of these accounts. Their common theme is that of the love that they felt with Meher Baba. I quote two more, which are connected and, I think, interesting.

Kim Tolhurst, a student of martial arts and Buddhism in London in 1931, became a lover of Meher Baba and one of his earliest Western followers. In *Glow International*, she describes her first meeting with Baba.

> Well, I went upstairs to his little room, which resembled a monastic cell because its stone walls were very thick. Baba was seated on a cot robed in white. I don't know what happened—I shall never know what happened. All I know is that I found myself on my knees at Baba's feet, crying as I think I have never cried before.
>
> The tears were streaming down my face. I don't think I was unhappy; I don't think I was happy. Perhaps the tears seemed to wash away all that had happened to me in the past, all that I had regretted. I was empty in a sense, yet filled with lightness and new dawn—fresh life. I felt clean and light. I don't know how long this weeping lasted; I couldn't tell you. It was timeless. Baba dictated on the board, which I heard Chanji interpret, "She is to stay near me." Somebody picked me up. I was put to bed and fell in a deep slumber. I can't explain what happened. It was a long, long time ago, but it is an impression which has remained very deep.
>
> I always loved Jesus Christ and it seemed to me that Baba was like the Jesus I had known as a child in the paintings depicting him. I felt this tremendous love, this tremendous compassion. Although there was a great deal to criticize in me and even be stern about . . . in his eyes there was nothing but understanding and compassion and no condemnation at all. I think it was that that won me over to him. However sensual one had been, however undutiful, ungrateful or careless—whatever one's faults were that he saw—it seemed as if he saw what one might become and drew this out.[7]

Tolhurst, who knew Christmas Humphreys, founder and president of the British Buddhist Society, told Humphreys of her meeting with Meher Baba and arranged for him to meet Baba, too. The British Buddhist Society had a major influence on introducing knowledge and appreciation of Buddhism to the West. In his autobiography, *Both Sides of the Circle*, Humphreys relates how he came to be a Buddhist. He had been raised a Christian and while attending college, in 1917, he learned that his beloved older brother had been killed in action during World War I. Humphreys believed in a loving, protective God and the shock and disillusionment surrounding his brother's death led him to search for the meaning of life and later to his practice of Buddhism. Humphreys remained a committed Buddhist and as a member of the Society wrote numerous books on Buddhism. In 1936, he met the Japanese Zen teacher, D. T. Suzuki, became his follower, and introduced Suzuki's writings to the West.

In his 1941 article entitled "The Man of Love," in the *Buddhist Society Journal*, Humphreys described his meeting with Baba.

[Meher Baba's] view was that emotions in the West are like a veritable jungle of untamed animals, and they must be released in order that the mind may come to terms with them. However the emotions are defined, they are one expression of the vast force of the human entity, and must be controlled even as the intellect must be trained and controlled before it becomes a first-class instrument. Meher Baba's emotion was love. I sat beside him cross-legged on a sofa and we talked on love, he through an alphabetical board, as he had taken a vow of silence. He literally radiated love. It was a physical sensation of warmth and I have never experienced anything like it. The effect on visitors varied from garrulous chatter to silence, from halting questions to halting tears. And what fascinated me, who am not an emotional person, is that the love was far above the emotional plane, nearer to the divine compassion which is the supreme quality of Mahayana Buddhism at its best.[8]

Among the many who met Meher Baba and were touched by his love were advanced souls on the spiritual path, called *masts*. As I described in Chapter 3, for more than a decade Baba and the mandali engaged in the painstaking and strenuous activity of seeking throughout India to find these "God intoxicated" souls. What was accomplished is difficult, if not impossible, to understand. We have only Meher Baba's laconic comments such as, "I work for them, and they work for me."

Masts appear to most people to be insane or mentally unbalanced. Yet, some masts have a regular following who see them as spiritually advanced and pay homage to them. In general, they do not communicate in a recognizable way.

When masts do speak, it seems to be a babble of meaningless words because they are detached from the physical world. Through the self-sustaining power of this disconnected state, the masts often remain indifferent to physical needs. Nevertheless, they remain healthy and frequently display an inner vitality and glow.

The mandali, for the most part, saw the masts as others did and heard the same incomprehensible utterances. On rare occasions, however, the mandali were startled by a brief moment of illumination of a mast's inner state. At these times, there would seem to be a connection in the statement of a mast to Meher Baba's identity. William Donkin, a chronicler of Baba's activities with the masts, recorded these statements in "Those Who Bear Witness."

MEHERABAD, CIRCA 1927–1928.

> In May 1946, a mast considered to be on the fifth plane was brought to Baba's house. When Baba came out he gazed at Baba's face, laughed with tears of joy in his eyes, and embraced Baba. Pointing to Baba, he then said to those standing by, "Look at this man's face and forehead. They shine as if the sun were there, can't you recognize who he is?"

Chatti Baba, a high mast from south India, spent more time than most masts with Baba.

One day in 1941, he said to a disciple of Meher Baba:

> You want to leave don't you, but what's the good of it; all the world is in Baba's power, so where will you go? Serve him now, he is the Ocean, because, one day when lots of people throng to see him, you may never get the opportunity of meeting him.

 Brahmanandji Mast of Mathura, in October 1946, touched Meher Baba's feet and said:

> Behold, how devoted love draws the Lord Krishna to me; the Perfect Master is here.

Also in 1946, Meher Baba contacted the mast Azim Khan Baba, who said:

> You are Allah; You have brought forth the creation, and once in a thousand years you come down to see the play of what you have created.⁹

In this chapter and in Chapter 11, I have gathered what I consider to be objective evidence that Meher Baba is not mad, not a charlatan, not an ordinary person, but rather that he is what he announced himself to be in messages such as "The Avatar's Call," "The Highest of the High," and the "Universal Message." Perhaps the best summing up for me from the most rational perspective that I can adopt in regard to his claim is in the following statement made to me by a Baba lover. We were walking along a trail at Myrtle Beach and only half seriously complaining to each other about the state of the world and the pressures and problems in our lives. In the facetious spirit of the conversation, I asked her, "So, is Meher Baba really God?" Her answer was a question in reply, "Who else could he be?"

∞ ∞ ∞

I have written that I came to believe in God through Meher Baba. For me, the fact that God exists and that Meher Baba is God are one and the same; that is, if Meher Baba is not God, then God doesn't exist. This statement, of course, is not true for most of the world's people who have come to believe in God through avenues other than Meher Baba. Most believers, not knowing anything about Meher Baba, would say *their* belief in God is correct and belief in Meher Baba is false, although God can and does work through all the channels, happenings, and vicissitudes of life to bring people to recognize His existence. Therefore, one might say that God can work through the false—perhaps even through misguided claimants to divine status—to bring people to the true.

If that is the case for someone like myself (as well as all other people who believe in Meher Baba), I have yet to be shaken loose from this falsity by God and led to a belief in God founded on a "true" basis. God has not seen fit to do this yet. But when and if it does happen, then presumably I would gain something that I don't have now or lose something that is standing in the way of truth. What would that be? Let me examine this question from the standpoint of Christianity.

Christians believe in providence—that happenings in the world, both positive and negative, are directed by God for our edification and eventual salvation. Through Meher Baba, I have come to believe in this, too. Christians believe that all human beings should live with one another in a community of agape or spiritual love. I believe that also. Christians believe that Christ will appear again and redeem the world. I believe that He has already come. (The matter of world redemption is a most mysterious one and a matter that I will address in the next chapter.) So, for the most part, and in what appears to me to be the most important respects, the Baba lover and the Christian believe in God in the same way. They share deep truths about the world. So what essential truth is lacking? Or what truth has this "false claimant" obscured?

Christians might point out:

- *You have been taught reincarnation and believe that the soul reincarnates through many lifetimes until oneness with God is attained.* We believe in one life and at death we either enter heaven or hell. Meher Baba explained that what is called heaven and hell really refer to the states of existence between incarnations. The heaven and hell quality of this experience occurs because, without the damping medium of the physical body, the spiritual and moral meaning of one's actions during embodied life are experienced by the soul in a more complete way. It is this experience that provides valuable knowledge in the after-physical-death state that serves as a positive and forward-looking foundation for the next incarnation.

- *You have not been taught the independent existence of evil, which in some of our sects we call the Devil.* True. Meher Baba has taught that what we call good and evil are relative terms for the range of duality in embodied life or the life of phenomena and form. Behind these diverse forms is the one Supreme Being.

- *By not believing that Christ is the only way to salvation, you will go to hell, not to heaven, when you die.* As for the question of being consigned to hell for not believing that

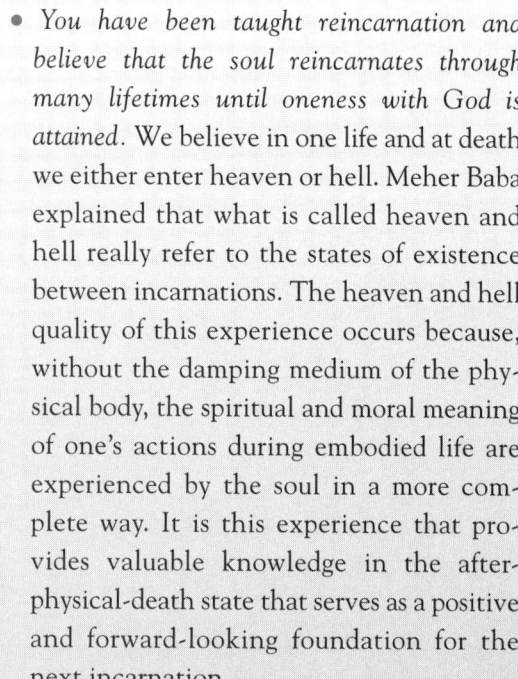

Christ is the only way, I do believe in Christ, but my belief is expanded and enlarged in the concept of the Avatar. Followers of Meher Baba may also believe in Buddha, Mohammed, Krishna, or other manifestations of the God-man. This is not for the purpose of an ecumenical "let's-all-get-along" convenience, but rather because Meher Baba said it is the Truth.

Finally, there is the subject of salvation through belief. Meher Baba said that what is critical for the soul is not belief—which can be seen as a mere assenting of the mind to a set of propositions—but rather "what one is"—one's character. Who am I? How do I conduct myself and treat others?

I am ever aware of my shortcomings in these areas, but I am thankful to my teacher, Meher Baba, who has enabled me to be mindful of this. If these teachings are in someway false, then Meher Baba is *radically* false (he cannot be just in some way false—when you say you're God, it's all or nothing). In the same way that I was open to him, I hope to be open to discovering his falsity.

This is not to say that belief has no value. That is not true at all. Certainly one's character and one's behavior is not divorced from one's beliefs. The cynical beliefs that principles have little or no meaning and that it is paramount to look out for number one and do whatever one can get away with would express one's character and be reflected in one's behavior. The reverse would be true if one believed that God resides in the seat of the soul and knows all. Real belief is more than skin deep and is reflected in who one is and what one does.

For me, the challenge to Meher Baba's divinity comes more from modern skepticism and atheism than from traditional beliefs and religions. The essential stance of the modern world views the question of whether Meher Baba is God as irrelevant and ridiculous because there is no God. For the secular modern, a belief in God results from a primitive tendency of the mind to be superstitious.

With the fall of the authority of the Christian Church during the Middle Ages, the Age of Enlightenment that followed is seen as the beginning of the modern era. The "enlightenment" meant enlightenment from superstition and the elimination of the primary superstition—a belief in God. In the modern era, God was replaced by *naturalism*—nature, as understood by science, is what the universe is. Nature, or existence, is what science understands it to be. There is no creator of the universe, no soul, certainly no reincarnation, and no life after death. Natural "laws" govern the universe. Phenomena do not have an inherent purpose. Whatever purpose we see is put there by our minds, and we should rid ourselves of the propensity to do so. Science does not believe in teleology or purpose within nature and replaces this purpose with a doctrine of natural causes. Even to call this purpose a "doctrine" is unacceptable to the scientific world, for it is seen not as a doctrine but as scientific truth.

As I have said, before coming to Meher Baba, the modern, naturalistic, and scientific perspective—personal enlightenment—made perfect sense to me. There was no belief in God, quite the opposite. If anything, enlightenment was a coming to believe in myself. No false notions about external forces of control and power; there was no such thing. There was just nature and the self—and in my case, myself.

Meher Baba changed all that, and the culmination of this change was my experience at Baba's tomb in 1980. I came to realize the false division that the modern mind places between itself and the outer world. For the modern man, enlightenment is a state of mind that has nothing to do with the world; the idea of God, if taken as anything more than a state of mind, is a deception.

What Meher Baba led me to see is that "true enlightenment" is coming to know one's true identity, which is God. This is why Meher Baba said: "Not only am I the Avatar, but you are all Avatars, only you do not know [experience] it." In enlightenment, the "mind" goes, and all spirituality in its best sense knows this. This mind is the division between inner and outer, and when God or Self-realization is attained, that artificial division snaps. The world and Self, true Self that is, are seen to be one. That is why in Hinduism (again, as in the spiritual case of all valid traditions), Krishna can be seen as "the big person that the universe is," or Supreme Being. Therefore, the universe is ultimately not a "thing," but a Self. And that is why these synchronicities or providential events that the spiritual aspirant (or the spiritual aspirant to be) is able to experience, occurs. That is why the true "enchantment" of the universe returns. It is all one Self. Purpose, therefore, is not imposed on the universe by the mind, but is the individual's own self-discovery of what really is.

Notice the word *Self* again. Previously, I said that from a secular perspective, there is just self and the world. Meher Baba has beautifully clarified this paradox and in so doing has shown where the modern comes close to being right. But that "close" is still so far away. I believe that Baba has come to close that gap. A way to see this is to note again how W. Y. Evans-Wentz, the modern scholar of Tibetan Buddhism, picked up on the profundity of Meher Baba's definition of God. When Evans-Wentz said that "no wiser definition of the term God has ever been formulated," he was referring to Baba's statement that "Philosophers, atheists and others may affirm or refute the existence of God, but as long as they do not deny the existence of their own being they continue to testify to their belief in God." What is this being? It is, of course, the self. For most of us in the modern world, this being, one's own being, the self, is misunderstood and misexperienced. We suppose Self to be the ego, the little me, the "I," which derives from our identification with the physical body and its attachments, and possessions. But if we were to experience ourselves—our Self— as we truly are, we would experience ourselves as Everything—that is, God. An explanation from Meher Baba helps in getting this across:

> It does not require a large eye to see a large mountain. The reason is that, though the eye is small, the soul which sees through it is greater and vaster than all the things which it perceives. In fact, it is so great that it includes all objects, however large or numerous, within itself. For it is not so much that you are within the cosmos as that the cosmos is within you.[10]

Begin to see God by seeing Him in all beings and things. Give without thought of return, serve without thought of reward. God is everywhere, in everything. Most of all He is right within yourself. You do not exist for the world—the world exists for you.[11]

All that I have said in the last two chapters is my exposition to the contemporary atheist or skeptic as to why Meher Baba is God, which is also to say that God exists. Meher Baba has clarified what God is for the modern world, cleared up previously accumulated misunderstandings, and is able through his mystical contact with us to progressively bring us to this realization. So, I still believe in enlightenment, but I now have a much better idea of what it is.

·13·13·13·13·13·13·13·13·13·

In the Augean Stables

Then also will the soul hear "the voice of the turtle dove," which surely denotes that perfect wisdom which the steward of the Word speaks among the perfect, the deep wisdom of God which is hidden in mystery.

ORIGEN

I turn now to the subtitle of this book, *Avatar of the Tortoise*. As I described earlier, I read the phrase "Avatars of the Tortoise" about a week before Meher Baba dropped his body when I was shown an essay by Jorge Luis Borges.

There is a paradox in the mythical race between the speedy Achilles and the tortoise. The tortoise is given a head start and whenever Achilles gets to where the tortoise was, the tortoise has moved a little bit ahead. Achilles gets ever closer to the tortoise, infinitely closer we might say, but never catches it. There are philosophical explanations why this paradox occurs, and they reveal the discrepancy between the concept of motion and that of fixed points (that is, time and space) as well as demonstrate the mathematical concept of an infinite series.

The synchronicity of reading that essay remained with me along with words from Meher Baba's discourse, "The Infinity of the Truth." In this discourse, Baba explains that God (Truth) is Infinite, has no boundaries, and permeates everything. This spiritual Infinite is not the same as the mathematical infinite; we misunderstand the Infinity of the Truth by identifying it with mathematical infinity. Mathematical infinity is a continual and never-ending adding of units. In his discourse Meher Baba said, "Each unit is false if it is taken to have separate and exclusive existence or importance."[1] It seemed that this discourse was a beacon of light shining on the tortoise paradox and revealing changes that humanity needed to make to surmount its seemingly insurmountable problems.

Meher Baba explained that in our daily reflection as well as our mathematical thinking, we naturally grant exclusive existence to units, which means anything that we single out is a single *thing*. However, the only Real and independent unit, or individual, is God. All other things (units) are only partial and fleeting reflections of the Only True One. Meher Baba's work is described as "bringing about this awareness." Continuing in this same discourse, Meher Baba said that awareness will "initiate a new way of thinking," in which "all relative values of comparison" will be discarded in "favor of the intrinsic worth of everything"—most significantly, people. We then will be able to accommodate and live the paradox that each individual will be "regarded as the totality itself." Everyone will be first "and no one will be second." This new way of thinking will be the solution to overwhelming social problems and complex issues because "life will be infinitely simple and integral."[2]

Meher Baba once said that he came to bring about a "revolution in consciousness," and that that is the "slowest revolution of all." Meher Baba, therefore, is both the Avatar *and* the tortoise. Baba said he has come to redeem or save the world. If he is doing it, his pace of action appears to be matching that of the tortoise.

As I contemplated the image of Meher Baba as a tortoise, I realized just how meaningful a metaphor this is. Not only is Meher Baba the tortoise in his imperceptible rate of speed in this business of world redemption, but the tortoise is a significant form in mythology. In the Indian tradition, the eternal form of the Avatar is called *Vishnu*, who is the Preserver of the universe. In the language of Sufism or Islamic mysticism, Vishnu has the name *Parvardigar*. Baba dictated a beautiful prayer that starts off with the words, "O, Parvardigar, the preserver and protector of all." Vishnu is the eternal form because the Avatar, of course, has successive incarnations in other forms, which in India are known as the "incarnations of Vishnu." Classic Indian tradition refers to "ten incarnations of Vishnu." Despite the fact that the later incarnations are human, such as Krishna and Buddha, the earlier ones are animal forms, such as a fish and a boar. Sure enough, I discovered after I had chosen the title of this book that one of these other animal incarnations of Vishnu is a tortoise. The general interpretation of the animal incarnations is that they project a concept of evolution thousands of years before Darwin. However, there is the added and most significant element that each of these prehuman forms, and thus all of evolution, is a process of Vishnu coming into Self consciousness. Meher Baba affirms and further explains this account of evolution and states that the contemporary theories of evolution "Fail to do justice to God's hand in the game."

According to Indian cosmology, the tenth incarnation of Vishnu has yet to occur. This incarnation is referred to in advance as "Kalki," or "the White Horse Avatar," who comes during the most destructive age in history, known as the *Kali Yuga*. In this connection, Mehera tells an interesting story in her book.

When Mehera was a school girl in Poona, at the Catholic Convent of Jesus and Mary, she and a friend snuck off one day from school to visit the revered saint Hazrat Babajan, who was reputed to be able to grant wishes. (She was the same Perfect Master who had given Merwan Irani the unveiling kiss a few years before.) As it so happened, Babajan was not sitting under her tree that day, but instead was seated behind the wall outside their school. Shyly, the two girls approached her with their wishes and, when it was Mehera's turn, she suddenly asked the kindly old woman for a horse. Years later, Mehera recalled Babajan's response:

[She] looked at me, gave a slight, very sweet smile, and nodded Her head. Then She looked up towards the sky. "Yes, He will be very beautiful. You will get a horse, and all the world will see Him and love Him." She spoke very softly and in Urdu, and I could not hear Her very well, but those words I caught.[3]

A few months later, Mehera got a surprise horse from her mother, one that was beautiful

WHILE IT'S NOT MEHERA'S WHITE HORSE, THIS PRECIOUS PICTURE GIVES US A SENSE OF THE UNIVERSALITY OF THE AVATAR ACROSS RELIGIOUS TRADITIONS. MEHERABAD HILLS, 1936.

and snow white. Not long after that, her mother took her to see Meher Baba for the first time, when he was still known as Merwan. Eventually, Mehera's white horse was given to Baba when Mehera went to live with the mandali. She had forgotten about her visit to Babajan and her wish until years later, and then recalled what Babajan had said, "All the world will see Him and love Him," and knew that Babajan was not referring only to her horse.

Another story specifically about Meher Baba and turtles took place during Baba's 1958 visit to Myrtle Beach. He was holding a meeting in the largest gathering place at the Center, known as the Barn. Suddenly, in a quite noticeable and amusing way, a turtle was seen walking across the Barn floor and making its way right up to Baba's feet. Years later a Baba lover, Bob Brown, commemorated this event in a charming children's book, *The Turtle's Darshan for All the Animals*.

Turning from mythologies and stories from India to that of Native Americans, who refer to the earth as "Turtle Island," is a creation story of a maiden or Goddess from Heaven falling from the sky and plunging toward the infinite waters below. This legend says that a turtle rose from the unbounded ocean and provided a landing place for the woman. In some versions of the story, the turtle's back is covered with earth. The gospel song, "He's got the whole world in his hands," could be paraphrased in indigenous cultures as "He's got the whole world on his back." Meher Baba touched on this idea when he once referred to the weight of the world as "the jest on my chest."

Strikingly close to this interpretation of Meher Baba's advent is a phrase from the "Song of Solomon," in which the welcome springtime is described as when "the voice of the turtle [or turtledove] will be heard again in the land." Indeed, springtime is what the Avatar promised to bring. Meher Baba said, "Avataric periods are like the springtide of creation. They bring a new release of power, a new awakening of consciousness, a new experience of life—not merely for a few, but for all."[4]

As a Baba lover, again and again I ask myself the question, "Is this happening now or is it still to come? In the Discourse "The Awakener," Meher Baba concludes with the following words in reference to suffering humanity:

> For the moment they must be patient. The wave of destruction must rise still higher, must spread still further. But when, from the depths of his heart, man desires something more lasting than wealth and something more real than material power, the wave will recede. Then peace will come, joy will come, light will come.
>
> The breaking of my silence—the signal for my public manifestation—is

not far off. I bring the greatest treasure it is possible for man to receive—a treasure that includes all other treasures, that will endure forever, that increases when shared with others. Be ready to receive it.[5]

Meher Baba gave this message in the late 1930s. Are we still waiting to receive it? In terms of our tortoise metaphor, it has been a long race. Will the Avatar really win it in the end? My hopeful answer comes in this final reference to tortoise mythology in Aesop's fable, *The Hare and the Tortoise*. In this story, the speedy rabbit plays Achilles' role. As we know in the fable, the rabbit, confident and arrogant about his prowess, sits down to take it easy with no concern for the tortoise, not yet visible on the horizon. Due to the rabbit's arrogance and indulgent rest, the turtle passes him and wins the race.

In our materialistic, competitive, violent, ever-quickening, and increasingly complex world, Meher Baba is not yet visible on the horizon—or on the radar. Most bets are on the rabbit. Yet, Baba says he has come to save the modern world. The Avatar has no need to come, but he does so for our sake. Our faith in Meher Baba is that like the tortoise, he will win the race for us.

I wrote earlier that after my trip to India in 1982, I believed that Meher Baba had already broken his silence and the results of that divine action were slowly beginning to manifest throughout the world. Many Baba lovers such as my friend, Ann, believe this is the case. Another disciple, who as a little boy in the 1950s met and grew up with Baba, justified this belief in the following manner. He said that Meher Baba "gave away the secret in the beginning." In the late 1920s, Meher Baba told some of the mandali that he was going to speak. So that they could hear him when he did so, he took them to a distant place that they could reach only after several days of walking. When they arrived, Baba had them stand around him in a circle at a distance of about fifty feet, with their backs to him. When he clapped his hands, they were to turn to him, and he would break his silence. Very dramatic. He clapped, they turned but heard nothing. Why hadn't he spoken, they asked? He said, through his usual means, "Do you not know that I am always speaking?"

For many Baba lovers, this is the secret. Meher Baba has come to enable us, once again, to hear his voice, the ever-present voice of God in our hearts. This, he said, is the voice of intuition. It is there, but in our age of skepticism, doubt, and disbelief, we are deaf to it. Meher Baba has also said, most beautifully:

> It is not through words that I give what I have to give. In the silence of your perfect surrender, my love which is

BABA IN A RELAXED MOOD, GESTURING. MEHERAZAD, JANUARY 1949.

always silent can flow to you—to be yours always to keep and to share with those who seek me. When the Word of my Love breaks out of its silence and speaks in your hearts, telling you who I really am, you will know that this is the Real Word you have always been longing to hear.[6]

There is no doubt that Meher Baba speaks in our hearts all the time, and he has come for us to know and experience this. But what about the world, I ask? Some might answer, "You are part of the world." I respond, "But what about the rest of the world?"

It is always possible that Meher Baba's love will spread around the world like a wildfire, inflaming the hearts of millions and billions, and a new age will arrive as Baba so many times recounted. But, as I write this, some thirty years after he dropped his body, it does not seem to me that this will be the case. The idea of a "Baba movement" and awareness of Meher Baba, so far, just doesn't seem to be happening. A movement—pretty much how the modern world sees the spread of religion—seems too superficial, too outward, and too much like religion—and we know that Baba did not come to start a new religion. It's been over seventy-five years since Meher Baba *began* his mission as the Avatar. Despite this modern world's instant communication and a period of time almost equal to the first century of Christianity, there's no religion yet. A new religion or a religious movement is hardly a concern.

I awoke one morning at the Center in Myrtle Beach and saw this issue in a new way. It is not whether Meher Baba has or has not broken his silence. We can, each of us, go back and forth on that one. The only issue is the redemption of the world. If Meher Baba is the Avatar, then that is his mission. So the heart of the matter comes down to faith in Meher Baba as the Avatar. How he will redeem the world is something we are not going to know until it happens. *That* is the secret he has not given away.

Does this all sound too passive? Meher Baba is going to redeem the world and it has nothing to do with us. That sounds like we are all supposed to sit back and let it happen. Such a concept certainly goes against my Western activist grain. In his "Universal Message," one line says, "There was and is no way out except through my coming in your midst. I had to come and I have come."[7]

When I read these words years ago, something bothered me, but I couldn't put my finger on it. Over time, I realized what it was and can now convey it better if I break Meher Baba's statement into two parts. The first part is, "There was and is no way out. . . ." On the surface, this surely strikes me as a very pessimistic message. No way out? Things can't be that bad.

Certainly, if we human beings pull together and take right actions, then we can pull ourselves out of this mess. This statement by Baba seems to put a damper on that idea and was one of the reasons why the breaking of his silence was so critical for me.

The second part of his statement, "except through my coming in your midst," along with the rest of the Universal Message seemed to refer to not only being here in physical form, but also to his breaking his silence. He continued, "All this world confusion and chaos was inevitable and no one is to blame." Well, I didn't like *that*—I thought there were a lot of people to blame. And the crux:

> I veil myself from man by his own curtain of ignorance, and manifest my Glory to a few. My present *avatāric* Form is the last Incarnation of this cycle of time, hence my Manifestation will be the greatest. When I break my Silence, the impact of my Love will be universal and all life in creation will know, feel and receive of it. It will help every individual to break himself free from his bondage in his own way.[8]

This seemed to mean that he needed to do something more than just be here. For me, the reinforcement of this was that world confusion and chaos seemed to continue unabated throughout Meher Baba's life and continues to date. In fact, I am not able to avoid the perception that it's getting worse. Therefore, his coming in our midst has not yet turned the tide.

There is one thing I am convinced of: The passage of time has confirmed for me the truth of the first part of the statement—"There was and is no way out." Pessimistic or not, I see it as true. (The challenge is that Meher Baba has not yet demonstrated that the second part is true.) For me, the play of events have confirmed the unpalatable truth that there was and is no way out and that is why it is so important to know about Meher Baba. As events around the world become more desperate, it will be increasingly harder to hold on to hope. Without hope, where are we and what are we? It is said that where there is life, there is hope. The inverse of this, then, is just as true—if there is no hope, we might as well be dead.

Meher Baba said in regard to himself, "Have hope." Baba is hope—pure hope. Please don't misunderstand this. One does not believe in Meher Baba as a way to cling to hope in otherwise despairing times. One believes in Meher Baba because one believes that he is God and that God exists. That existence brings hope. Hope is not the *reason* for believing in Meher Baba. Hope is the *result* of believing in Meher Baba.

Again, the matter of passivity. Does one do nothing and wait for Meher Baba to redeem the world? The answer is a resounding "No!" for several reasons. Hope is not a passive state; it takes work to maintain hope. That work is not limited to, but certainly includes, interaction with other people. It is important for people to know about Meher Baba if not directly, then indirectly. By *indirectly* I mean knowing about values, truth, love, principles, and hope itself. The best way to communicate hope is to be hopeful oneself.

The most essential reason for not being passive, however, is love. Meher Baba is love, and he has come to bring us this love. How can we love and not love others? Loving is not a passive state of watching the world become a place of misery, discord, and destruction. Love compels us to act.

As to the second part of his statement, "except through my coming in your midst," we don't yet know what this means in terms of world redemption—but we do know what it means in physical fact. Meher Baba has come in our midst. That is the phenomenal fact of our time and one that we can immediately grasp. Our job is to keep that grasp. Baba repeatedly told us to "hold on to my damaan," the hem of his garment. "Don't let it slip," he said. "Hold on tight to it with both hands." He meant that it is easy for it to slip away by losing faith in him. What seems like the nonredemption of the world is the instrument that can do this.

Just as love cannot be consistent with passivity in our own lives, it was not that way in Meher Baba's life. Baba has spoken of the creation of the world as a result of the active nature of love—"God is love and love must love . . ." and in order for God to love, all this has come into being.

So, the puzzle continues. Meher Baba has come to redeem the world. That he has come is a fact. That he is redeeming the world can be much in doubt—to me, the world appears to be getting worse all the time. *Gradualists* might say that the world is slowly getting better and that we just don't see the major effect. Maybe. But, if we don't see it, then can we know that it's happening?

As a guide, I contemplate Meher Baba's statements, such as "the wave of destruction must rise still higher, must spread still further." This process will reach its peak when "from the depths of his heart, man desires something more lasting than wealth and something more real than material power, the wave will recede. Then peace will come, joy will come, light will come." Baba has always connected the breaking of the wave at its peak with his work—"the one miracle I will perform;" "the breaking of my silence;" "the signal for my public manifestation."[9] As we can see, this is intrinsically related to humanity's readiness to hear this word. The picture is one of destruction—to use that word in its broadest sense, not just physical—reaching an *apex*. Meher Baba uses this word in another statement:

> Man cannot escape his glorious destiny of Self-realization, and no amount of suffering that he passes through on the way to it can ever be too much. After the apex of suffering has been reached, the time will soon come for mankind to have a deeper spiritual understanding, bringing it closer together in universal love and brotherhood in the bond of divine knowledge—the only knowledge worth having.[10]

I cannot deny that I see the world as moving toward the apex. Meher Baba placed this concept of the apex of destruction and suffering within the context of hope in his "have hope" messages. To fully comprehend this seeming contradiction of simultaneous destruction and hope, one must consider destruction part of God's work as well as construction. Meher Baba said that "destruction must precede construction."

Meher Baba said (as did the *Bhagavad Gita*) that the Avatar comes "when the wick of righteousness burns low," and destruction is threatening to overrun the world. At first, I saw this destruction as "anti-God," and God, in the form of the Avatar, comes to defeat what is anti-God. I had fallen into the intellectually tempting and classical error of dualism, known in Christian history as *Manichaeism*. *Manichaeism* is the belief that the world is a contest between good and evil—the forces of light and the forces of darkness—and that the darkness represents Satan, independent of the existence of God. Baba categorically repudiated this view because it places God on one side of a dualism, which is false. God is Infinite and as such cannot be on one side of any demarcation. Good and evil are ultimately relative terms, formed by our judgment, and are both contained within the absolute and infinite nature of God. In Meher Baba's words:

> If God were good rather than bad or bad rather than good, or if He were small rather than great or great rather than small, or if He were right rather than wrong or wrong rather than right, or if He were virtuous rather than evil or evil rather than virtuous, or if He were happy rather than miserable or miserable rather than happy—He would be finite and not infinite. Only by being above duality is God infinite.[11]

This is not easy for one to accept because it is natural and compelling to see God as "good." I had to stretch my mind to comprehend that this wave of destruction reaching an apex is as much God's work as is his redemption. For those of us in the West, this concept is difficult to grasp. In the Persian language, the words *jamal* and *jalal* convey the complementary (though opposite) phases of God's work. *Jamal* can be translated as beauty, sweetness, and peacefulness, and *jalal* as power, majesty, and wrath (what burns). Meher Baba uses these terms in his "Message of Cheer and Hope to the Suffering Humanity."

> There are always two aspects of Divinity, perpetually and eternally active in the affairs of the world. The destructive aspect of Divinity as expressed in Persian (*Shama-e-Jalal*) means "Self-Glorification," and the constructive aspect is called in Persian as "Self-Beatitude" (*Shama-e-Jamal*). The aspect of "Self-Glorification" by God, when it gets palpably active, entails suffering and destruction on a colossal scale . . . The aspect of divine "Self-Beatitude," when it asserts itself, brings in its wake peace and plenty. . . . The former is a negative method and the latter is a positive method and both these methods ultimately are instruments of divine Wisdom, to rouse humanity to their Divine Heritage, which is "Self-Realization."
>
> Further, both the aspects of God referred to just now not only affect humanity individually and collectively, but its intensity and force is directly in proportion to each other and they assert themselves in cyclic waves. Now that the Destructive phase is about to weaken, the aspect of "Divine Beatitude" is nearly due to come to the force; and to invite humanity to avail themselves of this Blessedness to come is my Divine Mission in life.[12]

For me, the key was to understand that the force of destruction is ultimately as much Meher Baba's work as is the force of construction associated with his "Word" and "manifestation." Mandali member Bhau Kalchuri, who is the author of the multivolume biography of Baba, *Lord Meher*, has written, at Baba's instructions, an account of the meaning of Meher Baba's manifestation entitled *Avatar of the Age: Meher Baba Manifesting*. The book is a series of short essays, and "The Highest Became a Sweeper," describes the Avatar coming into the world and finding it "full of dirt and filth," which is the spiritually unnatural human behavior that has accumulated.

The people have become accustomed to the dirt and filth and assume that it is natural. So the task of the Avatar is to set about cleaning each "room," that is, each mind, with his broom. As he sweeps, the dust rises as a thick dark cloud and the people, who are almost suffocated, become intensely conscious of their own filth. Humanity grows desperate. When the Avatar has swept away the majority of the dirt, only particles remain in the air. Then they gradually settle, the air becomes fresh and clear, and light follows. It is then that people will know that the Avatar has come and has cleansed the world.[13] Through Bhau's image, I understood for the first time that if the world still seems to be moving toward the apex of destruction, this very process is also part of Baba's work.

This metaphor, of God as "the sweeper," is in almost perfect parallel with the Hercules (or Herakles) story from Greek mythology. There are historical indications that Hercules is an Avatar figure, an heroic God-Man—the convergence of several similar figures into a single Greek figure. There is also evidence that his origins are oriental.[14] In the legend, Hercules performs a series of "Labors." In the fifth labor, he cleans out the Augean stables. Augeas had thousands of cattle and their stalls had not been cleared out for years. We can imagine the accumulation of dung. In the myth, Hercules diverts the course of two rivers making them flow through the stables in a great flood that washes them clean. To fully appreciate the significance of the parallel, both for Bhau's image and the light it sheds on the meaning of the Hercules legend, we should know that it is most unlikely that Bhau had this legend in mind when he wrote about the Highest becoming a sweeper.

And now my apologies to the gradualists. I am well aware that the title of Bhau Kalchuri's book uses the word *manifesting*, which implies a presently ongoing process. Does this deny and ignore Baba's statements about the apex? To me it would be foolish to say so as it would fly in the face of a major part of my experience in the world. What it does say is that there is room for disagreement about whether the apex has been reached. Maybe it has. Maybe it was Baba's life itself—or when he dropped the body—and what we are witnessing now is the dust in the air before it settles down. Whichever it is, is anyone's call.

And maybe how one sees it is a function of the diversities of human temperament. Meher Baba was exquisitely solicitous and responsive to that diversity, as only God can be. One thing we all can agree on: If Meher Baba is who and what he says he is, God in human form, then there is no cause for anything other than faith and its attendant handmaiden, Hope.

· 14 · 14 · 14 · 14 · 14 · 14 · 14 · 14 · 14 ·

More to Come

I played the vina until my heart turned into the same instrument.

INAYAT KHAN

If one already believes in God, does it matter then if one believes that Meher Baba is God? In other words, as a Christian if one already believes in Jesus, is there any further point in believing that Baba is Jesus?

This question was often asked of Meher Baba's mandali, although in India it was asked relevant to Krishna or perhaps Rama. The mandali never went around proclaiming that Meher Baba was the Avatar, and Baba would not allow them to do so. He said, "If I am what I am, I don't need publicity agents." Nevertheless, discussions pertaining to this question regularly occurred with people who were not Baba lovers. The mandali were asked directly, "I have Krishna, why do I need Meher Baba?" The mandali did not know how to answer, so Meher Baba gave them the following anecdote known as the "Quaker Oats" story.

In India, Quaker Oats is seen as a nutritious, wholesome, and popular breakfast cereal. A mother on rising one morning to prepare breakfast for her children found that her tin of Quaker Oats was almost empty. She quickly rushed to the grocer to buy another. When she entered the store, she saw that she was in luck—there was one tin left on the shelf. When she asked to buy it, however, the grocer refused again and again to sell it to her. She continued to insist on buying this last tin. Finally, the grocer interrupted and explained that he wanted to sell her a tin from a fresh shipment he had just received. Meher Baba then said,

> What mother is there who would insist on buying the old stock when she could purchase a tin of the fresh new stock? I am the fresh stock.... It is all Quaker

Oats, the ingredients are the same, but
I am the fresh stock.[1]

This story is also an excellent example of the natural and humorous way that Baba answered seemingly thorny questions.

If Meher Baba is Zoroaster, Rama, Krishna, Buddha, Jesus, and Mohammed come again, it makes no sense to reject the Beloved now in favor of his past form. At each appearance, the Avatar promised that he would come again. That message was part of every advent; the promise to come again, not only for those who are not believers, but also for those who have come to him through established religions. Meher Baba said that when the Avatar comes again, long-standing religions have often become like a cage. The Avatar comes to give us his uncaged real Self and to tell us again that this is *our* real Self as well. This is the message that is so often lost or obscured and even deemed a blasphemy as religions develop. The Avatar comes again to refresh our love for him, to restore his voice in our hearts, and to spiritually recharge our lives. Once again, we are given an opportunity to avail ourselves of this fresh presence. What would it mean for a lover of God to turn this down?

Meher Baba did not speak and stated that he did not come to teach, but to awaken. "You have been given enough words," he said, "It is now time to live them." Nevertheless, he did teach and this is important to know. Meher Baba's teaching served to clear up misconceptions, distortions, and omissions that crept into the record of his past messages. What one *is* and what one *believes* are not irrelevant. We can look upon Meher Baba's messages concerning reincarnation and the eternal existence of the soul as a vital corrective to the prevailing Western belief of one life followed by either heaven or hell or the materialist's concept of one life and then nothing.

Of fundamental importance is the concept that *we will all arrive at the goal*; it is inevitable—it is only a question of when. *We are God*, but that knowledge is veiled by impressions gathered through our journey of evolution and reincarnations. Therefore, there is nothing that we need to gain. It is already there within us. Rather than gain, it is a question of what we need to lose.

An accurate understanding of the spiritual realities of life was relevant to Meher Baba's mission:

> My panacea to the worried world is the effort on its part to get an answer to the questions of "whither and whence." The knowledge that all have the same beginning and the same end, with life on earth a happy interlude, will go a long way in making the Brotherhood of Man

a reality on earth, and this, in turn, will strike at the root of narrow . . . exploitation.[2]

In explaining the "whence and wither," Meher Baba said that the universe springs out of God at a tiny place known as the Om point. Because God is none other than the Real Self, the one Real Self in all, it can be said that the universe springs out of the Self (not to be confused with the lower self or ego). In other words, the Om point is in the Self. Science, in discovering the "big bang" in the twentieth century, began to develop a cosmology that is closer to the spiritual truth than the earlier Newtonian theory of a clockwork mechanical universe. The major element missing in the scientific theory of Creation is, of course, the concept that God (the Real Self) came first, before the creation of the universe.

At least one stumbling block for science in the above picture is its tendency to equate consciousness, and thus any idea of a Self, with the brain. From this perspective, it is absurd to say that the universe springs out of the Self because that would mean that it springs out of the brain, which would make no sense given that the brain is a physical product of the universe. What science needs to realize is that consciousness comes first and then matter. Therefore, consciousness cannot come from or be a product of the brain. Instead, the brain is a *medium* for consciousness, like a radio receiver is a medium for the program that it transmits.

Meher Baba said that there are many planets in the universe with life and a few with "human beings," which perhaps one may take to mean intelligent life. However, he said, the humans on other planets differ from beings on Earth in that some planets' humans have "100% head and no heart," others "75% head and 25% heart," and only Earth's humans have "50% head and 50% heart." Because of this balance (or potential for balance), Earth has a unique place in the universe; only on Earth can human beings begin the spiritual journey, and it is only on Earth that the Avatar incarnates. Therefore, the incarnation of the Avatar is not only the most significant event in human and Earth history, but in the entire universe as well.[3]

This then is the "Good News;" Meher Baba, the Avatar, has come to give a fresh dispensation of love to the weary world and to initiate a New Humanity "that will make the further spiritual advance of humanity safe and steady."[4] His being and his work, although essential and significant from 1894 to 1969, begins to unfold its real impact after his physical life was over, as with all previous appearances of the Avatar.

Meher Baba clearly stated that the effect of this appearance, in contrast to previous ones, will not be a new religion. He said that we have enough religions that have become like cages for the soul rather than liberating the soul, and

"DON'T WORRY." GURUPRASAD, MAY 1961.

he said that this will not happen again. Therefore, the effect of Meher Baba's appearance will not be a new religion, but rather a new humanity and a new world.

The Avatar is at work in everyone's life, whether they are aware of it or not, and the purpose of the Avatar's appearance is to bring us to that awareness. Meher Baba said, "When mankind becomes completely deaf to the thunder of His silence, God incarnates as man."[5]

In Meher Baba's statement of "whence and wither," he referred to the "worried world." Meher Baba's often expressed, "Don't worry, be happy," is a simple message that carries a deeper significance. I returned from a trip to India in the summer of 1989 to learn that a hit song by that name was spreading throughout the United States and the world. Hardly anyone knew at the time or knows today that this phrase came from Meher Baba and that the songwriter, Bobby McFerrin, heard it from friends who were Baba lovers—a perfect illustration of how Baba flies "below the radar." This catchy phrase became known worldwide in a flash, while the Avatar who authored it remains largely unknown even today. For me, this trivial example indicates how—when he is ready—Baba can make anything happen just like that—a flash from the eternal. The depth of this deceptively simple phrase is described by a Baba lover.

People without knowledge of Meher Baba interpret this wrongly, I think. They read, "Take it easy, be cool, you're not supposed to struggle. Just ignore what is troubling you and stay amused somehow." But that is not it at all, really.

A better interpretation would be something like this: the practice to which we are called is to choose happiness; to deliberately and intelligently, even bravely, through an act of internal will, exercise the innate power of our spirit to return, right now and in every moment to a state of complete sufficiency. . . . already happy . . . even when confronted with every apparent reason why we should retract from that happiness into doubt and self-concern.[6]

Also in the "whence and whither" statement, Meher Baba referred to life on Earth as "a happy interlude." That is, if we *practice* "Don't worry, be happy." But an interlude? Between what? Between the state of being "on the other side" (what Meher Baba calls the subtle and mental worlds—the place between incarnations) and being on Earth (the place between birth and death). Although this concept is basic to many native cultures as well as those religions that accept reincarnation, Western philosophical materialism and naturalism see it as a meaningless fantasy. From that perspective, life here is all there is. I am far from the only one to recognize that materialism denudes life of purpose and meaning. If, on the other hand, life on Earth is an interlude, it is not only the Avatar who is here on a mission. We all are—each one of us individually. Although we may not be clear as to what that mission is, our purpose is to find and carry it out. It is our responsibility to the other side—what indigenous people call "the ancestors."

To understand the Avatar's mission is to see it as his gift of awakening. To accept this gift enables us to come in tune with the Infinite as we play our individual part in the overall mission of "making the brotherhood of man a reality on earth."

How this will come about still remains Meher Baba's secret, but Baba has given an indication of *what* this condition will look like in terms of the issues of economics. In 1932, during the deepening economic depression, Meher Baba traveled to the United States. Although there were accounts in the newspapers and periodicals about the "Indian Messiah," Meher Baba agreed to only one interview, with reporter Fredrick Collins, for *Liberty* magazine. The question of material deprivation and the Depression were central. Part of the interview is as follows, with Meher Baba beginning:

> "Poverty, if cheerfully endured, and providing one does one's best to find work, develops humility and patience, and can greatly assist spiritual progress. It is a test of character. I know it is difficult to be cheerful when starving, but all worthwhile things are difficult." Baba concluded, "Even millionaires are unhappy unless they have learned to think and live rightly."
>
> "Would a general acceptance of your doctrine of love bring about a more equitable distribution of money?" Collins asked.
>
> "It must," Baba emphasized. "Suppose we all loved each other as deeply as we now love the one whom we love best. The most natural desire of love is to share what one has with the beloved. The desire to share with everyone would produce a condition in which it would be a disgrace, rather than an honor, for anyone to possess more than anyone else."
>
> Taken aback, Collins asked, "Do you expect to do this all at once?"
>
> "No, but sooner than you think. People will respond," Baba replied.
>
> "Why?"
>
> "They will have to."[7]

Later during this journey, an extensive article about Meher Baba appeared in the *Kansas City Evening Star*, which again focused on the Depression. The paper quoted Baba's close Western disciples Malcolm and Jean Schloss.

> All such social problems spring from self-interest. Self-interest is based on imperfect knowledge of the true nature of the self, which is an eternal reality, infinite in power and resources.
>
> Then all our social problems will be solved from the inside out, not the outside in. When you realize your identity with the whole of life, that your powers are infinite instead of finite, you will have no fear, no greed, no reason for

conflict with anything or anybody in life, and the attitude of men will be one of cooperation instead of competition. Man will give what they have instead of receive. Everybody's interest shall be as vital to you as your own, because we are all one great universal self.[8]

On this early tour of the West, Meher Baba stated as always that he had not come to start a new religion, but rather to "put them together like beads on one string." When asked about converting people, he replied that the task of one who loves God is to help the Christian become a better Christian, the Hindu a better Hindu, and so forth, but not to give them a new religion. There is no question of conversion.

We now see the resurgence of religion and spirituality, surprising observers who were convinced that in this modern age, God was dead. Although some aspects of this resurgence may be seen as a mixed blessing, something spiritual is clearly stirring. How will Meher Baba put these religions together like beads on one string? If Meher Baba's appearance is not to bring a new religion, then what is it? Could it be that the world's religions are the beads and Meher Baba himself the string? As the Avatar, perhaps his role is to show the connection and the unity among religions.

When Meher Baba's sister and close disciple, Mani, wrote her letters to give news of Baba to the rest of the world whenever he was in seclusion, she called them the "Family Letters," leading to the term, *Baba family*. I now look upon family, a good and loving family, as among the most important achievements of human society. The increasing experience of love that Meher Baba has brought to me, even me, has made this happen.

My sense is that Meher Baba has come to renew not only our individual families, but the human family. It is remarkable to see how this renewal occurs in the Baba community—so subtle it is almost impossible to describe and perhaps it can only be known by experiencing it.

I emphasize *subtle* because, like religion, at times the word *family* has had uncomfortable associations for some of us. Or, when hearing the phrase *Baba family*, perhaps one pictures something like an overly sentimental Norman Rockwell painting. Not so. Baba groups, meetings, and informal get-togethers have many of the same characteristics as any other group. There are rivalries and jealousies that one finds anywhere in human groupings. It is not an "ideal" society. But there *is* a certain quality that comes from the fact that all of us "are children of one father," as Meher Baba expressed at the East–West Gathering in 1962. Any group trying to live in this spirit will have this quality that is essential for healing humanity by restoring the human family. A materialistic and secular society does not have the basis for this healing because it rejects the existence of the "One Father," and thus the idea of a human family becomes an empty phrase. As a result, modern secular society has become a disaster that is not only destroying the social fabric of civilized existence, but the natural world as well.

To understand this problem, it is important to be aware of where it came from. Modern secularism was a response to the disaster produced by oppressive and murderous religions during the Middle Ages. Their "One Father" was claimed by various religious sects to be superior to others' "One Father." Meher Baba has come to heal and correct this breach by showing us that there is only One Father or Mother— but that he or she comes again and again (as Avatar) in human form, and the different images of the "Father" only reflect the different appearances. Meher Baba specifically addressed this issue when he spoke to those gathered from the East and the West to be with him at the 1962 Gathering:

> All religions of the world proclaim that there is but one God, the Father of all in creation. I am that Father.
>
> I have come to remind all people that they should live on earth as the children of the one Father until my Grace awakens them to the realization . . . that all divisions and conflicts and hatred are but a shadow-play of their own ignorance.
>
> Although all are my children they ignore the simplicity and beauty of this Truth by indulging in hatreds, conflicts and wars that divide them in enmity, instead of living as one family in their Father's house. . . . It is time they become aware of the presence of their Father in their midst and of their responsibility towards Him and themselves. . . .[9]

Despite the fact that Baba lovers are fallible human beings, they know and accept the above. That seems to make all the difference, even though it's still a subtle one. It is interesting to note in the above quote that Meher Baba refers to a future event in the phrase, "until my Grace awakens," implying that there is more to come.

In this book, I have examined Meher Baba's life and highlighted how my life connected with his. If you are learning about Baba for the first time by reading this book, then this is the beginning of the connection of your life with Meher Baba's, even if it turns out to be all the connection that there is.

If your connection with Meher Baba goes beyond this acquaintance and you seriously consider that Baba may be the Avatar, it is as if the stream of Meher Baba's life begins to interweave with the stream of your life. When this happens, the result is a natural unification. Each of us is a separate and unique individual. Yet, we become unified by becoming part of the one life that contains all other lives.

But it's much more than unification, and maybe unification is just a secondary effect. It is also a question of meaningfulness and especially a grand meaningfulness. Meher Baba's life, if it is the story of God once again putting in a direct appearance on earth, is also the story of the universe—how it came to be, why it came to be, and the Avatar's role in it. If we connect with that, then by becoming a part of Baba's story, our own story becomes part of the grand story of the universe. The healing of society, the human family, will come about by putting all of our stories together. When that happens, a sense of anomie, purposelessness, and meaninglessness blows away like obscuring smoke and enchantment returns.

Of course, one doesn't "come to Baba" to achieve these ends. It does not and cannot work that way. One comes to Baba only because one comes to believe that He is That. All else, then, follows.

So how does one continue to make contact with that stream? The overall answer is: however and in whatever way one is drawn to. This is consistent with the idea that one's individuality is of crucial importance. In spirituality, as Meher Baba has shown, one's individuality is not eliminated. Baba shows us real individuality and its Source. God is the ultimate individual—the only Real unit. As we strive to become one with God, we become one with our real Self. All other individuality is then seen as the false individuality of the ego. Thus, we cannot become one with God through a direct act of the ego. Meher Baba says we can only do it by loving God.

How do we love God? What is this God that we should love? I once heard Eruch say, "Is it the air, should we love the air?" Loving God and connecting with Meher Baba are the same thing. Love is individual. Romantic lovers always feel unique in their love even though it is a timeless universal phenomenon. Therefore, one's coming to Baba needs to be consistent with one's individuality. I don't mean to make this matter seem vague. There are steps, but how one takes these steps is an individual matter.

Books convey Meher Baba's words, despite his silence. Do his words speak to you? There are many pictures and films of Meher Baba throughout his life. Along with biographical material, discourses, and messages, the pictures and films establish the reality of his life, so that there can be no doubt that, at least as a human being, he existed. With the advance of computer technology and the Web, even more information about Meher Baba, his Centers around the world, and group activities can be accessed.

While the books and the pictures have an undeniable value, they are no substitute for the living stream of Meher Baba. Baba's life touched other lives, deeply, and those lives touched others, and this goes on and on. The physical centers of those streams are the places that Baba set up and intended as Centers, such as the Meher Spiritual Center in Myrtle Beach, South Carolina (his "Home in the West"); his tomb and the community surrounding it in Meherabad, near the city of Ahmednagar, India (his "Final Resting Place"); as well as the Center that he inspired and visited in Queensland, Australia. Baba lovers have local groups and meetings, and some groups such as in Los Angeles have set up local centers.

But most of all, we need to remember that Meher Baba said "my true center is in the hearts of my lovers." A fundamental reason for visiting the physical centers is to make renewed contact with that inner center within oneself.

Some followers of Meher Baba do not like the term *Baba lover*. They

THE AVATAR DIPPING HIS HANDS IN THE WATER
OF THE NARBADA RIVER, MARBLE ROCKS.
JABULPUR, DECEMBER 1938.

AVATAR MEHER BABA, WITH HIS LOVERS BY HIS SIDE, WALKS ON THE BEACH AT THE MEHER SPIRITUAL CENTER, MYRTLE BEACH.

may say, "I'm not a Baba lover, because I'm not able to love Baba. I don't know what love is, and especially love for God." So, maybe they are Baba "likers." Eruch said, don't worry about loving Baba. Just *try* to love Baba. So, maybe then we are all "Baba triers."

Whenever I become uncomfortable with the term *Baba lover,* I remind myself that it comes about because Meher Baba himself used that term to refer to us. What a bold phrase! It could only be said either by God or by the world's most supreme egotist. Baba didn't refer to us as his followers, but rather as his lovers.

Although from time to time within this book I have used the term *followers,* it is truly not a question of following Baba. It's a question of love, Divine Love. Baba said, "I have only one Message to give; and I repeat it, age after age, to one and all: LOVE GOD."[10]

I like the feel of the easy-going advice given by a Baba lover to a general audience in Minneapolis: "Read a couple of Baba books, hang out with him, and see what you think. I can only say that he is the Real Deal."

Good luck and remember—you are *not* on your own.

ENDNOTES

• PREFACE

1. Filis Frederick, editor, *The Awakener: A Journal Devoted to Meher Baba*, vol. 22, no. 1 (Hermosa Beach, CA), p. 34.

1 • FIRST CONTACT

1. *God in a Pill: Meher Baba on L.S.D. and the High Roads* (San Francisco: Sufism Reoriented, 1966), back cover.
2. Ibid., p. 1.
3. Ibid., pp. 2–4.
4. Ibid., pp. 4–5.
5. Peter Marin and Alan Y. Cohen, *Understanding Drug Use*, HarperCollins, 1971.
6. Meher Baba, *The Everything and the Nothing* (Myrtle Beach, SC: Sheriar Press, 1989), p. 1.
7. Francis Brabazon, "Introduction," ibid., pp. v–vii.
8. Philip Glass and Constance DeJong, *Satyagraha: M. K. Ghandi in South Africa 1893–1914*. New York: Standard Editions, 1980. Text adapted from the *Bhagavad Gita*, chap. 4, verses 7–8.
9. Meher Baba, "Baba's Call" in C. B. Purdom, *The God-Man* (Myrtle Beach, SC: Sheriar Press, 1971), p. 222.
10. Meher Baba, *Discourses*, 7th revised ed. (Myrtle Beach, SC: Sheriar Press, 1987), pp. 268–269.

2 • HOW I CAME TO BELIEVE

1. F. C. Happold, *Mysticism: A Study and an Anthology* (Baltimore, MD: Pelican Books, 1963), p. 130.
2. Meher Baba, *Gift of Love*, compiled by Perin Jasumani, (Ahmednagar, India: Avatar Meher Baba Trust, 1994), p. 1.
3. Rick Chapman, *Meher Baba: The Compassionate One* (Berkeley, CA: White Horse, 1987), pp. 25–26.
4. Norman O. Brown, *Love's Body* (New York: Random House, 1966), p. 266.
5. Meher Baba, "The Highest of the High" in C. B. Purdom, *The God-Man* (Myrtle Beach, SC: Sheriar Press, 1971), p. 211.
6. Matthew 6:24.
7. Meher Baba, *Discourses*, 7th revised ed. (Myrtle Beach, SC: Sheriar Press, 1987), p. 99.
8. Ibid., p. 101.
9. Ibid., pp. 368–369.

3 • HIS LIFE

1. Bhau Kalchuri, *Lord Meher*, vol. 1 (Asheville, NC: Manifestation, Inc., 1986), p. 163.
2. Ibid., p. 213.
3. Antonio Rigopoulos, *The Life and Teachings of Sai Baba of Shirdi* (Albany, NY: State University of New York Press, 1993), p. 30.

4. Bhau Kalchuri, *Lord Meher*, vol. 2 (Asheville, NC: Manifestation, Inc., 1986), p. 503.
5. Meher Baba, "Last Message on the Alphabet Board" in Don E. Stevens, *Meher Baba: The Awakener of the Age* (Myrtle Beach, SC: Companion Books, 1999), p. 125.
6. Bhau Kalchuri, *Lord Meher*, vol. 4 (Asheville, NC: Manifestation, Inc., 1989), p. 1403.
7. Meher Baba, *Messages of Meher Baba, Delivered in the East and the West*, compiled and published by Adi K. Irani, undated, pp. 90 and 93.
8. Bhau Kalchuri, *Lord Meher*, vol. 5 (Asheville, NC: Manifestation, Inc., 1990), p. 1656.
9. Ibid., p. 1650.
10. William Donkin, *The Wayfarers: Meher Baba with the God-Intoxicated* (Myrtle Beach, SC: Sheriar Press, 1988), pp. 151–157.
11. Ibid., p. 164.
12. Ibid., pp. 118–119.
13. C. B. Purdom, *The God-Man* (Myrtle Beach, SC: Sheriar Press, 1971), p. 166.
14. Ibid., p. 195.
15. Rick Chapman, *Meher Baba: The Compassionate One*, (Berkeley, CA: White Horse, 1987), p. 24.

4 • AT THE CENTER—
MEHER BABA'S HOME IN THE WEST

1. Kitty Davy, *Love Alone Prevails* (Myrtle Beach, SC: Sheriar Press, 1981), p. 372.
2. Ibid., p. 533.
3. Ibid., p. 604.
4. Personal telegram, 1968.

5. Mani S. Irani, *Eighty-Two Family Letters to the Western Family of Lovers and Followers of Meher Baba* (Myrtle Beach, SC: Sheriar Press, 1976), letter of September 9, 1968, p. 321.
6. Meher Baba, "The Universal Message" in C. B. Purdom's, *The God-Man* (Myrtle Beach, SC: Sheriar Press, 1971), p. 344.
7. Irani, letter of November 1, 1968, p. 328.

5 • DROPPING THE BODY

1. Mani S. Irani, *Eighty-Two Family Letters to the Western Family of Lovers and Followers of Meher Baba* (Myrtle Beach, SC: Sheriar Press, 1976). letter of January 26, 1969, p. 341.
2. Ibid., p. 342
3. Irani, letter of March 14, 1969, p. 345.
4. Irani, letter of August 26, 1969. p. 362.
5. Irani, letter of March 14, 1969, p. 342.
6. Meher Baba, 1954 Special Message, from a pamphlet, *Meher Baba Calling* (Ahmednagar, India: Meher Nazar Books, 1962).

6 • THE LAST DARSHAN

1. Filis Frederick, editor, *The Awakener: A Journal Devoted to Meher Baba*, vol. 13, no. 1–2. (Hermosa Beach, CA).
2. James Ivory, "Jai Baba!" *The New Yorker*, June 21, 1969, p. 31.
3. This issue is discussed further in Chapters 11 and 12.

4. Geoffrey Giuliano, *Behind Blue Eyes: The Life of Pete Townshend*, (New York: Penguin Group, 1996), p. 109.
5. Peter Townshend, "In Love with Meher Baba," *Rolling Stone*, vol. 71, November 26, 1970, pp. 25–27.

7 · WHEN I BREAK MY SILENCE

1. Meher Baba, "The Universal Message" in C. B. Purdom's, *The God-Man* (Myrtle Beach, SC: Sheriar Press, 1971), p. 344.
2. Meher Baba, *Why Meher Baba Is Silent*, (compiled and published by Avatar Meher Baba Poona Center, 1961), pp. 2–6.
3. Meher Baba, *Messages of Meher Baba, Delivered in the East and West*, (compiled and published by Adi K. Irani, undated), pp. 89–90.
4. Meher Baba, *Why Meher Baba Is Silent*, p. 15.
5. Ibid., p. 22.
6. Mani S. Irani, *Eighty-Two Family Letters to the Western Family of Lovers and Followers of Meher Baba* (Myrtle Beach, SC: Sheriar Press, 1976), letter of February 16, 1966, p. 247.
7. William Donkin, *The Wayfarers* (Myrtle Beach: Sheriar Press, 1987), Supplement, 30.
8. Tom and Dorothy Hopkinson, *Much Silence* (Bombay: Meher House Publications, 1974), p. 57.
9. Meher Baba, *Discourses*, 7th revised ed. (Myrtle Beach, SC: Sheriar Press, 1987), p. 3.

8 · THE MIRACLE WORKER

1. Bernard Gunther, *Sense Relaxation Below Your Mind* (New York: Collier Books/Macmillan, 1970).
2. Meher Baba, *Discourses*, 7th revised ed. (Myrtle Beach, SC: Sheriar Press, 1987), pp. 266–267.
3. Filis Frederick, editor, *The Awakener: A Journal Devoted to Meher Baba*, vol. 12, no. 1, (Hermosa Beach, CA), p. 57.

9 · THE MAGIC FLUTE

1. Bhau Kalchuri, *Lord Meher*, vol. 13–14. (Asheville, NC: Manifestation, Inc., 1999), p. 4591.
2. E. F. Schumacher, *Small Is Beautiful: Economics As If People Mattered* (New York: Harper & Row, 1973).
3. Mark Lutz and Kenneth Lux, *The Challenge of Humanistic Economics* (Redwood City, CA: Benjamin Cummings, 1979).
4. Charles H. Hession, "E. F. Schumacher as Heir to Keynes' Mantle," *Review of Social Economy*, vol. 44, no. 1 (1986), p. 8.
5. Ibid., pp. 8–9.
6. E. F. Schumacher, *A Guide for the Perplexed* (New York: Harper & Row, 1977), p. 139.
7. Werner Sichel and Peter Eckstein, *Basic Economic Concepts* (Chicago: Rand McNally, 1974), p. 15.
8. Meher Baba, *Messages of Meher Baba, Delivered in the East and West*, (compiled and published by Adi K. Irani, undated), p. 94.
9. Meher Baba, "Foundation Message," Universal Spiritual Center at Bangalore, in C. B. Purdom, *The God-Man* (Myrtle Beach, SC: Sheriar Press, 1971), p. 144.

10. Kenneth Lux, *Adam Smith's Mistake: How a Moral Philosopher Invented Economics and Ended Morality* (Boston: Shambhala, 1990).
11. Meher Baba, *Discourses*, 7th revised ed. (Myrtle Beach, SC: Sheriar Press, 1987), p. 5
12. C. S. Lewis, *Out of the Silent Planet* (1938), *Perelandra* (1943), and *That Hideous Strength* (1945). (New York: Scribner).
13. Ray Grasse, *The Waking Dream: Unlocking the Symbolic Language of Our Lives* (Wheaton, IL: Quest Books, 1996).
14. Meher Baba, *Discourses*, p. 31.
15. Morris Berman, *The Reenchantment of the World* (Ithaca, NY: Cornell University Press, 1981).

10 • Karma Sensitive Psychotherapy

1. P. Scott Richards and Allen E. Bergin, *A Spiritual Strategy for Counseling and Psychotherapy* (Washington, DC: American Psychological Association, 1997), p. 13.
2. A. C. Ewing, *The Fundamental Questions of Philosophy* (New York: Collier, 1962), pp. 152–153.
3. Peter Breggin, *Reclaiming Our Children* (Cambridge, MA: Perseus Books, 2000), p. 23.
4. Meher Baba, *Discourses*, 7th revised ed. (Myrtle Beach, SC: Sheriar Press, 1987), p. 81.

11 • Examining the Possibilities

1. Meher Baba, *The Everything and the Nothing* (Myrtle Beach, SC: Sheriar Press, 1989), p. 100.
2. Bal Natu, *More Conversations with The Awakener* (Myrtle Beach, SC: Sheriar Press, 1993), pp. 29–30.
3. Meher Baba, "The Highest of the High" in C. B. Purdom, *The God-Man* (Myrtle Beach, SC: Sheriar Press, 1971), p. 211.
4. Meher Baba, "Manonash Statement" in C. B. Purdom, *The God-Man* (Myrtle Beach, SC: Sheriar Press, 1971), p. 195.
5. Tom and Dorothy Hopkinson, *Much Silence* (Bombay: Meher House Publications, 1974), p. 57.
6. Meher Baba, *Discourses*, 7th revised ed. (Myrtle Beach, SC: Sheriar Press, 1987), p. 81.
7. C. B. Purdom, *The God-Man* (Myrtle Beach, SC: Sheriar Press, 1971), p. 212.
8. Bhau Kalchuri, *Lord Meher*, vol. 13–14 (Asheville, NC: Manifestation, Inc., 1998), p. 4879.
9. Mani S. Irani, "Foreword" in *Mehera* (East Windsor, NJ: Beloved Books, 1989), p. vii.

12 • Once in a Thousand Years

1. Meher Baba, "Baba's Call" in C. B. Purdom, *The God-Man* (Myrtle Beach, SC: Sheriar Press, 1971), p. 222.
2. Meher Baba, *Discourses*, 7th revised ed. (Myrtle Beach, SC: Sheriar Press, 1987), p. 21.
3. Bhau Kalchuri, *While the World Slept* (North Myrtle Beach, SC: Manifestation, Inc., 1984), p. 15.
4. Kitty Davy, *Love Alone Prevails* (Myrtle Beach, SC: Sheriar Press, 1981), p. 398.
5. Ibid., p. 400.
6. Ibid.

7. Naosherwan Anzar, editor. (*Glow International*, May 1993), p. 19.
8. Ibid., pp. 19–20.
9. William Donkin, "Those Who Bear Witness," *The Wayfarers: Meher Baba with the God-Intoxicated*. (Myrtle Beach, SC: Sheriar Press, 1988), pp. 151–157.
10. Meher Baba, *Life at Its Best* (San Francisco, Sufism Reoriented, 1957), p. 43.
11. Ibid., p. 47.

13 • IN THE AUGEAN STABLES

1. Meher Baba, *Discourses*, 7th revised ed. (Myrtle Beach, SC: Sheriar Press, 1987), p. 117.
2. Ibid., pp. 121–122.
3. Mehera J. Irani, *Mehera* (East Windsor, NJ: Beloved Books, 1989), p. 29.
4. Meher Baba, *Discourses*, p. 268.
5. Ibid., p. 270.
6. Mani S. Irani, *Eighty-Two Family Letters to the Western Family of Loveers and Followers of Meher Baba* (Myrtle Beach, SC: Sheriar Press, 1976), letter of June 15, 1965, p. 226.
7. Meher Baba, "The Universal Message" in C. B. Purdom, *The God-Man* (Myrtle Beach, SC: Sheriar Press, 1971), p. 344.
8. Ibid.
9. Meher Baba, *Discourses*, p. 270.
10. Meher Baba, *Life at Its Best* (San Francisco, CA: Sufism Reoriented, 1957), p. 50.
11. Meher Baba, *Discourses*, p. 384.
12. Meher Baba, *Messages of Meher Baba, Delivered in the East and the West* (compiled and published by Adi K. Irani, undated), pp. 71–72.
13. Bhau Kalchuri, *Avatar of the Age: Meher Baba Manifesting* (North Myrtle Beach, SC: Manifestation, Inc, 1985), p. 80.
14. Mark W. Padilla, *The Myths of Herakles in Ancient Greece* (Lanham, MD: University Press of America, 1998), p. 34 and p. 36, note 8.

14 • MORE TO COME

1. Eruch Jessawala, *That's How It Was: Stories of Life with Meher Baba* (Myrtle Beach, SC: Sheriar Press, 1995), pp. 274–275.
2. "43rd Birthday Message at Nasik," in Meher Baba, *Messages of Meher Baba, Delivered in the East and the West* (compiled and published by Adi K. Irani, undated), p. 9.
3. Meher Baba, *God Speaks*, 2nd ed. (NY: Dodd, Mead, 1973), p. 244.
4. Meher Baba, *Discourses*, 7th revised ed. (Myrtle Beach, SC: Sheriar Press, 1987), p. 3.
5. Meher Baba, "The Universal Message," C. B. Purdom, *The God-Man* (Myrtle Beach, SC: Sheriar Press, 1995), p. 345.
6. *Love Street Lamp Post* (Los Angeles, Oct.–Dec., 1999), p. 25.
7. Bhau Kalchuri, *Lord Meher*, vol. 4 (Asheville, NC: Manifestation, Inc., 1989), p. 1622.
8. Ibid., p. 1640.
9. C. B. Purdom, *The God-Man*, (Myrtle Beach, SC: Sheriar Press, 1971), p. 363.
10. Meher Baba, *Gift of Love: Sayings and Messages of Meher Baba*, compiled by Perin Jasumani, (Ahmednagar, India: Avatar Meher Baba Trust, 1994), p. 69.

BIBLIOGRAPHY

Adriel, Jean. *Avatar. The Life Story of the Perfect Master Meher Baba*. Santa Barbara, CA: J. F. Rowny, 1947.

Anzar, Naosherwan, editor. (*Glow International*, May 1993).

Avatar Meher Baba Poona Center. *Why Meher Baba Is Silent*. India: Avatar Meher Baba Poona Center, 1961.

Berman, Morris. *The Reenchantment of the World*. Ithaca, NY: Cornell University Press, 1981.

Breggin, Peter. *Reclaiming Our Children*. Cambridge, MA: Perseus Books, 2000.

Brown, Bob. *The Turtle's Darshan for All the Animals*. Myrtle Beach, SC: Sheriar Press, 1973.

Brown, Norman O. *Love's Body*. New York: Random House, 1966.

Brunton, Paul. *A Search in Secret India*. New York: E. P. Dutton, 1990 (first printing, 1937).

Chapman, Rick. *Meher Baba: The Compassionate One*. Berkeley, CA: White Horse, 1987.

Davy, Kitty. *Love Alone Prevails*. Myrtle Beach, SC: Sheriar Press, 1981.

Donkin, William. *The Wayfarers: Meher Baba with the God-Intoxicated*. Myrtle Beach, SC: Sheriar Press, 1988.

Ewing, A. C. *The Fundamental Questions of Philosophy*. New York: Collier, 1962.

Frederick, Filis, editor. *The Awakener: A Journal Devoted to Meher Baba*, vol. 12, no. 1, Hermosa Beach, CA.

Frederick, Filis, editor. *The Awakener: A Journal Devoted to Meher Baba*. vol. 13, no. 1–2. Hermosa Beach, CA.

Frederick, Filis, editor. *The Awakener: A Journal Devoted to Meher Baba*. vol. 22, no. 1. Hermosa Beach, CA.

Giuliano, Geoffrey. *Behind Blue Eyes: The Life of Pete Townshend*. New York: Penguin Group. 1996.

Glass, Philip and Constance DeJong. *Satyagraha: M. K. Ghandi in South Africa 1893–1914*. New York: Standard Editions, 1980.

Grasse, Ray. *The Waking Dream: Unlocking the Symbolic Language of Our Lives*. Wheaton, IL: Quest Books, 1996.

Gunther, Bernard. *Sense Relaxation Below Your Mind.* New York: Collier Books/Macmillan, 1970.

Hession, Charles H. "E. F. Schumacher as Heir to Keynes' Mantle," *Review of Social Economy*, vol. 44, no. 1 (1986).

Hopkinson, Tom and Dorothy. *Much Silence.* Bombay: Meher House Publications, 1974.

Irani, Adi K. comp. *Messages of Meher Baba, Delivered in the East and West.* undated.

Irani, Mani S. *Eighty-Two Family Letters to the Western Family of Lovers and Followers of Meher Baba.* Myrtle Beach, SC: Sheriar Press, 1976.

Irani, Mehera J. *Mehera.* East Windsor, NJ: Beloved Books, 1989.

Ivory, James. "Jai Baba!" *The New Yorker.* June 21, 1969.

Jasumani, Perin, comp. *Gift of Love: Sayings and Messages of Meher Baba.* Ahmednagar, India: Avatar Meher Baba Trust, 1994.

Jessawala, Eruch. *That's How It Was: Stories of Life with Meher Baba.* Myrtle Beach, SC: Sheriar Press, 1995.

Kalchuri, Bhau. *Avatar of the Age: Meher Baba Manifesting.* North Myrtle Beach, SC: Manifestation, Inc., 1985.

———. *Lord Meher: The Biography of the Avatar of the Age, Meher Baba.* Vol. 1. Asheville, NC: Manifestation, Inc., 1986.

———. *Lord Meher: The Biography of the Avatar of the Age, Meher Baba.* Vol. 2. Asheville, NC: Manifestation, Inc., 1986

———. *Lord Meher: The Biography of the Avatar of the Age, Meher Baba.* Vol. 4. Asheville, NC: Manifestation, Inc., 1989.

———. *Lord Meher: The Biography of the Avatar of the Age, Meher Baba.* Vol. 5. Asheville, NC: Manifestation, Inc., 1990.

———. *Lord Meher: The Biography of the Avatar of the Age, Meher Baba.* Vol. 13-14. Asheville, NC: Manifestation, Inc., 1999.

———. *While the World Slept.* North Myrtle Beach, SC: Manifestation, Inc., 1984.

Lewis, C. S. *Out of the Silent Planet.* New York: Scribner, 1938.

———. *Perelandra.* New York: Scribner, 1943.

———. *That Hideous Strength.* New York: Scribner, 1945.

Love Street Lamp Post (Los Angeles, Oct.–Dec., 1999).

Lutz, Mark and Kenneth Lux. *The Challenge of Humanistic Economics.* Redwood City CA: Benjamin/Cummings, 1979.

Lux, Kenneth. *Adam Smith's Mistake: How a Moral Philosopher Invented Economics and Ended Morality.* Boston: Shambhala, 1990.

Marin, Peter and Alan Y. Cohen, *Understanding Drug Use*, HarperCollins, 1971.

Meher Baba. *Discourses*, 7th revised ed. Myrtle Beach, SC: Sheriar Press, 1987.

———. *The Everything and the Nothing*. Myrtle Beach, SC: Sheriar Press, 1989.

———. *God Speaks*. 2nd ed. NY: Dodd, Mead, 1973.

———. *Life at Its Best*. San Francisco, Sufism Reoriented, 1957.

———. *Meher Baba Calling*. Ahmednagar, India: Meher Nazar Books, 1962.

Natu, Bal. *More Conversations with The Awakener*. Myrtle Beach, SC: Sheriar Press, 1993.

Purdom, Charles B. *The God-Man*. Myrtle Beach, SC: Sheriar Press, 1971.

Schumacher, E. F. *A Guide for the Perplexed*. NY: Harper & Row, 1977.

Schumacher, E. F. *Small Is Beautiful: Economics As If People Mattered*. New York: Harper & Row, 1973.

Sichel, Werner and Peter Eckstein. *Basic Economic Concepts*. Chicago: Rand McNally, 1974.

Stevens, Don E. *Meher Baba: The Awakener of the Age*. Myrtle Beach, SC: Companion Books, 1999.

Sufism Reoriented. *God in a Pill?: Meher Baba on L.S.D. and the High Roads*. San Francisco: Sufism Reoriented, 1966.

Townsend, Peter. "In Love with Meher Baba," *Rolling Stone*, vol. 71, November 26, 1970.

INDEX

Abdulla, Ramjoo (mandali), 37
Adam Smith's Mistake, ix, 116
Adriel, Jean, 140
Age of Enlightenment, 157
Ahmednagar, 5, 34
All Quiet on the Western Front, 16
Aloba (mandali), 107–108, 113
Alpert, Richard, 7–8
Amartithi, 106, 110
Andhra, 46
Apex of destruction, 169, 171
Arnold, Edwin, 30
Arrows of Flame, 38
Autobiography of a Yogi, 3, 9
Automobile accidents, 46–47
Avatar, 13–14, 18, 21, 31–33, 46, 105, 113, 124
Avatar, appearance of, 11, 13–14, 24, 58, 173
Avatar of the Age, 9, 32
Avatar of the Age: Meher Baba Manifesting, 170
Avatar of the Tortoise, 65–66
Avatar: The Life Story of the Perfect Master Meher Baba, 140
"Avatar's Call, The," 146
"Awakener, The" (Discourse), 163
Azim Khan Baba (mast), 42, 155

Baba family, 59, 178
Baba lover, as a term, 8, 181–182
Backett, Mary, 44 (photo)

Bankhead, Tallulah, 39
Be Here Now, 8
Behind Blue Eyes, 85
Belief
    Christian, 156
    Eastern versus Western influence, 105
    enlightenment, 157–158
    Manichaeism, 169
    naturalism, 157
    salvation through, 157
    science as system, 69
    Self, 159
    value of, 157
Bhagavad Gita, 13
Borges, Jorge Luis, 65–66
Both Sides of the Circle, 153
Brabazon, Francis (mandali), 11
Brahmanandji Mast, 155
British Bhuddist Society, 152
Brown, Bob, 163
Brown, Norman O., 20
Bruce, Virginia, 39
Brunton, Paul, 133
Bucke, Richard, 5
Buddha, 11, 14, 20, 24, 30, 58, 136, 151, 157, 173
Buddhism, 4–5, 135, 152–153, 158
Buddhist Economics, 113
Burleson, Dr. Ned, 151

Candles in the Rain, 85
Challenge of Humanistic Economics, The, 114
Chapman, Rick, 4, 7, 9, 48, 67, 72

Character, importance of, 157
Charlatan, refuting the concept of Meher Baba as, 137
Chatti Baba (mast), 154
Cohen, Alan, 4, 7, 9, 72
Colias, Nikos, 55
Collins, Frederick, 177
Cooper, Gary, 39
Cosmic Consciousness, 5

daaman, 57, 95
Dadachanji, Nariman (mandali), 38
Darshan, 47, 62, 110
Darwin, Charles, 69, 123
Davy, Katherine "Kitty" (mandali), 52–54, 54 (photo), 60, 96, 102–105, 104 (photo)
Deccan College, 30
DeLeon, Delia (mandali), 151
Deluded, Meher Baba as being, 133, 135, 137
Department of Justice, 62–64
Descartes, René, 69
Destruction, as part of God's work, 169–170
Deva (goddess), 29
Dimpfl, Lud, 67
Discourses, 10, 16, 135
Divine desperation, 108
Divine love, xi– xii, 60, 130, 140, 182
Divine will, 129
Donkin, William, 42–43, 154
"Don't Worry, Be Happy," 36, 45, 60, 175–176

Dreams, Meher Baba's mother's, 29
Dressler, Marie, 40
Dropping the body, 66–69, 71–72, 95

Earth, as unique in the universe, 174
East–West Gathering, 15, 47, 178–179
Ego, 124, 125
Enigmatic, Meher Baba as being, 133–134
Enlightenment, 4, 5, 158
Eswaran, Eknath, 4
Evans-Wentz, W. Y., 135, 158
Everything and the Nothing, The, 10–11, 19, 20
Evil, different views of, 156

Fairbanks, Douglas, 40
Family Letters, 59–62, 178
Fasts, Meher Baba's, 147
FBI, 67, 87
Frederick, Filis, 13 (photo), 13–15, 58, 109
Free Life, 45
Freud, Sigmund, 69, 123–125

Gamela yoga (yoga of labor), 34
Gandhi, Mahatma, 33, 38–39
Glimpses of the God-Man, 28
Glow International, 152
God In a Pill?, 4–6
God incarnate(s), 21, 85, 175
God intoxicated (see also masts), 41, 153

God Realization, 21, 96, 147, 149
God Speaks, 1, 6, 15, 18, 120, 135
Godspell, 86
Grant, Cary, 39
Gurdjieff, G. I., 115
Guruprasad, 77
Gustadji (mandali), 147

Hafiz, 4, 71
Hamirpur, 46
Hare and the Tortoise, The, 164
Hayakawa, S. I., 64–65
Haynes, Jane, 54, 55 (photo), 58
Hazrat Babajan High School, 37
Hazrat Babajan, 30–32, 37, 162
Heaven and hell, 156
Hercules, 171
"Highest Became a Sweeper, The," 170
"Highest of the High, The" (Discourse), 131, 137
Hoffman, Bruce, 85
Hollywood, 39–41
Hollywood Bowl, 40–41
Hope, viii–ix, xiii, 92, 167–171
Huma, as pseudonym, 30
Human beings on other planets, 174
Humanistic economics, 114–115
Humanistic psychology, 114
Hume, David, 123
Humor, as sign of Meher Baba's sanity, 136
Humphreys, Christmas, 152

Ideal life, 112
Indiana University at South Bend, 1, 17, 21–23
Individuality, in spirituality, 180
"Infinity of the Truth, The" (Discourse), 160
Intuition, 15, 88, 124, 127–128, 164

Intuition, in psychotherapy, 124
Irani, Adi K. (mandali), 96
Irani, Mani S. (mandali), 52–53, 59, 72 (photo), 75 (photo), 142 (photo), 144, 151, 178
Irani, Mehera J. (mandali), 52, 72 (photo), 78, 142–144 (photos), 144–145, 150, 162 (photo), 162–163
Irani, Meheru (mandali), 150
Irani, Merwan Sheriar (Meher Baba), 29
Irani, Rustom (mandali), 37
Irani, Sheriar Mundegar (Meher Baba's father), 28–30
Irani, Shireen Sheriar (Meher Baba's mother), 29–30
Ivory, James, 74

Jessawalla, Eruch (mandali), 77, 106–108, 110, 139 (photo), 139–140, 150 (photo)
Jesus Christ, 5, 11, 14, 18, 21, 24, 58, 136, 144, 152, 156–157, 173
Jesus Christ Superstar, 86
Jesus movement, 85–86

Kaaba, flooding of, 73
Kalchuri, Bhau (mandali), 28, 32–33, 96, 113, 148 (photo), 149, 170
Kali Yuga, 47, 162
Kalki, 162
Kansas City Evening Star, 177
Karkaria, Meherjee (mandali), 96, 150 (photo)
Karma Sensitive Psychotherapy, x, 125–128
Kher, Nana (mandali), 105
Krishna, 11, 14, 24, 58, 136, 144, 151, 157, 173

Lagoon Cabin, 54

Lama Govinda, 20
Last Darshan, 102
Last Sahavas, 72
Law Enforcement Assistance Administration, 62
Leary, Timothy, 7
Leavitt, Connie, ix–x, xiii
Lewis, C. S., 118
Liberty magazine, 177
Life Against Death, 20
Life on earth, as an interlude, 176
Light of Asia, The, 30
Living faith, 27
Living the Good Life, 87
Lord Meher, 28, 32, 113
Los Angeles Sahavas, 109
Love Alone Prevails, 151
"Lover and the Beloved, The," 10
Lover, of Meher Baba, x–xii
Love's Body, 20
LSD, 3
Lutz, Mark, 113–115

Mai, Godavri, 133
"Man of Love, The," 153
Mandali, 33, 106
Mani S. Irani (mandali), 52–53, 59, 72 (photo), 75 (photo), 142 (photo), 144, 151, 178
Manichaeism, 169
Mankato State University, 115
Manonash Statement, Meher Baba's, 134
Man-O-Nash, 45
Manzil-e-Meem, 33–34
Marx, Karl, 69, 123
Masts, 41–43, 153–154
Matchabelli, Norina (mandali), 50 (photo), 51–52, 54
Materialism, 121–122
McCuen, George, 57
McFerrin, Bobby, 176
Meaning of life, 119–120

Meditation, 3, 9
Meher Ashram, 36–37
Meher Baba, death of, 66–69, 71–72, 95
Meher Baba, meaning of name in English, 33
Meher Baba's tomb, 79
Meher Message, The, 38
Meher Prabhu (see *Lord Meher*)
Meher Spiritual Center, The, 15, 49–54, 58, 96, 181
Mehera J. Irani (mandali), 52, 72 (photo), 78, 142–144 (photos), 144–145, 150, 162 (photo), 162–163
Meherabad Hill, 104, 110
Meherabad, 34, 181
Meherazad, 59
Meheru Irani (mandali), 150
Mehta, Jamshed, 38
Merchant, Ismail, 74
"Message of Cheer and Hope to the Suffering Humanity," 170
Mohammed, 14, 24, 58, 73, 157, 173
Money, in Meher Baba's life, 141
Muni, defined, 20, 147
Myrtle Beach, South Carolina, 49–52
Myth of Mental Illness, The, 86

Narayan Maharaj, 31
Natu, Bal (mandali), 28
Naturalism, 157
Nearing, Scott and Helen, 87
New Humanity, 46, 68, 174
New Life, 44–45, 58
New Yorker, The, 74, 80, 86
Nietzsche, Frederich, 56, 69, 123
Nixon, Richard, 58, 63
Northeast Gathering, 109

Om point, 174
One father, 179

INDEX

Ordinary man, Meher Baba as, 140

Padri (mandali), 71
Parvardigar, 161
Passivity, arguments against, 167–168
Past lives, 125, 128
Patterson, Elizabeth (mandali), 47, 50 (photo), 51–52, 54 (and photo), 150
Perfect Master, 21, 31, 113, 124
Perfect saint, defined, 21
"Perfection" (Discourse), 124
Pickfair, 39
Pickford, Mary, 39–40
Pilgrim Center, 105
Pitts, Zasu, 54
Poona, India, 29, 46, 62, 102
Power, in Meher Baba's life, 142
Prague, Oklahoma, 46
Prasad (gift of God), 138
Prem Ashram, 37
"Problem of Sex, The" (Discourse), 24
Psychiatry, 121–122
Psychological disorders, 121–122
Psychology, 121–122
Publicity, Meher Baba's attitude toward, 58
Pukar (mandali), 97–98
Purdom, Charles B., viii–ix (photos), xi
Pure love, xi–xiii

Quaker Oats story, 172–173
Queensland, Australia, 181

Radhakrishnan, S., 115
Raja yoga, 9
Rajneesh, 102
Ram Dass (see Alpert, Richard), 8

Rama, 11, 14, 24, 58, 144, 173
Reason, 122–124
Reincarnation, 125, 156

Sadguru (see Perfect Master), 31
Safka, Melanie, 85
Sahavas, 47
Sai Baba of Shirdi, 31–32
Saint, defined, 21
Sangamner, India, 138
Sanskara (impressions), 33, 45, 125
Satara, India, 46
Schloss, Malcolm and Jean Adriel, 41, 177
Schroeder, Eric, 135
Schumacher, E. F., 113–115
Scientific naturalism, 120
Search in Secret India, A, 133
Seclusion Hill, 107–108
Self, higher versus provisional, 125
Self, in enlightenment, 158–159
Self-actualization, 114
Self-interest, in economics, 116
Self-Realization Fellowship (SRF), 3
Serving two masters, 22, 24
Seven planes of consciousness, 21
Sex, in Meher Baba's life, 143–144
Shaw, Darwin and Jeanne, 80, 82, 84–85
Sheriar Mundegar Irani (Meher Baba's father), 28–30
Shireen Sheriar Irani (Meher Baba's mother), 29–30
Silence Day Sahavas, 109
Silence, Meher Baba's, 18, 36, 46, 48, 55, 90, 92–95, 99, 147
Sitaram, 97–98

Sleep, conscious, 147
Sleep, dreamless, 147
Sleep, Meher Baba's, 147–150
Small Is Beautiful, 113–114
Smith, Adam, 116
Sobs and Throbs, 37
Spiritual authority, Meher Baba as, 131–133
Spiritual desperation, 107
Spiritual principles, in psychotherapy, 124
Sri Aurobindo, 98
St. Francis, 18
St. Theresa of Avila, 21
St. Vincent's High School, 29
Starr, Meredith, 37–38
Stevens, Don (mandali), 8, 9 (photo), 53 (photo), 72
Students for a Democratic Society (SDS), 17, 22
Subnis, Waman, 138
Sufi, 9
Sufi Center, 9, 65–67
Sufism Reoriented, 9
Suzuki, D. T., 153
Synchronicity, 23, 56, 130–131, 158
Szasz, Thomas, 86

Tajuddin Baba, 31
Telegram, The, 57
"Those Who Bear Witness," 154
Thus Spake Zarathustra, 56
Todd, Quentin, 41
Tolhurst, Kim, 152
Tommy, 55, 85
Tortoise, as metaphor, 160–161, 164
Tortoise, in mythology, 161
Townshend, Peter, 55, 85
Turtles, 163–164

Turtle's Darshan for All the Animals, The, 163
"Twelve Ways of Realizing Me," 107
2001, 56

Understanding Drug Use, 7
Union Jack, 29
Unpublished manuscript, Meher Baba's, 34, 38
Upasni Maharaj, 31–33, 38

Vishnu, 161–162

Washington Area Free Press, 60
Wayfarers: Meher Baba with the God-Intoxicated, The, 42
Weber, Max, 120
While the World Slept, 149
White Horse Avatar, 162
Who, The, 55, 85
Why Not Try God?, 40
Williams, Beryl, 56
Williams, Charles, 118
Wolkin, Adele, 57–58
Woodstock, 85
World's Fair, New York, 58
World's Fair, San Antonio, 55–57
Writing methods, Meher Baba's, 18

Yoga, 9
Yoga, gamela (yoga of labor), 34
Yogananda, Paramahansa 3, 9

Zeno of Elea, 66
Zoroaster, 14, 28, 56, 58, 173

The following publishers have generously given permission to use extended quotations from copyrighted works. *Discourses*, copyright 1987, Sheriar Press. *Gift of Love: Sayings and Messages of Meher Baba*, copyright 1994, Sheriar Press. *Glow International*, copyright May 1993, Beloved Archives. *God in a Pill: Meher Baba on L.S.D. and the High Roads*, copyright 1966, Sufism Reoriented. *The God-Man*, copyright 1971, Sheriar Press. *Eighty-Two Family Letters to the Western Family of Lovers and Followers of Meher Baba*, copyright 1976, Sheriar Press. *The Everything and the Nothing*, copyright 1989, Sheriar Press. *Life at Its Best*, copyright 1957, Sufism Reoriented. *Lord Meher*, vol. 2, copyright 1986, Manifestation, Inc. *Lord Meher*, vol. 4, copyright 1989, Manifestation, Inc. *Lord Meher*, vol. 5, copyright 1990, Manifestation, Inc. *Love Alone Prevails*, copyright 1981, Sheriar Press. *Meher Baba Calling*, copyright 1962, Sheriar Press. *Mehera*, copyright 1989, Beloved Books. *Messages of Meher Baba, Delivered in the East and the West*, undated, Sheriar Press. *Much Silence*, copyright 1974, Sheriar Press. *That's How It Was: Stories of Life with Meher Baba*, copyright 1995, Sheriar Press. *The Wayfarers: Meher Baba with the God-Intoxicated*, copyright 1988, Sheriar Press. *Why Meher Baba Is Silent*, copyright 1961, Sheriar Press. Used with the permission of the publishers.

PHOTO CREDITS: Cover—courtesy of MSI Collection; page xii—courtesy of Steve Edelman, Meher Prasad; page 2—courtesy of Lawrence Reiter, Manifestation, Inc.; page 9—courtesy of Don Stevens (photo given to Don Stevens by Mehera); page 13—courtesy of Sufism Reoriented; pages 34, 35, and 104—courtesy of Wendy and Buz Connor; pages 41, 42, 53, 79, 96, 107, and 182—courtesy of Meher Prasad and Sufism Reoriented; page 49—courtesy of Connie Leavitt; page 72—courtesy of Susan White; pages 75 and 76—courtesy of Meher Prasad, Sufism Reoriented, and Sheila Krynski; page 147—courtesy of Bhayya Panday; all other photos—courtesy of MSI Collection and Beloved Archives.